UNIVERSITY OF
WOLVERHAMPTON

CIRIA C630

London, 2006

Sustainable water management in land-use planning

Paul Samuels   HR Wallingford Ltd

Bridget Woods-Ballard   HR Wallingford Ltd

Chris Hutchings   HR Wallingford Ltd

John Felgate   SLPC

Peter Mobbs   WRc

Craig Elliott   CIRIA

David Brook   Consultant

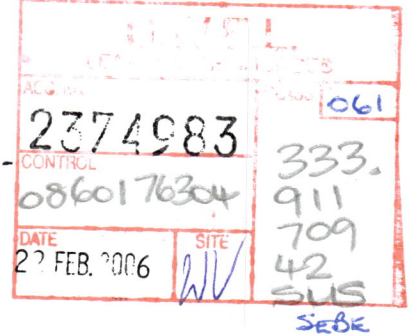

WITHDRAWN

CIRIA   *sharing knowledge ■ building best practice*

Classic House, 174–180 Old Street, London EC1V 9BP, UK
TELEPHONE   020 7549 3300   FAX 020 7253 0523
EMAIL   enquiries@ciria.org
WEBSITE   www.ciria.org

Sustainable water management in land-use planning

Samuels, P; Woods-Ballard, B; Hutchings, C; Felgate, J; Mobbs, P; Elliott, C; Brook, D

CIRIA

CIRIA C630   © CIRIA 2006   ISBN-13: 978-86017-630-5   RP627
                                          ISBN-10: 0-86017-630-4

This publication was produced in collaboration with the Environment Agency and forms EA R&D Technical Report W6-063/TR

British Library Cataloguing in Publication Data

A catalogue record is available for this book from the British Library.

Keywords		
Sustainable resource use, water infrastructure, water resources, water quality, urban drainage, sewerage		
Reader interest	**Classification**	
Land-use planning, water industry, water supply, water resources, water use, environmental regulation, provision and maintenance of sustainable water management systems	AVAILABILITY CONTENT STATUS USER	Unrestricted Technical guidance Committee-guided Land-use planners, water industry, environmental regulators, developers

Published by CIRIA, Classic House, 174–180 Old Street, London EC1V 9BP, UK.

Acknowledgements

Research contractor

This book has been produced as part of CIRIA Research Project 627. The detailed research was carried out by **HR Wallingford Ltd**, **SLPC** and **WRc**.

Authors

Paul Samuels FIMA MICE MCIWEM

A principal engineer at HR Wallingford, Dr Paul Samuels has 25 years of experience in river management and computational hydraulics. He has international experience in flood hydrology, hydraulic modelling of rivers, and development design and planning. Paul has written design guides and advice notes for CIRIA, the EA and others.

Bridget Woods-Ballard MICE MCIWEM

Bridget Woods-Ballard is a senior scientist at HR Wallingford specialising in hydrology for water resources assessments and flood prediction, hydrological and hydraulic modelling, development impact analysis and floodplain mapping. She also has a detailed knowledge of sustainable drainage system design and performance assessment.

Chris Hutchings MSc

Chris Hutchings, a group manager at HR Wallingford, has more than 15 years' experience of undertaking commercial and research projects in the water industry. His experience includes water supply/demand management studies for commercial developments and wastewater disposal projects for individual sites and whole catchments in the UK and overseas.

John Felgate MA MRTPI

John Felgate spent 12 years in town planning consultancy within an architecture/town planning practice before setting up Strategic Land Planning Consultants. He has since formed John Felgate Planning Consultancy Ltd and focuses on working with major development companies and landowners to identify and bring forward land for development.

Peter Mobbs MSc

A senior consultant with more than 12 years' experience at WRc, Peter specialises in demand management and benchmarking. His experience includes demand modelling, forecasting and least-cost planning. He also co-ordinated the UK water industry protocol for collaborative process benchmarking and has undertaken metric and process benchmarking exercises.

Craig Elliott MSc

Now the policy manager for flood risk management R&D at the Environment Agency, Craig previously led the Hydro-ecological Modelling Group at CEH Wallingford before joining CIRIA, initially as a research manager and then as an associate, leading CIRIA's research in the water sector. He has more than 16 years' experience of collaborative research into water and environmental issues, particularly water sustainability, surface water management and flood risk management.

David Brook OBE. PhD, CGeol, FlQ

David Brook is an independent consultant with over 30 years of experience in the mineral planning division of ODPM. He was responsible for Planning Policy Guidance notes on unstable land, flooding, pollution control and the environmental effects of mineral extraction.

Steering group	Following CIRIA's usual practice, the research project was guided by a steering group, as listed below.	
Chair	Martin Osborne	Earth Tech Engineering Ltd, now Ewan Group plc
Members	Caroline Bird	Hampshire County Council
	Catherine Bond	House Builders Federation
	Sarah Bowerman	Essex and Suffolk Water
	David Brook	ODPM
	Kathy Cooper	East Midlands LGA Environment Officers Group (RTPI)
	Danielle Cracknell	Anglian Water
	Sue Craddock	Thames Water
	Ian Heijne	WS Atkins (DTI)
	Christopher Mills	NHBC
	Ian Newberry	Three Valleys Water
	Mike Roe	WS Atkins (DTI)
	Gareth Rondel	Anglian Water
	Rob Westcott	Environment Agency
	Peter White	DWI (Defra)
	Richard Workman	South Gloucestershire Council
Corresponding members	Chris Blakeley	Environment Agency
	Robert Cunningham	RSPB (then Wiltshire Wildlife Trust)
	Hugh Howes	Environment Agency
	Simon Walster	Ofwat.

CIRIA managers　CIRIA's project managers for the project were Craig Elliott and Paul Shaffer.

Project funders　The project was funded by:

The Department of Trade and Industry

Environment Agency

Thames Water

Anglian Water

Hampshire County Council

Essex & Suffolk Water

Three Valleys Water.

Executive summary

This publication provides guidance on how water-related issues may be considered within the land-use planning process. It details the wide range of stakeholders, policies, processes and guidance that exist to foster sustainable water management. Many of these policies, processes and guidance are relatively recent. During the course of this project, new legislation was enacted in the Planning and Compulsory Purchase Act 2004. As planners become more aware of the issues and they are more fully addressed in local plans, the links between water management and land-use planning should improve. Nevertheless, there is still scope for improving sustainable water management through better collaboration between the stakeholders involved. This book aims to help this process by providing information on sustainable water management and identifying where it links in with planning policy. It also suggests how stakeholders can work to further sustainable water management within the land-use planning process in an appropriate and efficient manner.

The UK Government has set out objectives for levels of new housing development within the next 20 years through its Sustainable Communities Plan (ODPM, 2003a). The challenge inherent in these objectives is to balance the sustainable provision of water and wastewater services for people, agriculture, commerce and industry with protecting and improving the environment for the future. The ICE report *State of the nation 2003* (ICE, 2003) highlighted major successes in water management in 2002–3, but notes that, in identifying the need for 200 000 extra houses in the south-east of England, the Sustainable Communities Plan did not appear to take account of water requirements, or of the time taken to develop new sources of supply (up to 25 years to plan and provide a new reservoir, for example). This may make it difficult to ensure the sustainable provision of water to these new developments, at least in the medium term, although more sustainable options may be developed with time.

The planning system guides the development and use of land in the public interest. It aims to reconcile the needs of development and wider sustainability issues such as conservation, and to secure economy, efficiency and amenity in the use of land. Many pressures drive changes in the volume of water supplied and wastewater treated in the built environment and new development. These may include:

● demographic trends and societal expectations

● differential regional distribution and rate of change of employment and economic prosperity

● change in the climate and the associated hydrological and land surface processes.

By seeking to integrate the twin objectives of development and environmental protection, the planning system contributes to sustainable development. Indeed, this is now the statutory purpose of planning under the Planning and Compulsory Purchase Act 2004. The planning system is therefore an important independent tool for the promotion and facilitation of sustainable water management.

New development provides only about a 1 per cent per year increase in the total housing stock. This highlights the key role of the water utilities and sewerage undertakers and those who regulate them in managing water supplies and services to existing developments in a sustainable way outside the land use planning process. For new development (and redevelopment), the land-use planning process can play a major role in working with the

Environment Agency and water service providers in promoting sustainable water management. Some examples of the ways they can achieve this are given below.

1   Assisting the Environment Agency, water and wastewater service providers by maximising the time available to provide new services sustainably. The land-use planning process encourages consultation, and water and sewerage companies and the Agency are identified as "specific consultation bodies" that must be consulted during the preparation of and after submission/deposit of regional spatial strategies and local development documents. The earlier and more realistic the consultation, the sooner a practical and sustainable outcome can be developed. It is, for example, particularly important that stakeholders identify during the preparation of regional and local development plans, those areas where the marginal effect of new development has significant impacts (see the Basingstoke case study in Appendix 3). Relatively new options that could be considered include the use of inset appointments and/or local sewage treatment systems.

2   Promoting the use of sustainable drainage systems in new developments as the main option for surface water drainage so as to reduce any increase in flood and pollution risks downstream of a new development that may otherwise occur as a result of surface water runoff.

3   Managing development in areas at risk of flooding and avoiding it where possible.

4   Promoting the sustainable use of water resources, eg by helping to raise developers' awareness of sustainable water management. Where appropriate, environmental statements may be required, to review the issues and to identify potential impacts and mitigation measures. The latter may include the voluntary adoption of systems offering higher levels of water conservation than those that meet the Water Supply (Water Fittings) Regulations 1999.

Contents

Acknowledgements 3

Executive summary 5

List of figures 10

List of tables 11

List of boxes 12

Glossary 13

Abbreviations 16

1   INTRODUCTION 19

    1.1   Scope 19

    1.2   What is sustainable water management? 20

    1.3   The relationship between sustainable water management and the land-use
           planning system (England and Wales) 22

    1.4   Planning reform 22

    1.5   Structure of the guidance 23

    1.6   How to use the guidance 24

2   STAKEHOLDERS 29

3   PLANNING PROCESSES 37

    3.1   The land-use/spatial planning system in England and Wales 37

           3.1.1   Introduction 37

           3.1.2   Planning policies at a national level 38

           3.1.3   Regional planning 39

           3.1.4   Local development planning 42

           3.1.5   Planning applications and the development control system 45

           3.1.6   Environmental impact assessment 46

    3.2   Water resource planning 47

           3.2.1   Components of demand 48

           3.2.2   Water demand stakeholders, legislation and controls 49

           3.2.3   Water supply 51

           3.2.4   Water supply stakeholders, regulation and legislation 55

           3.2.5   Sustainability issues in water resource planning 57

    3.3   Wastewater planning 57

           3.3.1   Introduction 57

           3.3.2   Wastewater disposal 58

           3.3.3   Stakeholders in wastewater disposal 59

           3.3.4   Legislation and controls on wastewater disposal 59

           3.3.5   Surface water drainage 60

3.3.6   Stakeholders in surface water drainage 61

3.3.7   Legislation and controls on surface water drainage 61

3.3.8   Sustainability issues for waste water planning 62

4   PROCESS INTERACTIONS . . . . **.63**

4.1   Interaction between Environment Agency planning and land-use/spatial planning processes 63

4.2   Interaction between water company planning and land-use/spatial planning processes 66

4.3   Interaction between developers' planning and land-use/spatial planning processes 69

5   PLANNING ISSUES . . . . **.71**

5.1   Introduction 71

5.2   Challenge 1: meeting all stakeholder interests 72

5.2.1   Competing demands for water 72

5.2.2   Different regulatory objectives 73

5.2.3   Water management aspects of planning policy guidance 74

5.2.4   Meeting expectations of society, now and in the future 75

5.3   Challenge 2: addressing the uncertainties 76

5.3.1   Uncertainties in demand forecasting 76

5.3.2   Uncertainties in water resource availability 77

5.3.3   Uncertainties in operating at different planning scales 77

5.3.4   Uncertainties in implementing alternative design solutions 77

5.4   Challenge 3: timing issues 78

5.4.1   Land-use/spatial planning horizons and process duration 79

5.4.2   Environment Agency planning horizons 80

5.4.3   Water infrastructure planning horizons 80

5.5   Challenge 4: management at a catchment scale 81

5.5.1   Variation in management boundaries 81

5.5.2   Temporal and spatial dynamics of environmental quality 82

5.5.3   Sustainability of water transfers between catchments and new treatment technology 82

5.5.4   Impact of development on environmental quality 83

5.6   Challenge 5: education, communication and integrated planning 83

5.6.1   Routes of communication 84

5.6.2   Awareness and training 84

5.6.3   Integrated processes and policies 85

5.6.4   Confidentiality issues 85

5.6.5   Priorities 85

6   GUIDANCE **87**

6.1   Introduction 87

6.2   Guidance for land-use/spatial planners 90

    6.2.1   National planning policies 90

    6.2.2   Development planning 92

    6.2.3   Development control 93

6.3   Guidance for the Environment Agency 94

    6.3.1   National planning policies 94

    6.3.2   Development planning 95

    6.3.3   Development control 96

6.4   Guidance for water and wastewater service providers 97

    6.4.1   National level 97

    6.4.2   Development planning 98

    6.4.3   Development control 99

6.5   Guidance for house-builders and developers 100

    6.5.1   National level 100

    6.5.2   Development planning 101

    6.5.3   Development control 102

7   RECOMMENDATIONS **103**

APPENDICES **105**

A1   Stakeholders 105

    A1.1   Water management 105

    A1.2   Land-use planning 122

A2   Planning policies: guidance and good practice 127

    A2.1   Sustainable water use, supply and sewerage 128

    A2.2   Sustinable flood risk management 134

    A2.3   Environmental protection: general 138

    A2.4   Environmental protection: biodiversity 139

A3   Case studies 141

    A3.1   A sustainable development framework for the east of England 142

    A3.2   Sustainable water management in California: success stories 146

    A3.3   Flag Fen high-purity water production scheme 150

    A3.4   Challenges to sustainable water management: Basingstoke case study 154

    A3.5   Putting water into planning: "Water in Hampshire" 158

A4   Stakeholder web addresses 163

    A4.1   Web addresses for sustainable water management 163

REFERENCES **171**

Publications 171

Environmental and planning guidance 175

Legislation 175

Figures

Figure 1.1   Principal stakeholder organisations 20

Figure 1.2   Route map for land-use/spatial planners 25

Figure 1.3   Route map for Environment Agency staff 26

Figure 1.4   Route map for water supply and wastewater service providers 27

Figure 1.5   Route map for developers 28

Figure 2.1   Environment Agency regions of England and Wales, and areas managed by
               internal drainage boards 31

Figure 2.2   Water supply companies and sewerage treatment operators 32

Figure 2.3   Interaction of government organisations involved in land-use planning in
               England 35

Figure 3.1   The land-use/spatial planning process and changes resulting from the
               Planning and Compulsory Purchase Act 2004 37

Figure 3.2   Government office regions 40

Figure 3.3   Components of public water supply by volume 48

Figure 3.4   Water company planning to meet supply-demand balance 52

Figure 3.5   CAMS areas 53

Figure 3.6   CAMS process 54

Figure 3.7   Current indicative water resource availability: summer surface water 55

Figure 3.8   Wastewater planning 58

Figure 4.1   Interaction between EA and land-use/spatial planning processes 65

Figure 4.2   Interaction between water supply and land-use/spatial planning processes 67

Figure 4.3   Interaction between sewerage and land-use/spatial planning processes 68

Figure 4.4   Interaction between developers and land-use/spatial planning processes 70

Figure 5.1   Barriers to sustainable water management 71

Figure 5.2   Key stakeholder interests 72

Figure 5.3   Water resources and water users 72

Figure 5.4   Regulators in the water industry 73

Figure 5.5   Uncertainties in water management 76

Figure 5.6   Issues relating to alternative design solutions 77

Figure 5.7   Variability of planning programmes 78

Figure 5.8   Planning process timescales in Oxfordshire 79

Figure 5.9   Issues associated with catchment-scale management .81

Figure 5.10   Issues of communication and understanding 83

Figure 6.1   Summary of guidance on actions to address water sustainability issues 89

Figure 6.2   Incorporating water issues in development plans using existing guidance 91

Figure 6.3   Regional planning checklist . . . . .end of book

Figure 6.4   Development planning checklist . . . . .end of book

Figure 6.5   Development control checklist . . . . .end of book

Figure A1.1   Current interaction with the planning process 124

Figure A3.1   Flag Fen high-purity water treatment process schematic 152

Figure A3.2   Flag Fen microfiltration plant 152

Figure A3.3   Flag Fen reverse osmosis plant 153

Figure A3.4   Basingstoke alternatives 157

Tables

Table 2.1   Organisations involved in development, planning and water management . . .29

Table 2.2   Stakeholders in sustainable water management: national policy and
              regulation 30

Table 2.3   Stakeholders in sustainable water management: drainage 31

Table 2.4   Stakeholders in sustainable water management: water supply and sewerage . .32

Table 2.5   Stakeholders in sustainable water management: conservation 33

Table 2.6   Stakeholders: land-use/spatial planning and development (public sector) 34

Table 2.7   Stakeholders: land-use/spatial planning and development (private sector) 36

Table 3.1   National guidance covering water management and water sustainability
              issues 39

Table A3.1   Typical water quality delivered 151

Table A3.2   Typical sewage treatment works effluent quality 151

Table A3.3   Domestic poulation data for the Basingstoke sewerage catchment,
              1935–2011 155

Table A3.4   Basingstoke STW discharge consent, 1989–2005 156

Table A3.5   Selected "Water in Hampshire" actions and performance targets 160

Boxes

Box 6.1   Issues in achieving sustainable water management in new development 87

Box 6.2   Key steps for integrating water issues in spatial planning 88

Box 6.3   CIRIA guidance on technology for water sustainability 89

Box 6.4   National measures for the Environment Agency 94

Box 6.5   National initiatives in sustainable water management .98

Box 6.6   Recent water management initiatives 100

Box 6.7   Practical water conservation and water management solutions 102

Box A3.1   Water resources and quality issues 143

Box A3.2   Selected water sustainability challenges and key objectives within other
               issues 144

Box A3.3   Selected East of England sustainable development high-level objectives 145

Box A3.4   Water-related policy statements from the Hampshire County Structure Plan
               1996–2011 161

Glossary

Abstraction	The removal of water from any source, either permanently or temporarily
Abstraction charge	The charge payable to the Environment Agency under the terms of an abstraction licence
Abstraction licence	The authorisation granted by the Environment Agency to allow the removal of water from a source
Aquifer	A geological formation, group of formations or part of a formation that can store and transmit water in significant quantities
Areal	Related to the functions or characteristics of plots of land
Attenuation	Reduction in flow through natural or artificial storage that increases the duration of flow hydrograph
Biodiversity	The variety of life in all its forms, levels and combinations. Includes ecosystem diversity, species diversity and genetic diversity
Blackwater	The wastewater generated by toilets, kitchen sinks and dishwashers
Borehole	Narrow well-hole sunk into a water-bearing rock from which water may be pumped or the groundwater level measured
Brownfield site	Land that has been developed in the past (see *Previously developed land*)
Catchment	The area from which precipitation and groundwater will collect and contribute to the flow of a specific river
Coastal protection	Infrastructure developed to control coastal hazards
Combined sewer	A sewer designed to carry foul sewage and surface runoff in the same pipe
Common carriage	A way of encouraging competition by allowing third parties to access the water supply and sewerage infrastructure of a different water company
Commuted sum	A sum of money paid in the present, from a developer to the organisation adopting a development, to cover the costs associated with the maintenance of aspects of the development
Consumption	Water delivered billed less underground supply pipe losses. Consumption can be split into customer use plus total plumbing losses
Demand management	The implementation of policies or measures that serve to control or influence the consumption or waste of water (this definition can be applied at any point along the chain of supply)
Design criteria	A set of standards agreed by the developer, planners and regulators that the proposed system should satisfy
Drought order	A means whereby water companies or the Environment Agency can apply to the secretary of state or the Welsh Assembly Government for the imposition of restrictions in the uses of water and/or that allows for the abstraction of water outside the existing licence conditions
Economic level of leakage (ELL)	The level of leakage at which it would cost more to make further reductions in leakage than to produce the water from another source. Operating at ELL means the total cost to the customer of supplying water is minimised and companies are operating efficiently. In

	determining this it is important to include consideration of social and environmental costs as well as other costs
Effluent	Liquid waste from industrial, agricultural or sewage plants
Flood defence	Infrastructure developed to manage flood hazard
Floodplain	Land adjacent to a river that is subject to regular flooding
Flood risk mitigation	Reducing the consequences of flooding either by reducing vulnerability of communities to flooding and or by controlling the flood hazard
Flow regime	The pattern of varying flow rates within a river (usually measured as the daily mean flow in m^3/s)
Greenfield	Land that has never been developed, other than for agricultural or recreational use
Greywater	Wastewater from sinks, baths, showers and domestic appliances (excluding kitchen sinks and dishwashers)
Groundwater	Water within the sub-surface saturated zone (including aquifers)
Habitat	The customary and characteristic dwelling place of a species or community
Headroom	The difference between water available for use and annual average demand (distribution input) at any given point in time
Household	Group of one or more individuals who receive a common supply of water for domestic purposes where they are not occupying blocks of flats on single supply, institutions, factories, offices or commercial premises etc
Infiltration	The passage of surface water through the surface of the ground
Inset appointment	The legal process by which a water company may replace the existing supplier in a specific geographical area, eg a large industrial plant or housing project
Leakage	The sum of distribution losses and underground supply pipe losses
Level of service	Specific measures of services to customers
Load standstill	A restriction on the discharge conditions of a sewage treatment works
Main river	The watercourse shown on the statutory main river maps held by the Environment Agency and Defra. The Agency has permissive powers to carry out works of maintenance and improvements on these rivers
Marginal costs	An estimate of how total costs change as output is increased or decreased
Percolation	Infiltration to groundwater
Precipitation	Deposition of moisture including dew, hail, rain, sleet and snow
Previously developed land	Land that is, or was, occupied by a permanent structure (excluding agricultural or forestry buildings) and associated fixed surface infrastructure, including the curtilage of the development
Public water supply	Supply of water provided by the water undertaker
Rainwater harvesting	The collection and storage of rainwater for subsequent use
Ramsar site	A site designated for protection under the Ramsar Convention on the protection of wetlands of intentional importance
Recharge	Replenishment of groundwater storage in an aquifer
Recycling	The use of water for a second purpose, once it has undergone treatment or recovery processes

Reuse	The use of water that has already been used without treatment
Runoff	Water that flows over the ground surface to the drainage system. This occurs if the ground is impermeable or if permeable ground is saturated
Soakaway	A substrate structure into which surface water is conveyed, designed to promote infiltration
Source control	The control of runoff at or near its source
Specific consultation body	Body that must be consulted by regional planning bodies and/or local planning authorities when preparing regional spatial strategies and/or local development documents
Stakeholder	Person or organisation with a specific interest (commercial or professional) in a particular issue (political, regulatory, economic, financial, social, environmental etc)
Statutory	With a legally recognised status
SUDS	Sustainable drainage system: a sequence of management practices and control structures designed to drain surface water in a more sustainable fashion than some conventional techniques
Supply-demand balance	The balance between a company's available water resource and the demand for water by customers
Uprate	Increase capacity of water or wastewater network to meet increased demand
Waste minimisation	The reduction of waste by the adoption of more efficient and cleaner technologies or policies
Wastewater	Water used as part of a process, which is not retained but is discharged; includes water from sinks, baths, showers, WC and water used in industrial and commercial processes
Water conservation	Reduction in the amount of water used by limiting activities that use water or by ensuring that water is used more efficiently
Watercourse	Any natural or artificial channel that conveys surface water
Water efficiency	Reducing the amount of water to carry out a given task
Water resource zone	The largest possible zone in which all resources, including external transfers, can be shared and hence the zone in which all customers experience the same risk of supply failure from a resource shortfall
Water-stressed	The existence of a high risk of failure in satisfying demand with the available water resources
Water supply	Supply of water provided by the water undertaker
Water UK	An industry association representing all UK water and wastewater service providers
Wetland	Areas of marsh, fen, peatland or water, whether natural or artificial, permanent or temporary, with water that is static or flowing, that has a high proportion of emergent vegetation in relation to open water
Wholesome water	Water of a suitable quality for drinking
Yield	The reliable rate at which water can be drawn from a water resource

Abbreviations

ADA	Association of Drainage Authorities
AMP	asset management planning
BAP	biodiversity action plan
BATNEEC	best available techniques not entailing excessive cost
BedZED	Beddington Zero Energy Development
BRE	Building Research Establishment
CA	Countryside Agency
CAMS	catchment abstraction management strategy
CAP	Common Agricultural Policy
CCW	Countryside Council for Wales
CFMP	catchment flood management plan
CII	commercial, industrial and institutional
CIP	clean in place
Defra	Department for Environment, Food and Rural Affairs (from 2001)
DETR	Department for Environment, Transport and the Regions (1997–2001)
DOE	Department of the Environment (1970–1997)
DPD	development plan document
DTLR	Department of Transport, Local Government and the Regions (2001–2002)
DWI	Drinking Water Inspectorate
EA	Environment Agency (also referred to as the Agency)
EC	European Commission
EIA	environmental impact assessment
EIP	examination in public
ELL	economic level of leakage
EN	English Nature
EPSRC	Engineering and Physical Sciences Research Council
ES	environmental statement
EU	European Union
FRA	flood risk assessment
GLA	Greater London Authority
GO	government office
GOL	Government Office for London
GPG	good practice guidance
HA	Highways Agency
HBF	House Builders Federation
HCC	Hampshire County Council

HWCG	Hampshire Water Consultative Group
HWS	Hampshire Water Strategy
ICE	Institution of Civil Engineers
IDB	internal drainage board
IPPC	integrated pollution prevention and control
LA	local authority
LA21	local Agenda 21
LCC	London County Council
LDD	local development document
LDF	local development framework
LDS	local development scheme
LEAP	local Environment Agency plan
LGA	Local Government Association
LPA	local planning authority
MF	microfiltration
mg/l	microgrammes per litre
Mld	megalitres per day
MPG	minerals planning guidance note
MWD	Metropolitan Water District
NGO	non-governmental organisation
NHBC	National House Building Council
NNR	national nature reserve
ODPM	Office of the Deputy Prime Minister (from 2002)
Ofwat	Office of Water Services
ONS	Office of National Statistics
PCC	per-capita consumption (consumption per head of population)
PE	public examination
PLC	public limited company
PPG	planning policy guidance note
PPS	planning policy statement
RBMP	river basin management plan
RDA	regional development agency
RO	reverse osmosis
RPB	regional planning body
RPG	regional planning guidance
RSPB	Royal Society for the Protection of Birds
RSS	regional spatial strategy
S106 TCPA 1990	A section within the Town and Country Planning Act 1990 that allows a planning obligation between a developer and a local planning authority to be legally binding. This should not be confused with Section 106 of the Water Industry Act 1991, which relates to the right to connect to public sewers

SCB	specific consultation body
SCI	statement of community involvement
SDB	supply-demand balance
SMP	shoreline management plan
SPD	supplementary planning document
SPG	supplementary planning guidance
SSSI	site of special scientific interest
STW	sewage treatment works
SUDS	sustainable drainage system
UDP	unitary development plan
UKWIR	United Kingdom Water Industry Research Ltd
ULFT	ultra-low-flush toilet
WCED	World Commission on Environment and Development
WDM	Water Demand Management Team within the Environment Agency's Water Resources Function
WFD	EC Water Framework Directive (2000/60/EC)
WFRs	Water Supply (Water Fittings) Regulations 1999 (SI 1999/1148)
WRc	Water Research Centre
WRMU	Water Resource Management Unit
WRP	water resources plan
WWTW	wastewater treatment works

1   Introduction

1.1   Scope

This guidance highlights the importance of water management issues in land-use planning in England and Wales (Northern Ireland and Scotland are subject to different legislation and are not covered by this publication). Guidance is presented for all stakeholders in the land-use planning process, from regional planning to the submission and determination of planning applications. Since water is essential to all life, the management of water plays a key role in sustainable development.

The guidance is written on the premise that water is a renewable but finite natural resource. Water is also an economic good, the supply and disposal of which is of fundamental importance to the economy and to sustaining and improving the quality of life of all citizens and businesses. Although the ability to engineer an adequate supply of water is not in question, in some areas of the UK future demand may exceed existing local resources – even, in extreme cases, regional ones. Instead, the questions relate to the long-term sustainability of how this is done, the timescales involved, the environmental consequences of the supply and treatment options, and the economics of the managed water cycle. The key stakeholders in water management and planning are shown in Figure 1.1 and more detail is provided in Chapter 2.

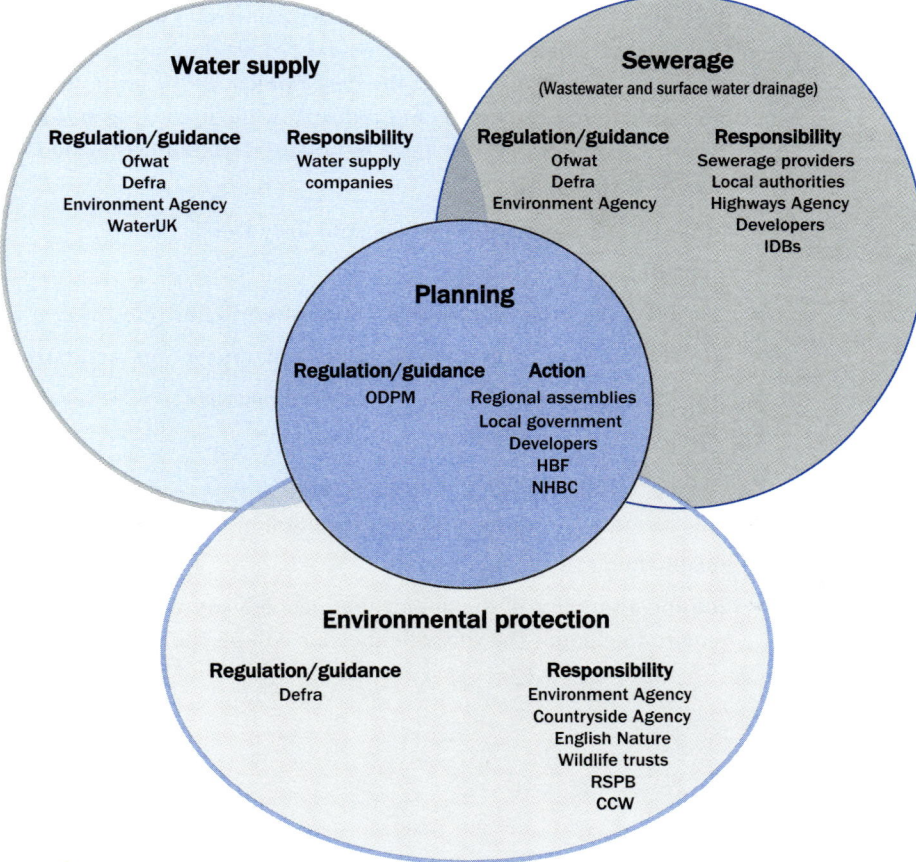

Figure 1.1   *Principal stakeholder organisations*

This guide has been prepared to assist a range of organisations, including:

- regional-scale planning in the government offices for the regions (GOs) and Welsh Assembly Government, and by the regional planning bodies (RPBs)
- the planning functions in all tiers of local government
- the Environment Agency
- the water supply and sewerage providers
- developers and their agents, consultants, and trade and professional bodies.

Water management cuts across many interests and businesses, and a strong theme of this guide is the need for timely communication between all parties involved. By including information on all stakeholders' concerns and activities, it is hoped that the book will foster a better understanding of the complexity of the principles involved and provide practical help in identifying key issues.

Sustainable development may be facilitated through partnerships between those responsible for managing our environmental resources and those involved in anticipating and responding to societal needs. The guide draws on a wide range of experience, but there are few easy answers to many of the issues raised and this publication will not be the last word on the subject. Understanding and experience of how the land use planning system may help to deliver more sustainable development continues to evolve as planners, in common with others, learn how to deliver more sustainable solutions for our environment.

1.2   What is sustainable water management?

In the context of this guide, water management covers water supply, wastewater treatment, surface water drainage and environmental protection. Sustainable water management is the management of water to support the development of the economy, providing water for people, agriculture, commerce and industry, while protecting and improving the environment for the future. Issues that may need to be considered in delivering the sustainable management of water include:

- effective management of the demand for water
- the efficient use of water
- ensuring the protection of rivers and groundwater resources
- processing wastewater to an adequate and appropriate standard
- the protection of floodplains and their functions
- the use of sustainable drainage systems
- reducing point-source pollution at source
- alleviation and treatment of diffuse pollution
- maintaining river water quality
- raising awareness of the impact that people's consumption of water has on the environment and the vital role they have to play in sustainable water management.

The Government wants sustainable development to be at the heart of policy-making (DETR, 2000a). The national strategy is defined in *A better quality of life: a strategy for sustainable development in the UK* (DETR, 1999a). In answering the question "What is sustainable development?", the strategy (Paragraph 1.1) states:

> *At its heart is the simple idea of ensuring a better quality of life for everyone, now and for generations to come. A widely accepted definition internationally is "development which meets the needs of the present without compromising the ability of future generations to meet their own needs".*

> *Our common future* ("The Brundtland Report"), WCED, 1987

In this context it is important to understand that the word "development" is used in a much broader sense than just construction of the built environment, as sustainable development interconnects social, economic and environmental issues. The strategy (Paragraph 1.2) identifies the need to meet four broad objectives.

1   Social progress that recognises the needs of everyone.

2   Effective protection of the environment.

3   Prudent use of natural resources.

4   Maintenance of high and stable levels of economic growth and employment.

In expanding these four objectives, the strategy specifically identifies water as an example of a renewable resource that "should be used in ways that do not endanger the resource or cause serious damage or pollution".

Reconciling the water needs of the natural environment with the demands of society poses many difficult challenges. The environment is under pressure from many directions: increased housing, increased population density (particularly in the south-east of England) and extended road networks all compete with the expectations of a population of rising affluence for an improved quality of life. In addition, the realisation and uncertainties of future climate change place additional pressure to adopt a precautionary approach to water management.

Many stakeholders have an interest in the management of the water environment. The public, as end-beneficiaries and consumers, create the demand for a high-quality water supply, and it is for them that the environment is conserved both now and in the future. Developers respond to the demand for new housing and the development plans that drive the requirement for new supply, drainage and wastewater treatment infrastructure. The water supply and sewerage providers have the responsibility to provide this infrastructure via sustainable and environmentally acceptable routes. In England and Wales the Environment Agency has a duty to protect and improve the environment and has powers to regulate abstractions from and discharges to controlled waters. The Agency also undertakes consultation and provides guidance on many environmental aspects of the land-use planning process. Other organisations with interests in, for example, wildlife or the countryside also play an active part in advising on and promoting environmental issues.

1.3 The relationship between sustainable water management and the land-use/spatial planning system (England and Wales)

The land-use/spatial planning system controls development and the use of land in the public interest. It is a plan-led system, requiring forward planning through development plans, and it gives plan policies pre-eminence in the determination of applications for planning permission. This permission is required for all development, as defined in the Town and Country Planning Act 1990. Separate but generally parallel legislation applies in Scotland and Northern Ireland.

The planning process has always been the means of addressing important societal issues at a regional and local scale. In the 1970s, land-use planning was dominated by social concerns; in the 1980s economic concerns came to the fore; and through the 1990s the environment had a rapidly rising profile. The concept of sustainability emerged in the late 1980s, came to prominence following the Rio Summit in 1992, and since then has risen in profile dramatically. Sustainability now plays a pivotal role within government policy.

Government guidance – such as PPG1 Para 5 (DoE, 1997), PPG12 Para 4.1 (DETR, 2000b), and GPG22 *Planning for sustainable development – towards better practice* (DETR, 1998a) – recognised that the planning system can make a major contribution to the achievement of the Government's objectives for sustainable development. The new planning policy statement, PPS1 (ODPM, 2005a), identifies sustainable development as the core principle underpinning planning. Since water is crucial for public well-being, agricultural production, industrial output and the quality of the natural environment, sustainable water management is an important component of sustainable development and so could be advanced in part through similar policy initiatives.

Published in December 2000, the Water Framework Directive (WFD; 2000/60/EC) is being implemented in the UK under the Water Environment (Water Framework Directive) (England and Wales) Regulations 2003. It recognises the interconnectedness of all parts of the water cycle and provides a new system for planning and managing the water environment in a more integrated and sustainable way. The successful implementation of the WFD will require closer collaborative working among all those organisations whose duties and interests interact with the water environment.

The Environment Agency has a statutory duty to secure the proper use of water resources and provides guidance and recommendations on this as part of its role as consultee to the land-use planning process. It will also be the competent authority for the implementation of the WFD. Water companies have a statutory duty to promote the efficient use of water, environmental good practice and the use of cost-effective solutions.

1.4 Planning reform

During the preparation of this guidance, the government initiated a programme of reform of the planning system with the aim of simplifying and speeding up the planning process and increasing public engagement. A Green Paper (DTLR, 2001b) proposed many changes to the planning system in England, receiving more than 16 000 responses. The Transport, Local Government and the Regions Select Committee (2002) also reported on the Green Paper and the Royal Commission on Environmental Pollution issued a report on environmental planning (RCEP, 2002). The resulting Planning and Compulsory Purchase Act 2004 reflects the government response to these exercises and makes significant changes to the planning system.

The changes contained within the Act do not alter the principles of this guidance but, if anything, strengthen the need for it. The changes include:

- introducing sustainable development as a statutory purpose for planning
- adopting a spatial planning approach, which extends beyond conventional land-use planning
- regional planning guidance (RPG) is replaced by a statutory regional spatial strategy (RSS) prepared by the regional planning body (RPB)
- subject to transitional arrangements, county structure plans are abolished, taking some issues into sub-regional planning and others into local development planning
- subject to transitional arrangement, local plans and supplementary planning guidance are replaced by local development frameworks (LDFs). An LDF is a portfolio of local development documents (LDDs) comprising development plan documents (DPDs), supplementary planning documents (SPDs) and a statement of community involvement (SCI)
- requiring local planning authorities (LPAs) to submit a local development scheme that identifies the LDDs it intends to produce and the time-lines for doing so
- reviewing all planning policy guidance notes, distinguishing national policy from guidance scheme
- requiring RPBs and LPAs to report annually on the achievement of RSS and LDS targets, identifying any remedial action necessary.

In addition, the ODPM is reviewing all PPGs to distinguish national policy from guidance in shorter, sharply focused PPSs, accompanied where necessary by technical annexes and practice guidance on implementation of those policies.

1.5 Structure of the guidance

The guide includes six main chapters, which are supported by four appendices.

Chapter 2 describes the stakeholders in both water management and land-use planning, together with their roles, responsibilities and interaction.

Chapter 3 summarises the land-use/spatial planning system in England and Wales, with details of all levels of development planning and development control. This chapter also describes the water management planning processes, including supply, surface water and wastewater disposal, and environmental protection. This is to inform planners on the processes and organisations with which they need to interact.

Chapter 4 covers the interactions between the planning processes of the water companies, the Environment Agency and the developers on the one hand and the land-use/spatial planning process – from national through to development control level – on the other. Flow charts are used to illustrate these process interactions.

Chapter 5 identifies the issues that continue to present challenges to the integration of sustainable water management practices within new development. These challenges include the wide-ranging interests and priorities of the organisations involved, the uncertainties inherent in future forecasts of demand and availability, the temporal and spatial scales important to the organisations, the physical and environmental processes, and the lack of formalised and well-established lines of communication.

Guidance and decision support for selected stakeholders are presented in **Chapter 6**, and recommendations for the future are included in **Chapter 7**.

Appendix 1 provides further details on the main stakeholders. **Appendix 2** contains examples of planning policies that seek to promote water sustainability. Case studies of examples of development where the land use planning process has supported the implementation of sustainable water management practices are presented and discussed in **Appendix 3**. **Appendix 4** provides selected relevant website addresses for stakeholders and relevant publications.

1.6   How to use the guidance

The following four pages provide route maps to this document, to support the following stakeholder groups:

- land-use/spatial planners
- developers and their agents
- Environment Agency
- water supply and wastewater service providers

in finding their way quickly to the most relevant parts of the document. The route maps (Figures 1.2 to 1.5) are distinguished by differing tones for the background to the text boxes, as indicated in the key below.

     Background information

     Possible solutions

     Specific actions that can be taken by each stakeholder group

     Land-use/spatial planners – decision support tools;
other stakeholders – potential future actions.

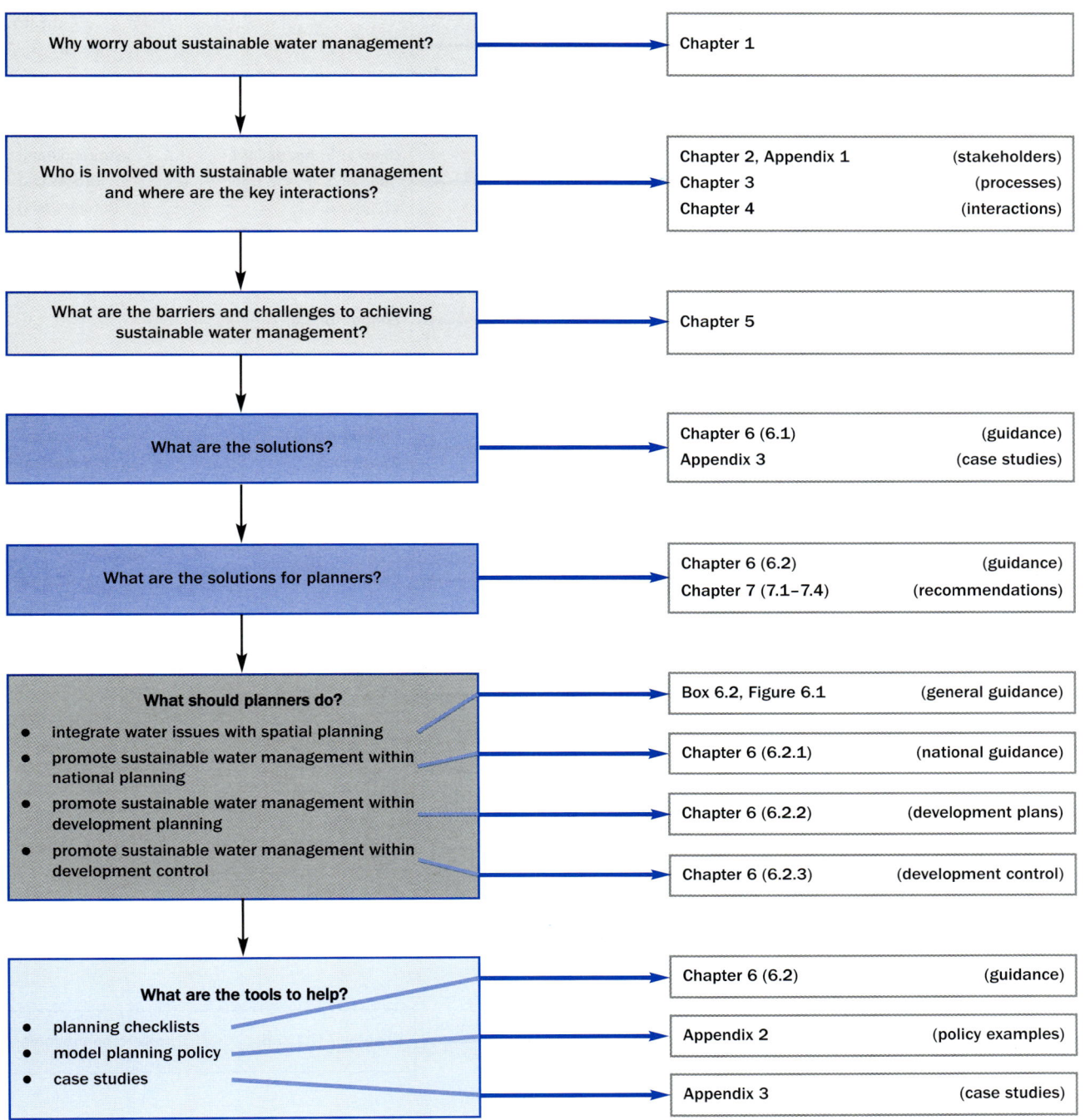

Figure 1.2   *Route map for land-use/spatial planners*

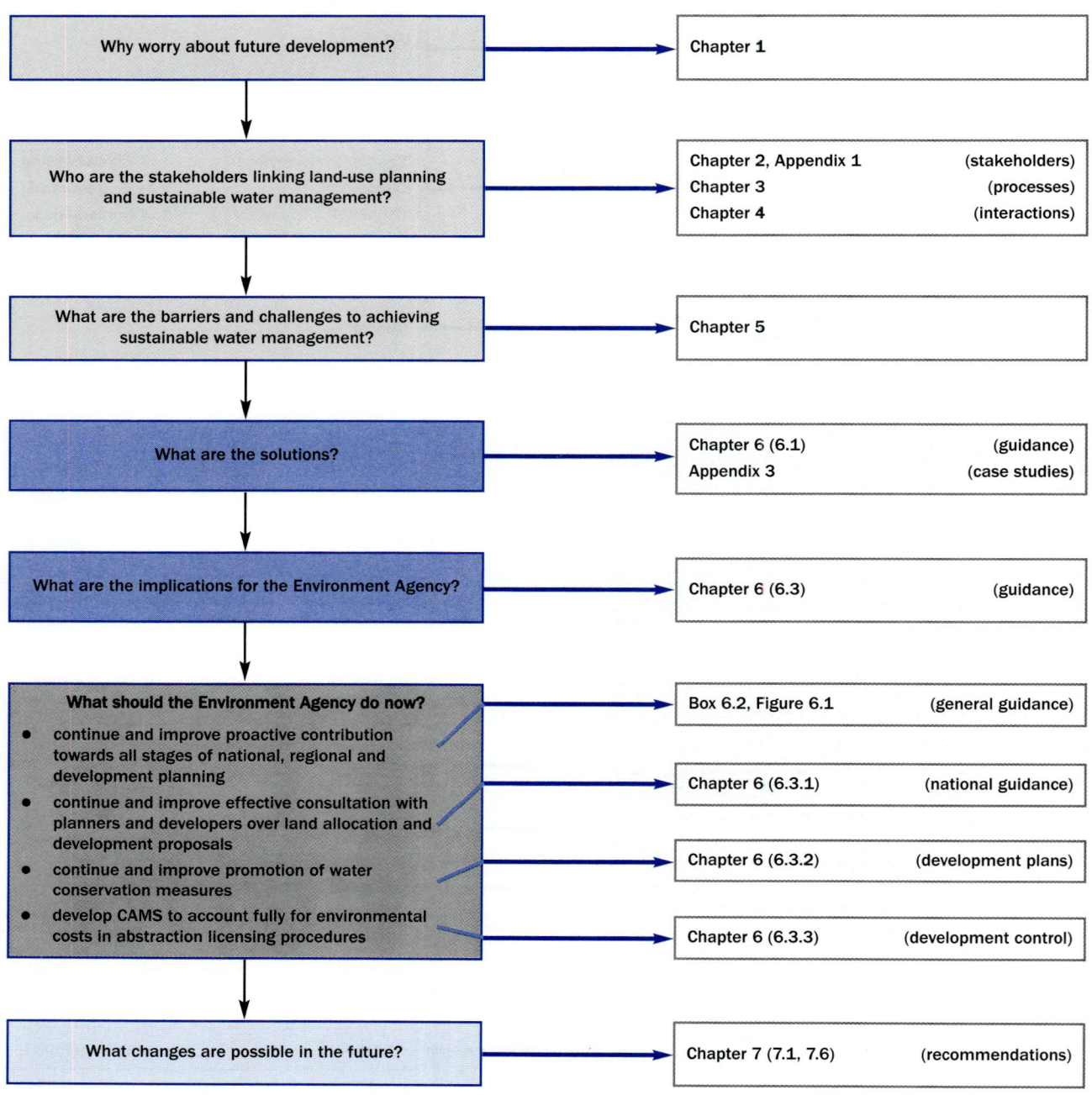

Figure 1.3   *Route map for Environment Agency staff*

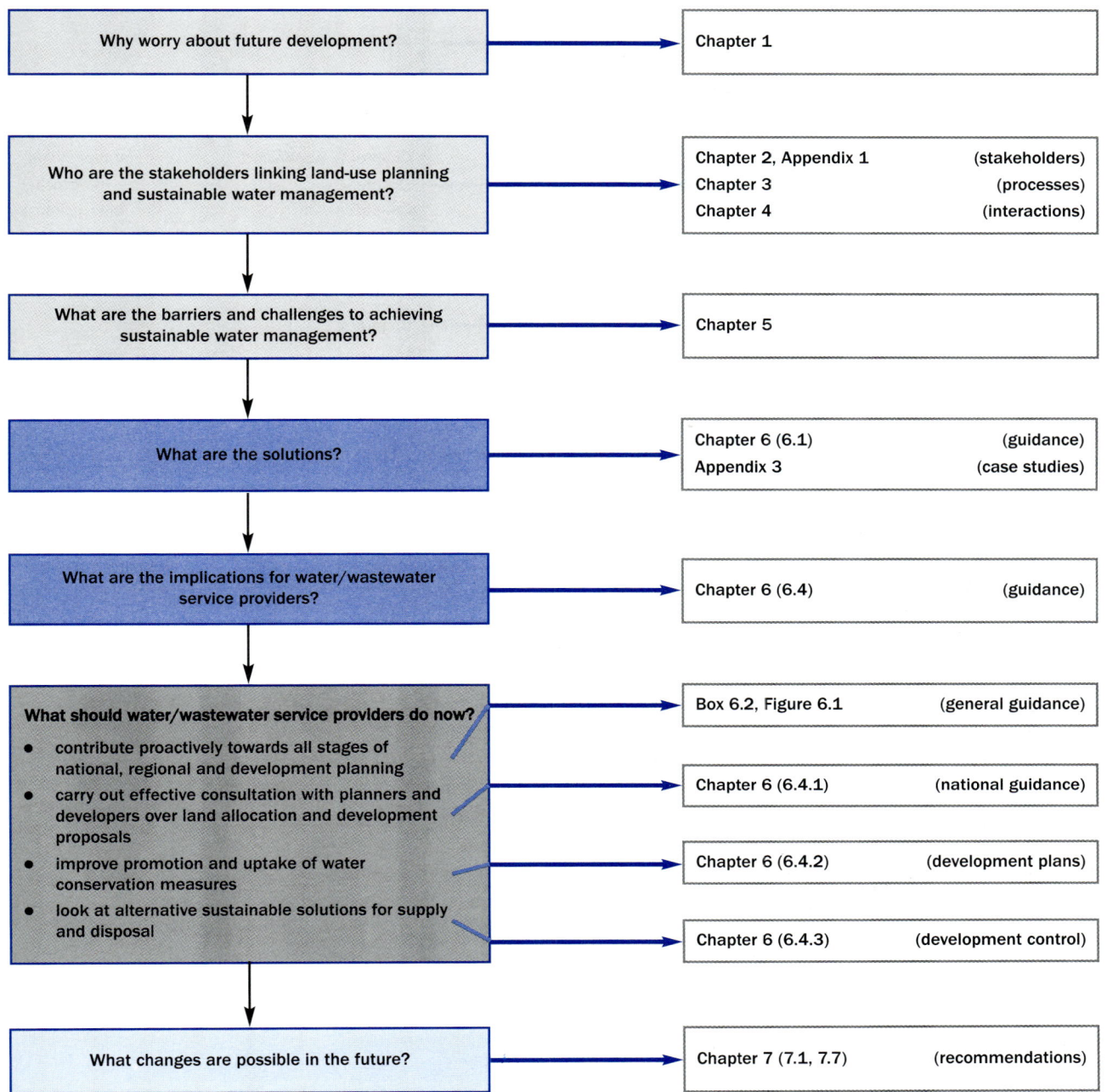

Why worry about future development?	Chapter 1
Who are the stakeholders linking land-use planning and sustainable water management?	Chapter 2, Appendix 1 (stakeholders) Chapter 3 (processes) Chapter 4 (interactions)
What are the barriers and challenges to achieving sustainable water management?	Chapter 5
What are the solutions?	Chapter 6 (6.1) (guidance) Appendix 3 (case studies)
What are the implications for water/wastewater service providers?	Chapter 6 (6.4) (guidance)
What should water/wastewater service providers do now? • contribute proactively towards all stages of national, regional and development planning • carry out effective consultation with planners and developers over land allocation and development proposals • improve promotion and uptake of water conservation measures • look at alternative sustainable solutions for supply and disposal	Box 6.2, Figure 6.1 (general guidance) Chapter 6 (6.4.1) (national guidance) Chapter 6 (6.4.2) (development plans) Chapter 6 (6.4.3) (development control)
What changes are possible in the future?	Chapter 7 (7.1, 7.7) (recommendations)

Figure 1.4   *Route map for water supply and wastewater service providers*

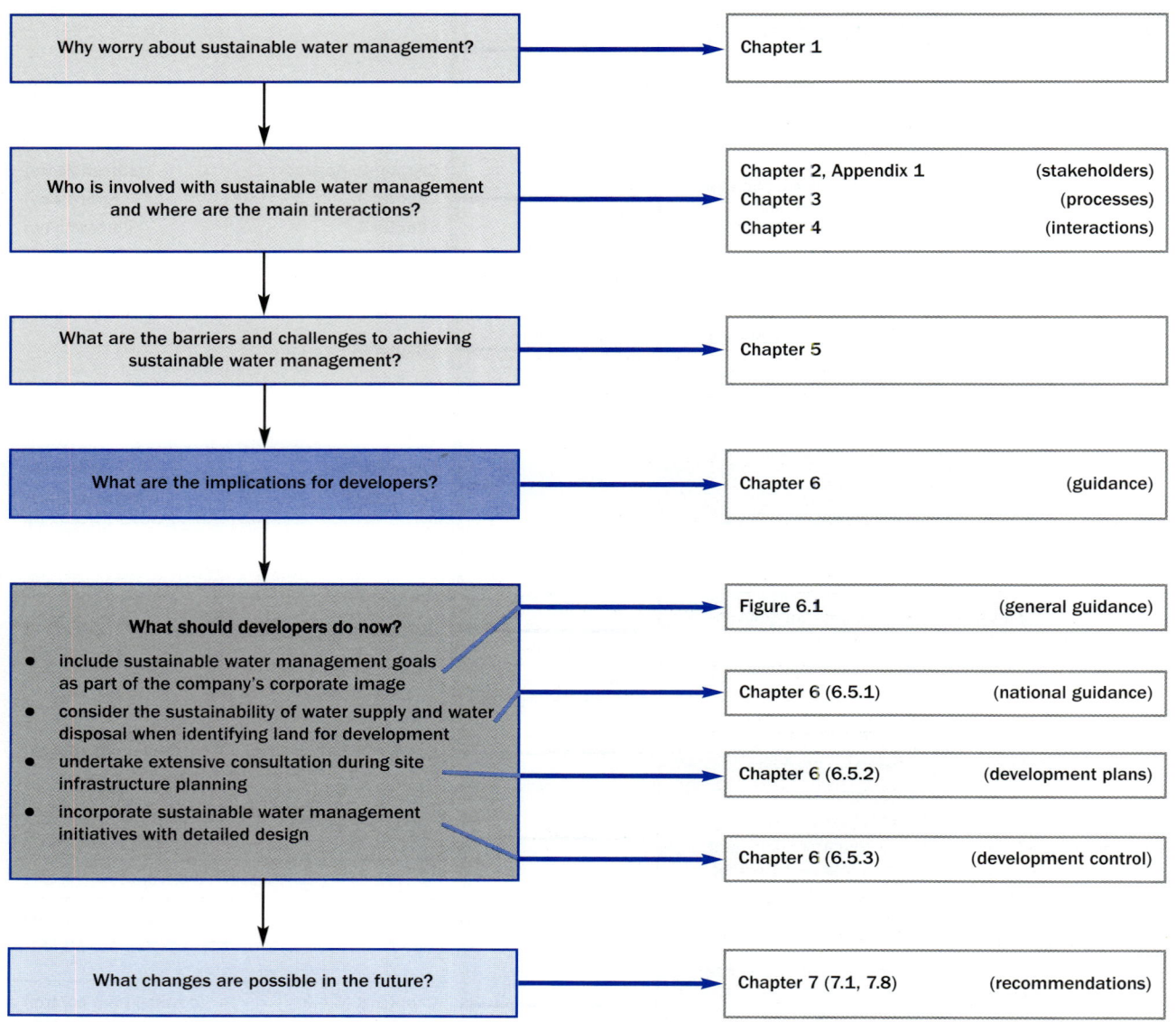

Figure 1.5 *Route map for developers*

2 Stakeholders

There are many stakeholders whose diverse interests span both sustainable water management and land use planning and development.

Table 2.1 *Organisations involved in development, planning and water management*

Organisations	Sector
Central government (Defra, ODPM, Ofwat, Welsh Assembly Government)	Public sector
Countryside Agency	
Countryside Council for Wales	
English Nature	
Environment Agency	
Highways Agency	
Internal drainage boards	
Local government (planning and drainage services)	
The London Mayor and regional assemblies	
Planning Inspectorate	
Campaign for the Protection of Rural England	Independent
Developers	
Independent consultants	
House Builders Federation	
Local wildlife trusts	
National House Building Council	
RSPB	
Water companies	
Water UK	

Tables 2.2 to 2.5 describe the public-sector and independent stakeholders with responsibilities for sustainable water management and summarise their function, structure and current level of interaction within the planning hierarchy. Tables 2.6 and 2.7 describe the stakeholders in the land-use/spatial planning process, while the interrelationship of the various tiers of government is represented in Figure 2.3. Appendix 1 provides additional information on the roles, responsibilities and interests of the principal stakeholder organisations.

Table 2.2   *Stakeholders in sustainable water management: national policy and regulation*

Organisation	Functions	Organisation structure	Authority	Interaction with planning system
Department for Environment, Food and Rural Affairs (Defra)	Policy in England and Wales, including: • drinking water quality • water quality in rivers, lakes and estuaries • groundwater • reservoir safety • flood and coastal defence • climate change • sponsorship of Environment Agency and English Nature.	Separate ministerial portfolios for: • food • environment • rural affairs. Departmental structure for specific areas of policy.	Secretary of State for Environment, Food and Rural Affairs responsible to Cabinet and Parliament. Departmental ministers with responsibilities for agriculture, flood defence etc.	Consultee on use of agricultural land. Consultee (through government offices for the regions (GOs) on regional spatial strategies (RSSs) and local development documents (LDDs).
Environment Agency (EA)	The Agency aims to protect and enhance the environment and to make a positive contribution towards sustainable developments in England and Wales. Water management functions of the Agency include: • water resources regulation and planning • water quality regulation and planning • flood defence and drainage, maintenance and operations in statutory main rivers • conservation and recreation.	Head office in Bristol that provides national guidance and policy and develops consistent processes. Eight regional offices (Figure 2.1). Teams in 26 area offices (and groups of areas where issues are common or strategic) undertake operational activity and implement national policy and process.	Powers and duties set out under the Environment Act 1995 and related legislation. Regulation and executive action on water resources, land, water and air quality, flood and coastal defence and flood warning, waste management, navigation, fisheries, conservation and recreation (see Appendix 1).	Statutory consultee on structure plans (to 2004), defined planning applications and environmental impact assessments (EIAs). Consultee on development plans (to 2004). Advises regional planning bodies (RPBs) (to 2004). Specific consultation body (SCB) for RSSs and LDFs.
Welsh Assembly Government	The remit of the Transport, Environment and Planning Group of the Welsh Assembly Government includes: • water supply, sewerage services • water industry matters • drinking and environmental water quality • sponsorship of Environment Agency in Wales • flood and coastal defence • climate change.	Elected subject committees reflecting the balance of political groups develop policies. Regional committees report on the needs and interests of their localities. The Assembly Government has around 3000 staff, working at some 30 sites throughout Wales.	Devolved authority in Wales. Responsibility for delivery of executive functions lies with Assembly ministers. Cabinet minister for the environment responsible to the elected Assembly members. Link to national government through the Secretary of State for Wales.	Consultee.

Figure 2.1 *Environment Agency regions of England and Wales, and areas managed by internal drainage boards (shaded) (Defra)*

Table 2.3 *Stakeholders in sustainable water management: drainage*

Organisation	Functions	Organisation structure	Authority	Interaction with planning system
Highways Agency (HA)	Maintains and improves the trunk road and motorway network in England, and aims to minimise its impact on natural environment.	HA manages 19 maintaining agencies under term contracts. County councils and unitary authorities have Agency powers to act on behalf of HA.	Executive agency of Department for Transport for England only. The Welsh Assembly Government is responsible for the highway network in Wales.	Statutory consultee on structure plans (to 2004). SCB on LDDs. Has powers of direction on planning applications.
Internal drainage boards (see Figure 2.1)	Drainage and flood defence for low-lying land in England and Wales. Regulation of watercourses, apart from designated main rivers.	IDB areas cover a range of sizes, each run by a board of nominated and elected members. The Association of Drainage Authorities (ADA) provides national co-ordination.	Set out in the Land Drainage Acts 1991 and 1994 covering maintenance, improvement and operation of drainage systems, conservation, revenue raising	Consultee
Local authority drainage departments	Drainage, flood alleviation and regulation of watercourses, apart from designated main rivers.	Technical services departments of some larger district and unitary authorities.	Particular responsibilities in drainage districts. Set out in the Land Drainage Act 1991.	Consultee

Table 2.4   *Stakeholders in sustainable water management: water supply and sewerage*

Organisation	Functions	Organisation structure	Authority	Interaction with planning system
Drinking Water Inspectorate (DWI)	Assesses and regulates drinking water quality in England and Wales.	Inspectorate based centrally in London.	The Secretary of State for Environment, Food and Rural Affairs and the Welsh Assembly Government have powers and duties under the Water Industry Act 1991 to regulate the quality of public drinking water supplies. Enforcement and prosecution powers are delegated to the chief inspector of the DWI.	
Office of Water Services (Ofwat)	Economic regulation of the water supply and sewerage companies in England and Wales. Ensures that customers' interests are protected.	Central office only, under the Director General of Water Services.	Established under the Water Act 1989.	Indirect. Involved in the development of national policy affecting water.
Water supply and wastewater service providers	Provide public services for wholesome water supply and wastewater disposal and treatment.	There are 30 companies in England and Wales, most of which are PLCs (see Figure 2.2). Each company operates in one or more geographic areas with its own office structure.	Authorities established under the Water Act 1989 and duties laid out in the Water Industry Act 1991 include: • to maintain an efficient public supply of wholesome water • to provide water to all persons on demand • to provide public sewerage system.	SCB for RSSs and LDDs. Consultee. Companies may interact with the planning system individually or via Water UK.

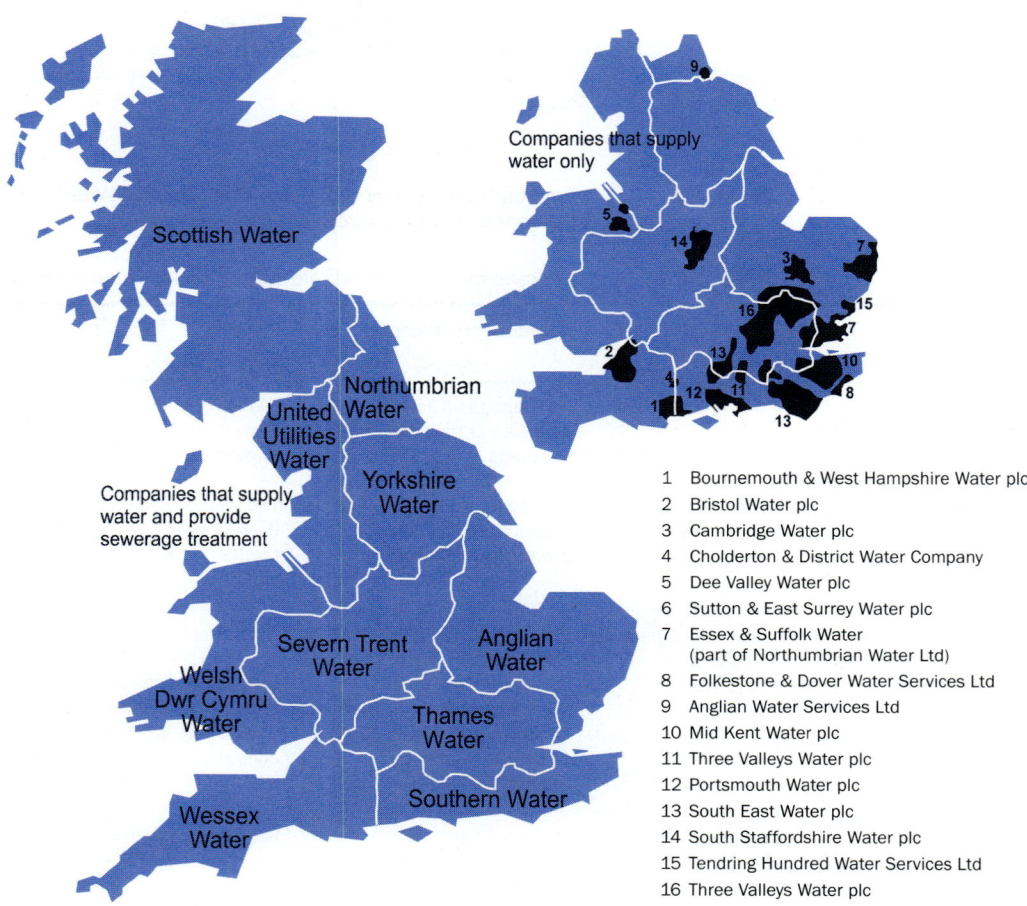

Figure 2.2   *Water supply companies and sewerage treatment operators (DoE/Defra)*

1 Bournemouth & West Hampshire Water plc
2 Bristol Water plc
3 Cambridge Water plc
4 Cholderton & District Water Company
5 Dee Valley Water plc
6 Sutton & East Surrey Water plc
7 Essex & Suffolk Water (part of Northumbrian Water Ltd)
8 Folkestone & Dover Water Services Ltd
9 Anglian Water Services Ltd
10 Mid Kent Water plc
11 Three Valleys Water plc
12 Portsmouth Water plc
13 South East Water plc
14 South Staffordshire Water plc
15 Tendring Hundred Water Services Ltd
16 Three Valleys Water plc

Table 2.5   *Stakeholders in sustainable water management: conservation*

Organisation	Functions	Organisation structure	Authority	Interaction with planning system
Campaign to Protect Rural England (CPRE)	Campaigns to protect the English countryside.	A national, regionally based, charity.	No formal powers; seeks to achieve objectives by reasoned argument and through the strict application of planning law.	Monitors local planning lists and may comment on planning applications.
Countryside Agency (CA)	CA is primarily an advisory and promotional body that aims to: • conserve and enhance the countryside • promote social equity and opportunity for countryside dwellers • research and advice • influence others. Liaises with the CCW.	Eight regions based on GOs. Defra provides financial support through grant-in-aid.	Formed by merger of the Countryside Commission and parts of the Rural Development Commission not transferred to RDAs in 1999. No formal powers under legislation.	Informal consultee on policy development. SCB for RSSs and LDDs.
Countryside Council for Wales (CCW)	Functions in Wales similar to those of EN and CA. Liaises with EN and CA.	Staff in 16 offices throughout Wales across five regions and operational field staff. CCW council members are responsible to Welsh Assembly Government for providing effective leadership, for setting its policy, and for ensuring that it meets its objectives.	Sponsored by the Welsh Assembly Government.	Informal consultee on policy development.
English Nature (EN)	English Nature's functions are to: • advise on nature conservation • designate sites, eg SSSI, NNR • license workers with protected species • support research • offer grants for conservation. Liaises with the CCW.	EN has a head office and 22 local teams whose job is to deliver nature conservation in their local area. EN also has regional-level interests through lead local teams, headed up by a regional co-ordinator for each of the eight regions and London. Development of regional policy at the national level is led from the office in Peterborough.	Established by Environmental Protection Act 1990. Sponsored by Defra. Powers under several Acts.	Statutory consultee on structure plans, consultee on others (to 2004). SCB for RSSs and LDDs. Statutory consultee for proposals on or near designated sites and for EIAs.
Local wildlife trusts	Manage nature reserves. Promote wildlife issues. Produce baseline surveys. Deliver advice to landowners. Advise on planning issues that impact management of the wider countryside. Water For Wildlife officers provide advice on water and wetland issues, including mitigation works for protected species, river restoration and wetland restoration. Many trusts run local Agenda 21 projects that raise public awareness on sustainability.	These 47 independent charities operate through a UK operations centre that co-ordinates matters of national importance.	Independent charities having defined (non-commercial) objectives. Can designate local wildlife sites.	Advisory consultees. May receive delegated role from EN on local consultations.
Royal Society for the Protection of Birds (RSPB)	Protection and conservation of birds and other wildlife. Undertakes surveys and research.	England is divided into six regions to deliver the objectives.	Independent, membership-based registered charity.	Consultee.

Table 2.6   *Stakeholders: land-use/spatial planning and development (public sector)*

Organisation	Functions	Organisation structure	Authority	Interaction with planning system
Office of the Deputy Prime Minister (ODPM)	Oversees the planning system in England; responsible for policy, research, approval of plans and major planning decisions. The ODPM issues: • planning policy guidance, • minerals planning guidance • regional planning guidance.	Central administration in London. Regional offices for English regions.	Deputy Prime Minister as First Secretary of State. Junior ministers with responsibilities for housing, local government etc. Must be notified of plans before adoption and certain planning applications.	Has powers to call in plans and applications at all levels for review and determination. Approves and issues RPG/RSS. Appoints inspectors for examinations in public (EIP)s, local plan inquiries and planning inquiries. Decision powers on appeals recovered from the inspector.
Welsh Assembly Government Transport, Planning and Environment Group	Oversees the planning system in Wales, responsible for policy development by research and casework. Reviews secondary legislation. Supervises the Planning Inspectorate in Wales. Develops the National Spatial Planning Framework.	Offices located in Cardiff and regionally in Wales. The Planning Division is part of Transport, Planning and Environment Group. The Planning Division has seven branches.	Cabinet Minister for the Environment responsible to elected Assembly members. Link to national government through the Secretary of State for Wales. Devolved authority in Wales.	Assembly Government advises on requests for intervention in the development control process. Assembly Government issues guidance to local planning authorities throughout Wales.
Regional assemblies and regional planning bodies	Prepare draft regional strategies/planning guidance.	Various regional centres (see Section 3.1.3).	Drafts approved by ODPM following EIP.	SCB for LDDs.
London Mayor London Assembly	Prepares spatial development strategy (London-wide plan). Advises the London Mayor.	Based in London. Permanent staff comprise the Greater London Authority.	Can issue direction of refusal to local authorities.	SCB for LDDs by London boroughs. Consulted on strategic planning applications.
Planning Inspectorate	The Planning Inspectorate provides independent and impartial advice on the resolution of planning issues and determines appeals and applications on behalf of the secretary of state on the use of land, natural resources and the environment.	The Planning Inspectorate is based in Bristol.	The chief inspector of planning is appointed by ODPM.	Inspectors: • determine appeals in transferred cases and report to secretary of state on "recovered" appeals and "call-ins" • hold local plan inquiries and sit on panels for EIPs.
Local authorities	Promote the economic, environmental and social well-being of their area. Develop county structure plans, local plans, unitary plans (Levels 1 and 2) (to 2004) and transitional period. Prepare and issue LDDs. Determine planning applications.	Two-tier (county and district) or unitary authorities, as determined after local consultation in 1990s. Each will have a planning department and possibly area teams. Parish and town councils.	Councils consist of elected members. Cabinet structure being introduced to modernise local administration. Councils have planning committees that consider planning issues and applications. Powers and duties in legislation including Town and Country Planning Act 1990, as amended. Parish and town councils have limited powers.	SCB for RSSs. County, district and unitary authorities are responsible for implementation of planning policy, determining planning applications. Parish and town councils are consultees. SCBs for RSSs and LDDs.

The various government bodies work within the planning systems at a variety of levels. Figure 2.3 illustrates this for the main government bodies with interests in sustainable water management issues.

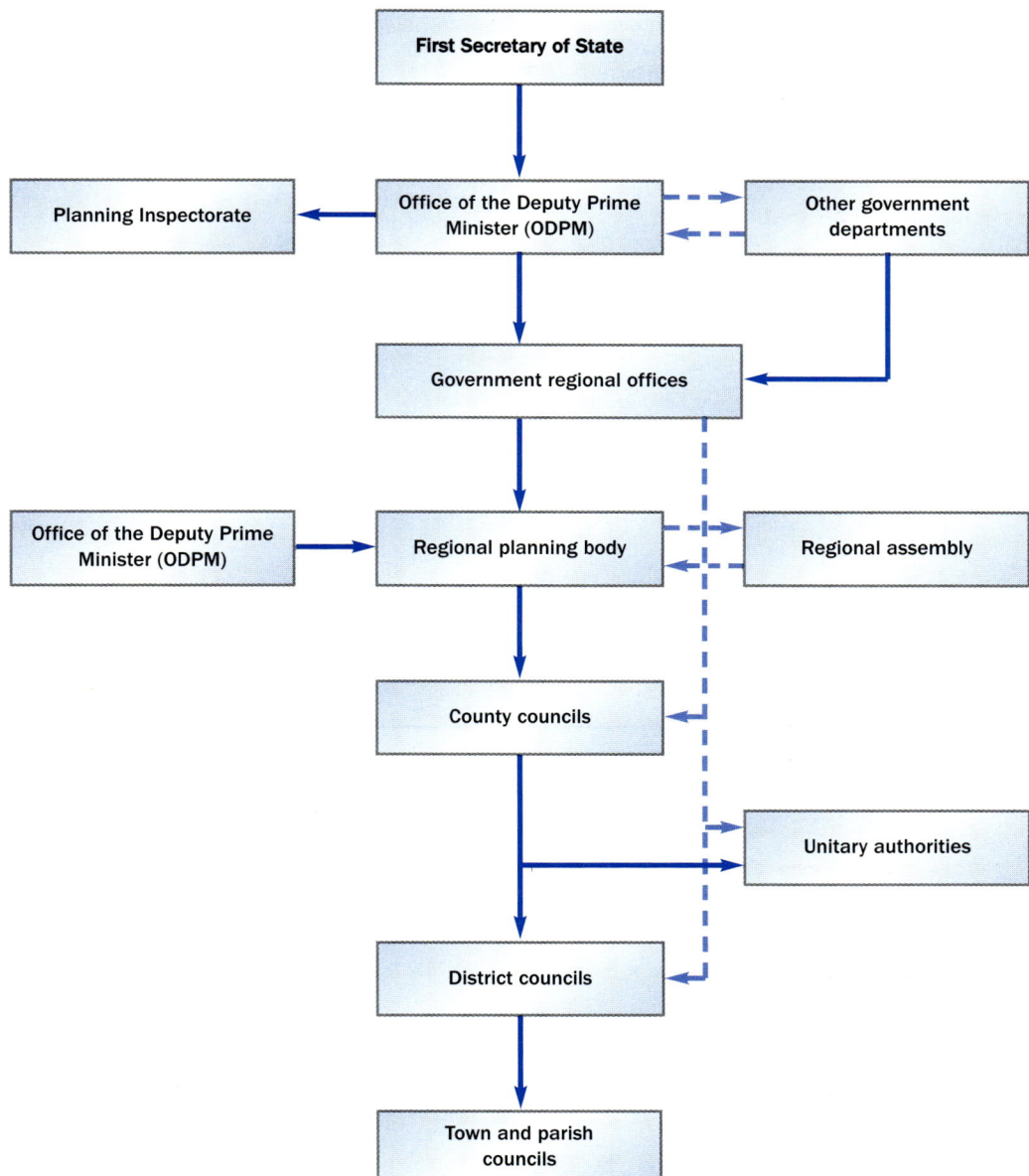

Figure 2.3   *Interaction of government organisations involved in land-use/spatial planning in England*

Table 2.7 *Stakeholders: land-use/spatial planning and development (private sector)*

Organisation	Functions	Organisation structure	Authority	Interaction with planning system
Trade associations, including the HBF and the NHBC (see below).	Trade associations represent the interests of private-sector builders and developers.	Each organisation has its own structure.	Independent organisations.	Indirect.
• **House Builders Federation (HBF)**	The HBF co-ordinates research on the implications of national planning issues for its members.	The HBF is based in London, with regional offices structured to match the GOs. Planning advisers are based in each regional office.		HBF has a committee on plan preparation and revision.
• **National House Building Council (NHBC) and similar organisations**	The NHBC advises on building control and design and is an "approved inspector" under the Building Act 1984.			NHBC is not directly involved in planning but influential on building control and design.
Developers (and their professional advisers and agents)	Deliver new housing, commercial developments etc guided by the local plan. Fund essential infrastructure under S106 TCPA 1990 agreements. Contribute to water supply and drainage infrastructure costs through commercial negotiations with the service providers.	Diverse – from single-site companies to large property companies and house-builders.	Independent organisations.	Submit planning applications. Voluntary input to structure, unitary and local plans (now RSSs and LDDs) according to local land ownership and options. Partners in preparation of planning and development briefs (now supplementary planning documents – SPDs) for major developments.

3   Planning

3.1   Land-use/spatial planning system in England and Wales

3.1.1   Introduction

Planning shapes the places where people live and work and good planning ensures that the right development occurs in the right place at the right time. It operates in the public interest through a system of plan preparation and control over the development and use of land under the Town and Country Planning Act 1990, as amended by the Planning and Compensation Act 1991 and the Planning and Compulsory Purchase Act 2004. The planning system helps to deliver homes and buildings, investments and jobs while protecting and enhancing the natural and historic environment and conserving the countryside and open spaces as a resource for all. It is designed to reconcile the benefits of development with the economic and environmental costs it can impose, while ensuring social equity. Sustainable development is the core principle underpinning planning and the overall aim is to enhance the quality of life now and for future generations.

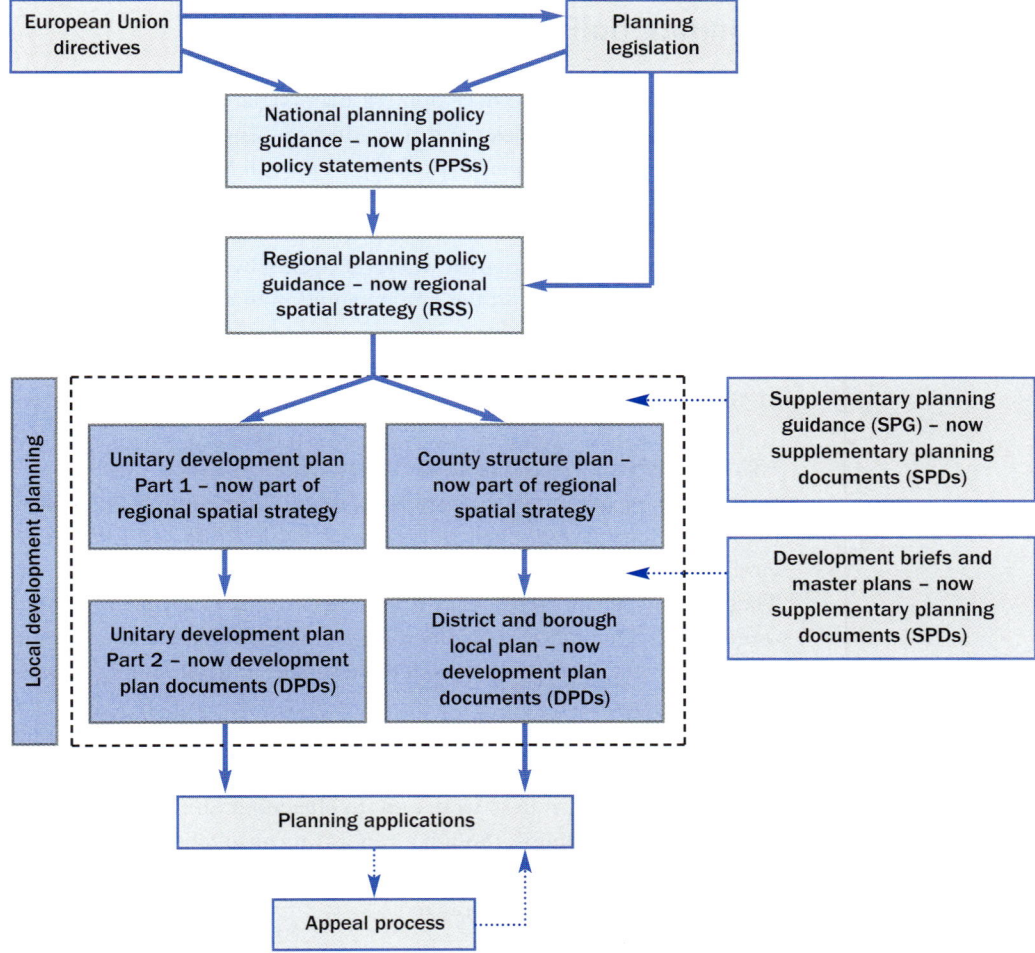

Figure 3.1   *The land-use/spatial planning process and changes resulting from the Planning and Compulsory Purchase Act 2004*

The system is plan-led, with national policies and regional and local development plans acting as the framework for sustainable development. Within that framework, decisions can be complex and often inherently political, and the framework needs to foster consistent, predictable and prompt decision-making. Figure 3.1 above illustrates the components of the planning process and the changes resulting from the Planning and Compulsory Purchase Act 2004.

The planning system comprises two main areas of activity:

● developing strategic policies and plans (development planning)

● determining individual planning applications submitted by developers, businesses and householders (development control).

These two components of planning are closely interconnected, as the decisions made by local authorities on planning applications should conform to the development plan, which now comprises the regional spatial strategy (RSS) issued by the secretary of state and development plan documents (DPDs) issued by local planning authorities (LPAs) as part of their local development framework (LDF). Development plans should conform to government plans and policies at a national level. Councillors are responsible for the adoption of plans and for decisions made on planning applications by local authorities, taking advice from officers of the council and reports from the Planning Inspectorate. The first secretary of state has powers to intervene in the preparation of DPDs, to call in departures from the development plan and to determine appeals against LPA decisions.

3.1.2   Planning policies at a national level

There is no country-wide development plan or national spatial strategy, but the Government has issued advice on policies and procedures in England as planning policy guidance notes (PPGs) and circulars. Separate provisions apply in Scotland, Wales and Northern Ireland. Existing PPGs are being reviewed and replaced by planning policy statements (PPSs), which are intended to provide more concise, clearer and better-focused statements of national planning policy – accompanied where necessary by technical annexes and good practice guides (GPGs) to advise on the implementation of those policies. Some of these policy guidance notes include water management and water sustainability issues, as shown in Table 3.1. Several mineral planning guidance notes (MPGs) and the new mineral policy statement, MPS2 (ODPM, 2005b), also contain reference to water management issues.

Policies in PPGs/PPSs and circulars are strategic guidance; they do not encompass regional or local variations (although the principles set out in them may be applied differently according to local circumstances). Their purpose is to guide RPBs and LPAs in preparing regional and local development plans and in dealing with planning applications and to guide developers. They provide a consistent policy framework within which planning and investment decisions can operate. The policies contained are not mandatory, but the Planning Inspectorate and secretary of state give them considerable weight in dealing with appeals against the refusal of planning permission.

PPGs and PPSs are subject to full public consultation, but there is no formal public forum for objections to be heard in person, and no obligation on the secretary of state to give reasons for rejecting representations, though a report on consultation responses is generally prepared before publication. Once issued, planning guidance has no fixed timescale, but remains in force until replaced or withdrawn.

Table 3.1   *National guidance covering water management and water sustainability issues*

Number	Title
C03/99	*Planning requirements in respect of the use of non-mains sewerage incorporating septic tanks in new development (DETR, 1999d)*
C02/99	*Environmental impact assessment (DETR, 1999b)*
C17/91	*Water industry investment: planning considerations (DOE, 1991)*
PPG1	*General policy and principles – withdrawn in 2005 and replaced by PPS1*
PPS1	*Delivering sustainable development (ODPM, 2005a)*
PPG3	*Housing (DETR, 2000e)*
PPS10	*Planning for sustainable water management*
PPG11	*Regional planning (DETR, 2000c) – withdrawn in 2004 and replaced by PPS11*
PPS11	*Regional spatial strategies (ODPM, 2004a)*
PPG12	*Development plans (DETR, 2000b) – withdrawn in 2004 and replaced by PPS12*
PPS12	*Local development frameworks (ODPM, 2004c)*
PPG20	*Coastal planning (DOE, 1992a)*
PPG23	*Planning and pollution control (DOE, 1994a) – replaced in 2004 by PPS23 and Annexes 1 and 2*
PPS23	*Planning and pollution control (ODPM, 2004g)*
Annex 1	*Pollution control, air and water quality (ODPM, 2004f)*
Annex 2	*Development on land affected by contamination*
PPG25	*Development and flood risk (DETR, 2001a) – under review 2005*
GPG13	*Development plans – a good practice guide (DOE, 1992c)*
GPG15	*Environmental appraisal of development plans – a good practice guide (DOE, 1993)*
GPG16	*Evaluation of environmental information for planning projects – a good practice guide (DOE, 1994b)*
GPG18	*Local development plans and unitary development plans – best practice (DOE, 1992b)*
GPG20	*Planning and development briefs – a guide to better practice (DETR, 1998b)*
GPG22	*Planning for sustainable development – towards better practice (DETR, 1998a)*
GPG23	*PPG13 – guide to better practice (DOE and DoT, 1995)*
GPG24	*Preparation of environmental statements for planning projects that require environmental assessment – a good practice guide (DOE, 1995)*
GPG25	*Sustainability appraisal of regional planning guidance – good practice guide (DETR, 2000d)*

3.1.3   Regional planning

England is divided into eight planning regions (see Figure 3.2), which in April 2001 were aligned generally with the government office (GO) boundaries. Exceptions are national parks that cross GO boundaries, which are allotted to only one GO, plus London. In each region a regional planning body (RPB) was responsible for preparing draft regional planning guidance (RPG) and for consulting the public and other interested parties. In London, the mayor is responsible for preparing a spatial development strategy. Following examination in public (EIP), an independent panel report was prepared for the secretary of state, who then issued the RPG for that region. Up to 2000, the RPB took the form of a standing conference of local authorities, but the RPB is now the regional chamber (known as the regional assembly), not to be confused with proposed elected regional assemblies. At least 60 per cent of the RPB must be representatives of those authorities that are planning authorities within the region, ie county, district and metropolitan district councils, national park authorities and the Broads Authority, and at least 30 per cent from bodies other than those authorities.

From 2004, the latest version of the RPG as issued by the secretary of state constitutes the RSS, and the RPB is responsible for drafting, consultation on and sustainability appraisal of revisions to the RSS, in whole or in part. Following consultation on draft revisions, EIP, a report by the EIP panel and consultation on proposed changes arising from the EIP, the RSS revisions will be approved and issued by the secretary of state.

In contrast to RPGs, which were strictly "planning" documents, the RSS adopts a spatial planning approach that goes wider than traditional land-use planning. It brings together and integrates policies for the development and use of land with other policies and programmes that influence the nature of places and the ways that they function. Although policies have to be related to the development and use of land, they are not restricted to policies that can be implemented by the grant or refusal of planning permission.

——— = English Regional Boundaries
G.O.L. = Government Office for London

Figure 3.2   *Government office regions*

The RSS, which incorporates a regional transport strategy, provides a broad spatial development strategy for the region, with policies and proposals for the whole of a region and for specific areas within the region, where necessary. It addresses regional or sub-regional (not local) issues and takes into account identification of the scale and distribution (by district) of the provision of new housing, priorities for the environment and issues of transport, infrastructure, economic development, agriculture, minerals extraction and waste management. The RSS, like RPGs before them, should conform to national policy set down in PPGs/PPSs, but should provide spatially specific policies applying national policies to the circumstances of the region. Where there is regional need to depart from national policies, this must be fully justified. RSS should also be consistent with and supportive of other regional frameworks and strategies, and any inconsistencies should be fully justified.

RPGs covered a timescale of 15–20 years ahead. RSSs cover a similar 15–20-year period, but recognise the need to look beyond the end of this period in certain instances because relevant forecasting horizons are longer-term. Historically, RPG has undergone a comprehensive periodic overhaul, usually at intervals of between five and 10 years. PPG11 (Paragraph 2.11 – DETR, 2000c) introduced a process of continuous, but more selective, review. This is maintained with the change from RPG to RSS (PPS11, paragraph 2.1 – ODPM, 2004a). Selective review and update of particular parts of the strategy can therefore occur in response to monitoring information or new policy imperatives. This is strengthened by the requirement for RPBs to report annually on the achievement of RSS targets, identify remedial action and trigger further revisions where appropriate. The timescale for selective review should be much shorter than that of a comprehensive review.

Regional planning must consider government objectives for sustainable development and, under PPG11 (Section 2), a sustainable development appraisal of regional planning guidance was required. The Planning and Compulsory Purchase Act 2004 requires that RSS should be subject to sustainability appraisal, incorporating the requirements of the Strategic Environmental Assessment (SEA) Directive (2001/42/EC) – transposed by the Environmental Assessment of Plans and Programmes Regulations 2004. The sustainability appraisal report must accompany the submission of draft RSS revisions to the secretary of state. The good practice guide to sustainability appraisal of RPG (DETR, 2000d) provides illustrations of objectives and targets to include in a sustainability appraisal. Water issues among them are:

- maintenance and improvement of the quality of ground, river and sea waters, with various suggested targets on quality measurements

- a suggested target to reduce the annual loss of flood storage to nil by 20xx (the date target to be set in the RPG)

- ensuring that water is used efficiently to meet needs while reducing environmental impact and resource depletion

- suggested targets to extend the use of greywater to x per cent of residential properties and y per cent of commercial property by 20xx (percentages and dates to be determined in each case)

- reduce to zero by 20xx all new development that would entail damage to river flows, new reservoir construction or significant aquifer depletion (date target to be set in each case).

The ODPM consulted in September 2004 on guidance on the sustainability appraisal of RSSs and LDFs (ODPM, 2004b).

PPG11 (Paragraph 2.34) identified the need to consider, with the Environment Agency and the water industry, the implications of different policy or spatial options for the provision of major new water resources; and in turn what their environmental effects may be in order to ensure sustainable development. For example, large new water users should be located where abstraction will not put supplies to other users or the local environment at risk. PPG11 (Paragraph 2.33) discussed the need to consider the impact of climate change in the region on its natural and human resources, using the most recent climate scenarios available from the UK Climate Impact Programme. The spatial strategy should take account of the need to avoid new development in areas that increase vulnerability and should consider possible adaptation options for vulnerable areas. Furthermore, PPG12 (Paragraph 6.20) (DETR, 2000b) stated:

> the availability of water resources will be a factor taken into account by Regional Planning Conferences in preparing proposals in RPG for the distribution of development in a region.

While these PPGs have now been superseded by the new PPS11 and PPS12 (ODPM, 2004a and c), the principles of good practice remain and they also provide the context, within which most current RSSs and development plans have been prepared. Annex A to PPS11 advises on policy and guidance on topics to be covered in an RSS; specific reference on water issues is made to the Water Environment (Water Framework Directive) (England and Wales) Regulations 2003, *Water resources for the future* (EA, 2001a) and *Directing the flow: priorities for future water policy* (Defra, 2002). The spatial planning approach now taken in RSS and the need for consistency with other regional framework strategies will strengthen the consideration of regional water strategies in the RSS. Examples of water policies in current regional planning guidance are presented in Appendix 2.

Consultation takes place both with stakeholder bodies and with the public at the project brief and draft guidance stages and PPG11 encouraged a consensus approach at these stages. Stakeholders recommended for consultation included statutory environmental bodies such as the Environment Agency and relevant commercial organisations including water utility companies, but there were no statutory consultees. The Town and Country Planning (Local Development) (England) Regulations 2004 contain a list of "specific consultation bodies" (SCBs) that the RPB must involve in preparing a draft RSS revision. This includes English Nature, the Environment Agency and water and sewerage companies. The RPB is also required to prepare, publish and keep under review a statement of public participation. A pre-submission consultation statement must accompany the submission of draft RSS revisions to the secretary of state. Consultation after submission, the EIP and consultation on proposed changes after the panel report provide further opportunity for representations on revisions to the RSS before approval and issue by the secretary of state.

3.1.4   Local development planning

Until 2004, the development plan comprised strategic structure plans prepared by county councils, sometimes in association with one or more unitary authorities, and detailed site-specific local plans, often with additional non-statutory supplementary guidance (SPG), prepared by district councils. In areas of single-tier local government (metropolitan district councils, London boroughs and unitary authorities), Parts 1 and 2 of the unitary development plan (UDP) were the equivalents of structure and local plans. County councils and single-tier authorities also had responsibility for preparing minerals and waste local plans.

The Planning and Compulsory Purchase Act 2004 abolished structure plans (and Part 1 of UDPs) and transferred the strategic planning function to the RSS with its new statutory status. County councils retain the preparation of minerals and waste DPDs. Local plans (and Part 2 of UDPs) are being replaced by local development documents (LDDs), which will comprise the local development framework (LDF), a non-statutory, informal term for the portfolio of documents that collectively delivers the spatial planning strategy for the LPA's area. Like the RSS, LDDs take a spatial planning approach that is wider than traditional land-use planning and are subject to sustainability appraisal incorporating the requirements of the SEA Directive and to annual monitoring. All LDDs must be in general, but not necessarily strict, conformity with the RSS or, in London, the spatial development strategy; variations must be individually justified.

The LDF comprises development plan documents (DPDs) that are, along with the RSS, part of the development plan and supplementary planning documents (SPDs), which expand policies contained in a DPD or provide additional detail. The LDF also includes:

- the statement of community involvement (SCI), which sets out the standards to be achieved by the local authority in involving the community in the preparation, alteration and continuing review of all LDDs and planning applications

- the local development scheme (LDS), the local authority's programme for production of LDDs, identifying those that will be DPDs, with complete time-lines for their production
- the annual monitoring report on achievement of targets and any need for change
- any local development orders and/or simplified planning zones.

DPDs include a core strategy, site-specific allocations of land, area action plans for areas where significant change or conservation is needed, and the adopted proposals map. The core strategy sets out the spatial vision and strategic objectives for the LPA's area, the spatial strategy, core policies (including criteria-based policies to establish the framework for assessing any unforeseen proposals and priorities for preparing action plans) and a monitoring and implementation framework with clear objectives for achieving delivery. All other DPDs must be in conformity with the core strategy. The adopted proposals map expresses geographically the adopted development plan policies of the LPA. It should identify areas of protection, illustrate locations and identify sites for particular land-use and development proposals included in any DPD and set out areas to which specific policies apply.

Structure and local plans (and UDPs) were subject to two- or possibly three-stage public consultation (pre-deposit, statutory first deposit and revised deposit stages) followed by EIP, for structure plans or local plan inquiry. The panel/inspector's reports were not binding on the LPA. Statutory consultees for structure plans included the Environment Agency and an advisory list of consultees. There were no statutory consultees for local plans, but there was an advisory list of consultees. All DPDs are subject to rigorous procedures of community involvement, consultation and independent examination, and adopted after receipt of the inspector's binding report. The Town and Country Planning (Local Development) (England) Regulations 2004 list SCBs that must be consulted. These include the RPB, the Environment Agency, English Nature and water and sewerage undertakers operating in the LPA area (see Annex E of PPS12). While not subject to independent examination, SPDs are subject to minimum requirements for consultation.

Adopted structure and local plans, and UDPs will retain their development plan status and automatically become "saved" policies for a three-year transitional period from commencement of the Act or the date of adoption, whichever is the later. Structure plan policies will be saved for three years unless revisions of the RSS published by the secretary of state replace them in whole or in part and/or the secretary of state directs extension of the three-year period. LPAs are expected to bring forward LDDs to replace saved local plan policies in accordance with their LDS. For plans in preparation, work on proposals that have not reached first deposit stage will cease. Where the statutory notice of deposit of a structure plan, local plan or UDP has been published, the proposals will continue through to adoption, though structure plan authorities may decide, in consultation with the RPB, to redeploy the appropriate expertise on sub-regional elements of the RSS and withdraw the structure plan.

Old-style development plans were required to include policies for the conservation of natural beauty, the improvement of the environment, and traffic management; also they were required to have regard for the economic, environmental and social well-being of the community. There were no equivalent requirements relating to water management or any associated issues. However, PPG12 urged local authorities to implement the land use aspects of sustainable development, and to "take environmental considerations comprehensively and consistently into account". Relevant environmental considerations identified in PPG12 (Paragraphs 4.4 and 4.5) included the following water issues:

- policies for coastal protection, flood defence and land drainage
- the need to protect groundwater resources from contamination or over-exploitation
- the need to evaluate water resource availability in determining location of new development.

Section 6 of PPG12 (Paragraphs 6.18 to 6.21) discussed the implications of development plans on utilities infrastructure. Specific issues identified were:

- the need for utilities to consider implications outside the area bounded by the plan
- the wider environmental effects on increased demand for water resources and emissions to water and that these may affect other authorities' areas
- the possible need for additional water supply and sewerage infrastructure such as reservoirs, pipelines or treatment works
- implications for the environment from land used for the additional infrastructure and the consequences of additional abstraction and discharges
- the availability of water resources between or even within districts may be a factor in determining the location of development within districts
- the adequacy of existing infrastructure may well influence the timing of development; this may particularly be the case if new water resources need to be developed
- the need for early consultation with the water companies and the Environment Agency.

Annex B to PPS12 confirms these issues and adds the importance of climate change in relation to, among other things, pressure on water resources and the risk of inland and coastal flooding. Guidance can be found in *Planning and climate change – a guide to better practice* (ODPM, 2004d). The adoption of a spatial planning approach, sustainability appraisal and the need for general conformity with the RSS and proper regard to other relevant plans, policies and strategies will strengthen the consideration of water management issues in LDFs.

Examples of existing structure plans that incorporate coverage of water issues include:

1   The Hampshire Structure Plan (adopted 2000) has policies against development that would lead to the deterioration in the quality of groundwater or surface water, and to prevent development in flood risk areas.

2   The Essex Structure Plan (adopted 2001) seeks to locate development where water supply is adequate, where it would cause no threat to existing water resources and where water resources can be provided within the plan period at an acceptable environmental cost.

3   The Hertfordshire Structure Plan Review (deposit draft 2003) requires development to take full account of the need to protect, and where appropriate enhance, water resources and the activities and ecology that depend upon them.

4   The Oxfordshire Structure Plan Review (deposit draft 2003) aims to restrict development to loctions where adequate water resources already exist or can be provided without harm; it also includes a specific policy for any new reservoir proposals.

Water issues are included in many local plans at various levels of detail and have strengthened since the implementation of the latest revision of PPG12. Examples include:

1   South Bedfordshire Local Plan Review (adopted 2004) contains policies to prevent development that would need to abstract water from surface or groundwater where such abstraction poses an unacceptable threat to the quality of these existing sources.

2   Rother District Council Local Plan (revised deposit draft 2003) seeks to refuse permission for development unless the infrastructure and services required to service the development are available or will be provided.

3   South Cambridgeshire Local Plan (adopted 2004) aims to protect watercourses and other water supplies from contamination due to development in areas without mains sewerage.

4   Welwyn Hatfield Local Plan (revised deposit draft 2002) includes a requirement for new development to incorporate water conservation measures, rainwater-recovery systems, and permeable surfaces to reduce runoff.

All of the plans above contain some form of policy against development in floodplains or other areas of flood risk. Most adopted local plans, and draft plans that are more than two to three years old, contain much less policy content dealing with water-related topics. Nevertheless, as with structure plans, there is still little explanation in any of these local plans as to how water issues have actually influenced the development proposals and land allocations within the plan itself. It is important to note that the coverage of water issues will vary according to local circumstance, so the examples above may not be transferable to other areas. In addition, the incorporation of water issues into such plans is developing and may be subject to review to ensure that they are both appropriate and effective. Further examples of water policies within current structure and local plans are presented in Appendix 2.

3.1.5   Planning applications and the development control system

All development, as defined in the Town and Country Planning Act 1990, is subject to the grant of planning permission on application to the LPA. However, agricultural land-use changes – such as improvement of pasture or change from pasture to arable – that may have water management implications are not classified as development under the Act. In addition, certain developments, including development for agricultural purposes, such as land drainage, agricultural reservoirs and irrigation water abstraction boreholes, and some developments by water and sewerage undertakers has deemed planning permission under the Town and Country Planning (General Permitted Development) Order 1995. Permitted development rights may be removed and an application for planning permission be required by a direction from the LPA where it considers that their imminent implementation is likely to cause harm. The wider spatial planning approach and the required sustainability appraisal of RSSs and LDFs may highlight the significance of some permitted development in relation to sustainable water management. It may, therefore, strengthen the arm of LPAs in requiring specific applications for these developments in some circumstances.

District councils deal with most planning applications, except for those types of major application, including minerals and waste disposal, that are classed as county matters. Certain bodies are defined as statutory consultees, which must be consulted on relevant types of planning applications and normally have 21 days within which to make their comments. The Environment Agency is a statutory consultee for some applications, defined in the Town and Country Planning (General Development Procedure) Order 1995, and for all applications subject to EIA and an informal consultee on many others. Water and sewerage undertakers are not statutory consultees, but they are often consulted informally. LPAs must consider all material considerations when determining applications, and the various guidance documents indicate the significance of such considerations, including those related to sustainable water management, in national policy terms. LPAs may grant permission subject to such conditions as they think fit, provided they are relevant, precise, enforceable, related to planning and reasonable in all other ways.

Under the plan-led system, where the development plan (RSS and DPDs) contains relevant policies, applications for planning permission should be determined in accordance with the development plan for the area unless "other material considerations" indicate otherwise. SPDs do not form part of the development plan but they are material considerations. If the planning authority wishes to grant planning permission for any development that departs from the development plan, it must show clear reasons for doing so and notify the secretary of state of its intention. In London, the mayor must also be consulted. The secretary of state may then, at his/her own discretion, decide to call in the planning application for his/her own determination, usually following a public inquiry.

Where the local planning authority refuses planning permission, or there is non-determination within eight weeks, the applicant may appeal to the secretary of state, either by written representations, or by requesting a hearing or a public inquiry. The applicant may also appeal against any conditions attached to a planning permission. The appeal is determined by an inspector appointed to act on behalf of the secretary of state unless it is recovered for policy reasons for determination by the secretary of state.

3.1.6 Environmental impact assessment

Planning applications for certain types of major development projects fall within the scope of the Town and Country Planning (Environmental Impact Assessment) (England and Wales) Regulations 1999, which transpose the European Directive on Assessment of Environmental Effects (85/337/EEC, as amended by 97/11/EC). They require an environmental impact assessment (EIA) and the applications must be accompanied by an environmental statement (ES). Guidance on the EIA process is contained in Circular 02/99 and in good practice guidance (DETR, 1998a). The definition of the types of development that fall within the Regulations is complex, and often may have to be determined with expert legal or other specialist opinions. If the proposed development is of a type that comes within the Regulations, various factors have to be considered by the LPA in deciding whether an EIA is required in each case. These include the characteristics of:

- the development, including its use of natural resources, the production of waste, pollution and nuisances, and the risk of accidents
- the location, including particular regard for certain types such as wetlands, coastal zones and other environmentally sensitive areas
- the potential impacts.

Should there be disagreement about the need for an EIA, an applicant may request a screening direction from the secretary of state.

The list of matters on which information required to be covered in an ES includes (among other things) soil, water, air, climate, flora and fauna, the inter-relationships between these, and any proposed mitigation measures. The LPA may issue a scoping opinion to guide the developer on the information that should be included within the ES. The overall aim of the ES should be to provide as systematic and objective account as possible of the significant environmental effects to which the project is likely to give rise. The ES should include a non-technical summary alongside sufficient information to enable those who wish to verify its conclusions and identify sources of information if they wish to do so.

The DETR guidance also highlights the need for fuller and earlier consultation by the developer with bodies that have an interest in the likely environmental effects of the development proposal. In particular, it notes that if important issues are not considered at a very early stage, they may well emerge when a project's design is well advanced, necessitating rethinking and causing delay. Ideally, the EIA should start at the stage of site selection and (where relevant) process selection, so that the environmental merits of practicable alternatives can be properly considered. The implementation of the SEA Directive (2001/42/EC) and the incorporation of its requirements in the sustainability appraisal of RSSs and LDDs increase the likelihood of the environmental impact of particular developments being considered earlier in the planning and development process.

When the LPA rules that an EIA is required, the relevant statutory consultees (which include English Nature and the Environment Agency) will be notified and the developer informed accordingly. This places an obligation on the consultees to provide any relevant information in their possession on request from the developer. On receipt of the environmental statement the LPA must consult the Agency and other statutory consultees for the relevant planning application. Other consultations may be undertaken at the council's discretion. It is not just the development itself that may require an EIA; any associated water management projects needed as a result of the proposals (eg water transfer infrastructure, wastewater treatment works, additional boreholes) will also be subject to environmental assessment. EIAs may also be required under other legislation, such as the Environmental Impact Assessment (Land Drainage Improvement Works) Regulations 1999 or the Water Resources (Environmental Impact Assessment) (England and Wales) Regulations 2003.

Issues relevant to water sustainability that may need to be covered in the environmental statement include:

- purpose and physical characteristics of the project
- land-use requirements and other physical features of the project: during construction, when operational and after use has ceased (where appropriate)
- type and quantities of raw materials, energy and other resources consumed by any production processes and operational features of the project
- discharges to water arising from any production processes and operational features of the project
- main alternative sites and processes considered, where appropriate, and reasons for the final choice
- information on the physical characteristics of the site and its environment, eg flora and fauna and their habitats, aquifers, watercourses, shoreline, including the type, quantity, composition and strength of any existing discharges
- information on the policy framework associated with the site, eg statutory national or international designations such as national parks and Ramsar sites
- assessment of effects including those on the drainage of the area, changes to hydrographic characteristics, such as groundwater and watercourses, coastal or estuarine hydrology and water quality
- assessment of the effects arising from the consumption of materials, including water
- assessment of the effects on other developments associated with the project, eg sewers
- where significant adverse effects are identified, a description of the measures to be taken to remedy these effects and the likely effectiveness of these measures.

In addition to the above, the environmental effects of a development during its construction and commissioning phases should be considered separately from the effects arising while it is operational. Where the operational life of a development is expected to be limited, the effects of decommissioning or reinstating the land should also be considered separately.

3.2 Water resource planning

The Environment Agency is responsible for ensuring the proper use of water resources in England and Wales. As part of this process, water service providers are required to plan their likely water resource availability and water demand under various climatic scenarios and to manage their water supplies to secure levels of service, particularly in a dry year and at peak demand. The development of water resources plans is an iterative process between the Agency and water supply companies designed to manage water resources to protect the long-term future of the environment while encouraging sustainable development. As part of this process the Agency has produced *Water resources for the future* (Environment Agency, 2001a), a long-term strategy for water resources that looks 25 years ahead and considers the needs of both the environment and society. The Agency also provides a range of information (accessible via the Agency website) including:

- monthly reports on the water resources situation for England and Wales
- annual reviews of water company resource plans, based on submissions from all of the water companies in England and Wales
- water company drought plans (setting out in advance the short-term operational steps that should be taken to manage the consequences of drought)
- water resource planning guidelines
- information on saving water and demand management
- catchment abstraction management strategies (CAMS).

3.2.1 Components of demand

Water demand is the sum of all potential uses of water resources within a given area. There are many different demands on water resource systems, including:

- public supply for domestic, commercial, agricultural and industrial use (including leakage)
- the needs of fisheries, forestry, recreation, navigation and hydropower
- the needs of the environment.

In terms of water provision, Figure 3.3 provides an overview of the component parts of public water supply. It should be noted that the values for each component of demand are presented on a general basis and these are likely to vary in specific areas, for example, distribution losses are much higher in some parts of London than elsewhere in England and Wales.

During years that are drier than average, there may be difficulties in meeting demand in some parts of the country because of:

- the uneven distribution of water resources in England and Wales
- under extreme conditions, the yields available from existing sources supplying particular areas failing to match patterns of demand
- the uncertainty of predictions of where, when or for how long a drought may occur
- the potential impacts of climate change
- a forecast (albeit uncertain) increase in total demand.

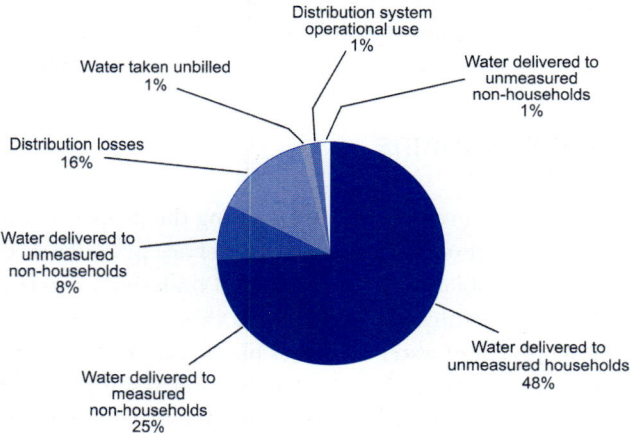

Figure 3.3 *Components of public water supply by volume (Ofwat)*

During hot, dry weather, demand for water may increase, in which case water companies have to match their declining stocks of water with the potentially rising demands of their customers. Although water companies have arrangements in place to collect, store and transfer water to cope with normal fluctuations in rainfall, in a drought these arrangements may not be enough to ensure full supplies for an indefinite period. A shortage of rainfall over a period may mean that water in storage or water available for abstraction from rivers or the ground is less than desirable. To manage the potential impacts of these events, water companies have developed drought management plans, which have been reviewed by the Environment Agency. These set out the actions a water company should take to manage the situation and ensure security of public water supply, and include steps designed to manage demand. The latter may include intensive promotion of water efficieciency and hosepipe bans. In reviewing the plans, the Agency considers potential impacts, identifies potential mitigation measures, and identifies any further actions required to improve the plans. The Agency has developed drought management plans for those hydrological systems for which it has operational responsibilities.

Regional variation in the forecasts of important macro-environmental factors such as population growth and climate change suggest that demand will rise at differing rates. The highest growth being predicted is for those areas that are already water-stressed, which may make drought management more difficult. To further assist in the management of these issues the Environment Agency (2001a) has also developed its 25-year strategy for the management of water resources.

All new houses in England are metered, with customers paying for their water and sewerage services based on the volume supplied. The key drivers of household demand are property type and occupancy. Therefore, the accurate prediction of demand within a new development will need to consider the split of flats, terraced, semi-detached and detached properties along with predicted occupancies. The amount of water an individual uses is dependent on such factors as the water fittings and appliances in the home, personal behaviour and the climate.

3.2.2 Water demand stakeholders, legislation and controls

Water supply companies need to estimate current and future water demand and develop water resource plans to ensure a strategy for secure, efficient and sustainable service provision. These plans are submitted to the Environment Agency for assessment and are also considered as part of water companies' strategic business plans by Ofwat. The companies have a statutory duty to manage leakage and to promote the efficient use of water, and many of their initiatives can be found in detail on their company websites. Each company provides water efficiency proposals as part of its five-year business plan and the regulator monitors annually the implementation of the proposed measures. Ofwat requires water companies to provide information on water savings and reductions in consumption and progress reports on implementing water efficiency initiatives, such as the use of cistern devices, self-audits and educational programmes. Ofwat seeks to ensure that companies' water efficiency plans are developed as part of an integrated least-cost plan (alongside reducing leakage or developing new resources) to meet demand.

The Environment Agency has a statutory duty to conserve, redistribute and augment water resources, and to secure their proper use. It works with the water companies and others to manage demand in domestic and commercial properties. The Agency will grant permission for new or additional abstractions only where water companies have reduced leakage to its economic level and implemented cost-effective demand-management measures. The Agency has policies to encourage the efficient use of water, and promotes measures to reduce water use and use water wisely. The National Water Demand Management Centre (now the Water

Demand Management Team within the Agency's Water Resources Function) was established in 1993 to help achieve sustainable water use; the team's aim is "to provide a focus for information and expertise to ensure acceptance of water conservation throughout society". As a centre of expertise it provides a "one-stop shop" for anyone wanting general information and technical advice on any aspect of water demand management and water conservation. Further information is given in Appendix 1.

Broad-scale planning decisions will strongly influence future demand levels across the country through the distribution of new development and housing, regionally and locally. Within England and Wales, the conservation of water supplied and its protection from contamination are regulated in general by the Water Supply (Water Fittings) Regulations 1999, which it is the statutory duty of the water companies to enforce under the Water Industries Act 1991. Formal Defra guidance on the Regulations is available from the Defra website and is incorporated, together with further information, into the Water Regulations Advisory Scheme's *Water regulations guide* (WRAS, 2000). In addition, guidance published by DETR (1999c) also provides details of the design and installation of water fittings and the performance specifications for materials and fittings. *The water fittings and materials directory* is produced twice a year by the WRAS as a reference directory for approved fittings materials and appliances. The Government announced plans to raise national standards for water conservation, seeking to reduce consumption in new developments by 20 per cent or more by 2005. This is likely to be achieved by extending the coverage of the Building Regulations 2000 to promote water efficiency and through the development of a Code for Sustainable Buildings, which will set higher aspirational standards than the minimum requirement that is set in regulations.

Developers may be able to reduce levels of demand arising from a new development by appropriate choice of water fittings and appliances within buildings even though they may not be covered by regulation. For example, installing rainwater harvesting devices as well as dual-flush toilets, low-flow showers and taps that exceed the requirements of the Water Supply (Water Fittings) Regulations 1999 and rainwater harvesting devices may help to reduce water consumption in any domestic or industrial property, but may incur additional costs and maintenance requirements and enhancements to the drainage specification. It is important to note that their effectiveness is dependent on user behaviour, which, if unsuitable, could reduce or negate potential savings. This may be less of an issue in certain types of development, for example public or industrial buildings where responsibility and maintenance procedures can be clearly set out.

Local authorities may have a useful role to play in demand management (which could increase in the future if the coverage of water fittings within the Building Regulations is strengthened). In particular they could foster a culture of innovation by increasing awareness of water sustainability issues (including demand management) among developers. Although it would not be appropriate to include water demand management techniques that go beyond the Water Supply (Water Fittings) Regulations 1999 as a planning condition, the developer could consider them as mitigation options in environmental statements if they were more aware of them and had easy access to independent, practical guidance on their installation and use. However, the LA would need to take into account whether any such savings can be guaranteed to be permanently applied (or applied for the time required to develop additional resources) and considered reasonable. As the first point of contact with developers, LAs could also help this process by making developers aware of information sources such as the Environment Agency's Savewater web pages within <www.environment-agency.gov.uk> (EA, 2002a) and CIRIA's publications, eg *Rainwater and greywater use in buildings. Best practice guidance* (Leggett *et al*, 2001).

3.2.3   Water supply

A plentiful supply of water is usually taken for granted in England and Wales, although water availability per person is actually low by international standards. However, direct costs of water to the user are relatively low. Charges for abstractions from surface and groundwater systems are calculated on an annual authorised volume of water (rather than a fixed charge for each unit of the actual quantity taken) and are based on the costs incurred by the Environment Agency in managing these resources. In some cases this cost may be as low as 0.5–1 penny per cubic metre of water, depending on location, the time of year and the use to which it is put. Consumers of tap water supplies pay more to cover the costs of the supply company, which include the costs of treating and transporting the water.

It is feasible for water companies to supply water anywhere in England and Wales. However, in many locations new supplies may be prohibitively expensive, require the transport of water over long distances, be politically sensitive or have adverse environmental impacts that cannot be mitigated. To maintain supplies of water, the water companies must balance future demand against the available resource. The key to water resources planning is the management of the water available. If supply is greater than demand, there should be no need to develop new sources of water. If supply is less than demand, now or in the future, a solution will be needed. This could include the development of new resources, additional leakage control and wider use of water-efficient fittings. These solutions will need to enable adequate drought management planning (see Section 2.3.1) and take into account the potential impacts of climate change on future resource availability, while also balancing uncertainties associated with future demands and future infrastructure investment requirements.

To ensure that water demand is met in a sustainable manner, the water companies follow a "twin-track" approach. This involves encouraging the efficient use of water while implementing timely proposals for sustainable resource development as appropriate. Water companies deal with uncertainty through applying "headroom" (an additional allowance) to their long-term water resources plans, assuming that the uncertainty (and subsequently headroom) will increase through the planning period. Short-term uncertainty over security of supply during extreme dry weather events is then managed through drought contingency planning.

This strategic planning is undertaken by water companies in close consultation with the regulators and in response to regulatory requirements. As part of the five-year periodic review of company performance, each water company must submit to Ofwat its business plan, which includes a supply-demand balance (SDB) projection (Figure 3.4) within its water resources plan (WRP). These have a 25-year horizon, are submitted to the Environment Agency every five years and are reviewed annually. Additionally, both the SDB and WRP provide base information for the company's submission on the economic level of leakage (ELL) as required by Ofwat on a five-yearly basis in line with Ofwat price reviews.

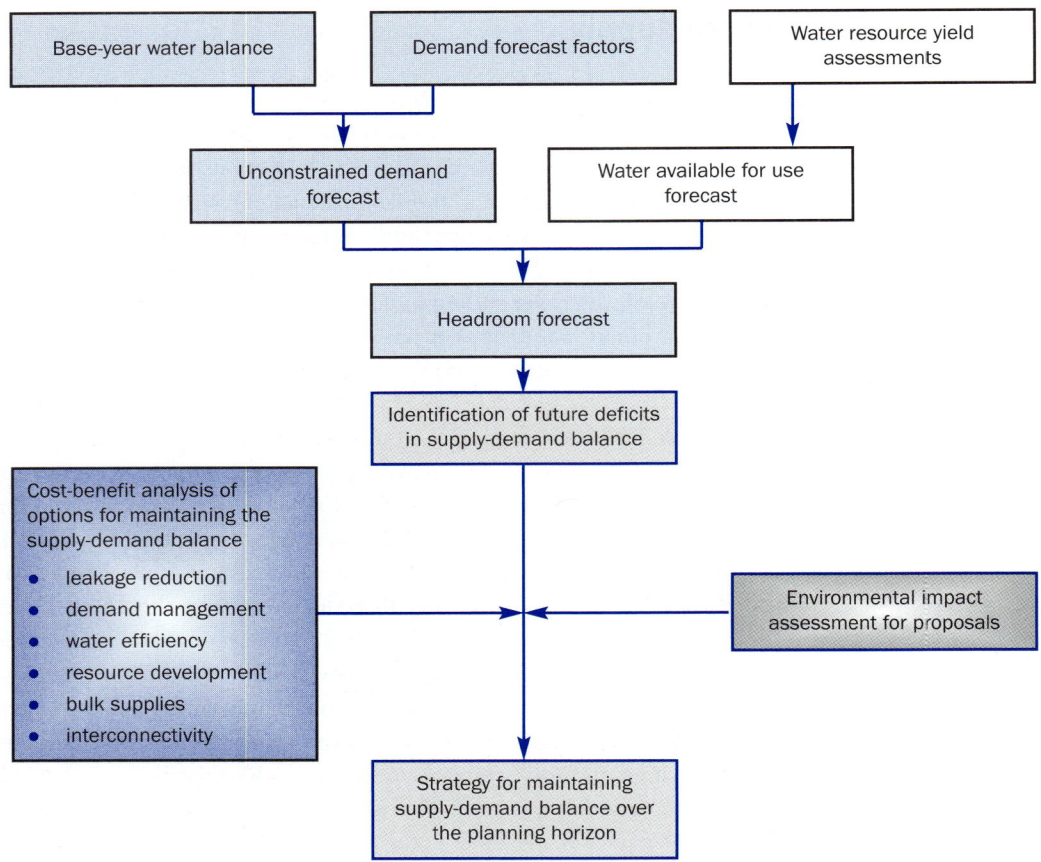

Figure 3.4   *Water company planning to meet supply-demand balance*

Companies base their WRPs on discrete water resource zones. These are geographical areas containing customers that can be supplied from a single source or a group of sources. In each zone, the plan will consider the present and future yield of existing sources, particularly with reference to the Agency's overall strategy for environmental sustainability. If the predicted headroom is going to be unacceptably low in the future, the WRP proposes options for the development of additional resources. In undertaking its duty to manage water resources, the Agency determines whether applications for new resources are reasonable and whether abstractions are environmentally acceptable.

Much of the existing pattern of abstraction is historical, reflecting the needs of users over the last 30 years. Under present abstraction licensing arrangements and legislation, further allocation of resources within a given catchment is by the Environment Agency, which must have "particular regard" to abstractions for the needs of public water supply. Any abstractor with a legitimate need for water can have an allocation, provided that there is water available in the catchment. The availability of water is determined by both the environmental needs of the catchment and the legal requirement to protect the abstraction rights of other water users. If there is no water available, a potential new abstractor will be refused a licence, even if the need for water appears pressing.

In the paper *Taking water responsibly* (DETR and WO, 1999) the Government outlined its decisions on changes to the abstraction licensing system. Foremost was the proposal for the development of catchment abstraction management strategies (CAMS).

The objectives for CAMS are:

- to publish information on water resources availability and licensing within a catchment

- to provide a consistent and structured approach to local water resources management, recognising both abstractors' reasonable needs for water and environmental needs

- to provide the opportunity for greater public involvement in the process of managing abstraction at a catchment level

- to provide a framework for managing time-limited licences

- to facilitate licence trading.

For the resource assessment within CAMS, the catchment areas are divided into water resource management units (WRMUs), which define the largest subdivision of the catchment that can be managed in the same way. These are shown in Figure 3.5.

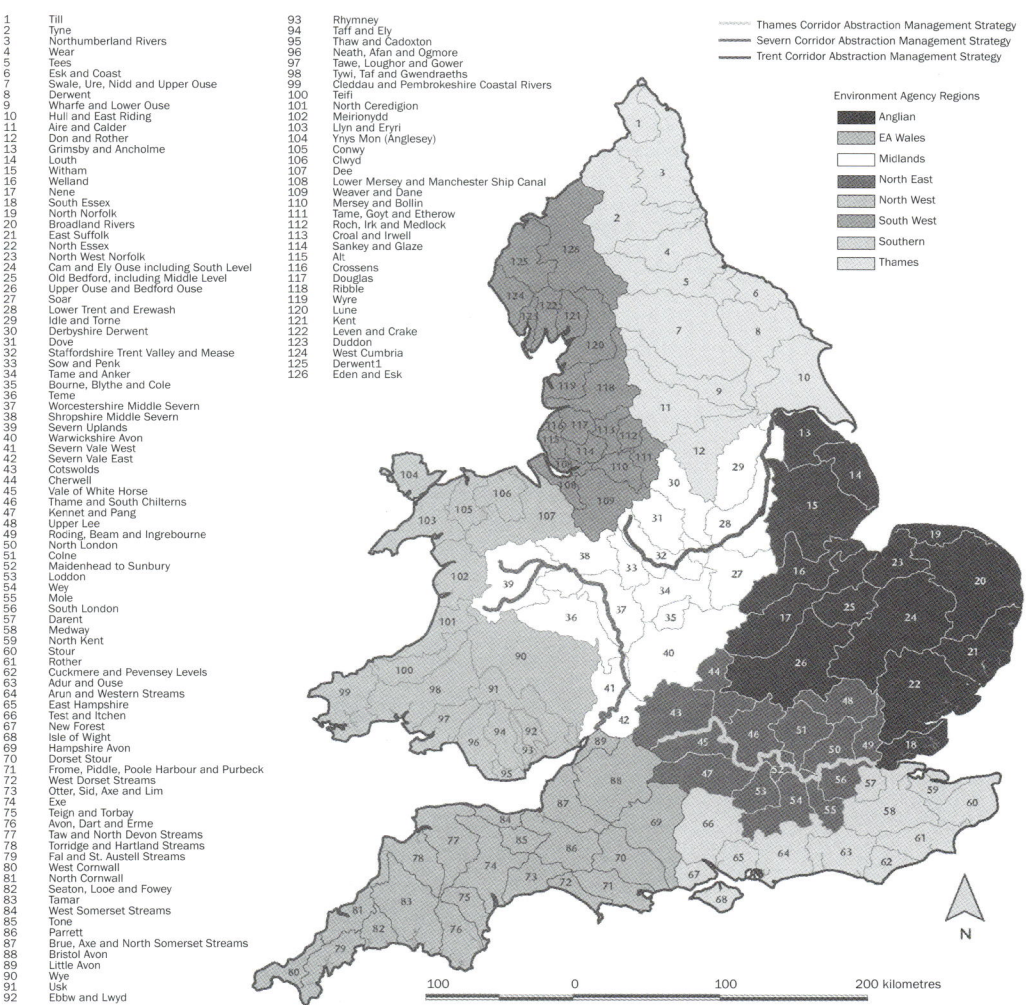

1	Till	93	Rhymney
2	Tyne	94	Taff and Ely
3	Northumberland Rivers	95	Thaw and Cadoxton
4	Wear	96	Neath, Afan and Ogmore
5	Tees	97	Tawe, Loughor and Gower
6	Esk and Coast	98	Tywi, Taf and Gwendraeths
7	Swale, Ure, Nidd and Upper Ouse	99	Cleddau and Pembrokeshire Coastal Rivers
8	Derwent	100	Teifi
9	Wharfe and Lower Ouse	101	North Ceredigion
10	Hull and East Riding	102	Meirionydd
11	Aire and Calder	103	Llyn and Eryri
12	Don and Rother	104	Ynys Mon (Anglesey)
13	Grimsby and Ancholme	105	Conwy
14	Louth	106	Clwyd
15	Witham	107	Dee
16	Welland	108	Lower Mersey and Manchester Ship Canal
17	Nene	109	Weaver and Dane
18	South Essex	110	Mersey and Bollin
19	North Norfolk	111	Tame, Goyt and Etherow
20	Broadland Rivers	112	Roch, Irk and Medlock
21	East Suffolk	113	Croal and Irwell
22	North Essex	114	Sankey and Glaze
23	North West Norfolk	115	Alt
24	Cam and Ely Ouse including South Level	116	Crossens
25	Old Bedford, including Middle Level	117	Douglas
26	Upper Ouse and Bedford Ouse	118	Ribble
27	Soar	119	Wyre
28	Lower Trent and Erewash	120	Lune
29	Idle and Torne	121	Kent
30	Derbyshire Derwent	122	Leven and Crake
31	Dove	123	Duddon
32	Staffordshire Trent Valley and Mease	124	West Cumbria
33	Sow and Penk	125	Derwent1
34	Tame and Anker	126	Eden and Esk
35	Bourne, Blythe and Cole		
36	Teme		
37	Worcestershire Middle Severn		
38	Shropshire Middle Severn		
39	Severn Uplands		
40	Warwickshire Avon		
41	Severn Vale West		
42	Severn Vale East		
43	Cotswolds		
44	Cherwell		
45	Vale of White Horse		
46	Thame and South Chilterns		
47	Kennet and Pang		
48	Upper Lee		
49	Roding, Beam and Ingrebourne		
50	North London		
51	Colne		
52	Maidenhead to Sunbury		
53	Loddon		
54	Wey		
55	Mole		
56	South London		
57	Darent		
58	Medway		
59	North Kent		
60	Stour		
61	Rother		
62	Cuckmere and Pevensey Levels		
63	Adur and Ouse		
64	Arun and Western Streams		
65	East Hampshire		
66	Test and Itchen		
67	New Forest		
68	Isle of Wight		
69	Hampshire Avon		
70	Dorset Stour		
71	Frome, Piddle, Poole Harbour and Purbeck		
72	West Dorset Streams		
73	Otter, Sid, Axe and Lim		
74	Exe		
75	Teign and Torbay		
76	Avon, Dart and Erme		
77	Taw and North Devon Streams		
78	Torridge and Hartland Streams		
79	Fal and St. Austell Streams		
80	West Cornwall		
81	North Cornwall		
82	Seaton, Looe and Fowey		
83	Tamar		
84	West Somerset Streams		
85	Tone		
86	Parrett		
87	Brue, Axe and North Somerset Streams		
88	Bristol Avon		
89	Little Avon		
90	Wye		
91	Usk		
92	Ebbw and Lwyd		

Thames Corridor Abstraction Management Strategy
Severn Corridor Abstraction Management Strategy
Trent Corridor Abstraction Management Strategy

Environment Agency Regions

Anglian
EA Wales
Midlands
North East
North West
South West
Southern
Thames

Figure 3.5   *CAMS areas (Environment Agency, 2001b)*

The "resource availability" status is a classification system developed to indicate the relative balance between committed and available resources, indicating whether further abstraction may be possible and highlighting areas where action is needed to reduce current abstraction. The key elements of the CAMS process are presented in Figure 3.6 (overleaf). A CAM strategy may take up to two years to develop, depending on the complexity of the issues within a catchment and the availability of information. For all CAMS, the period of formal consultation will be three months.

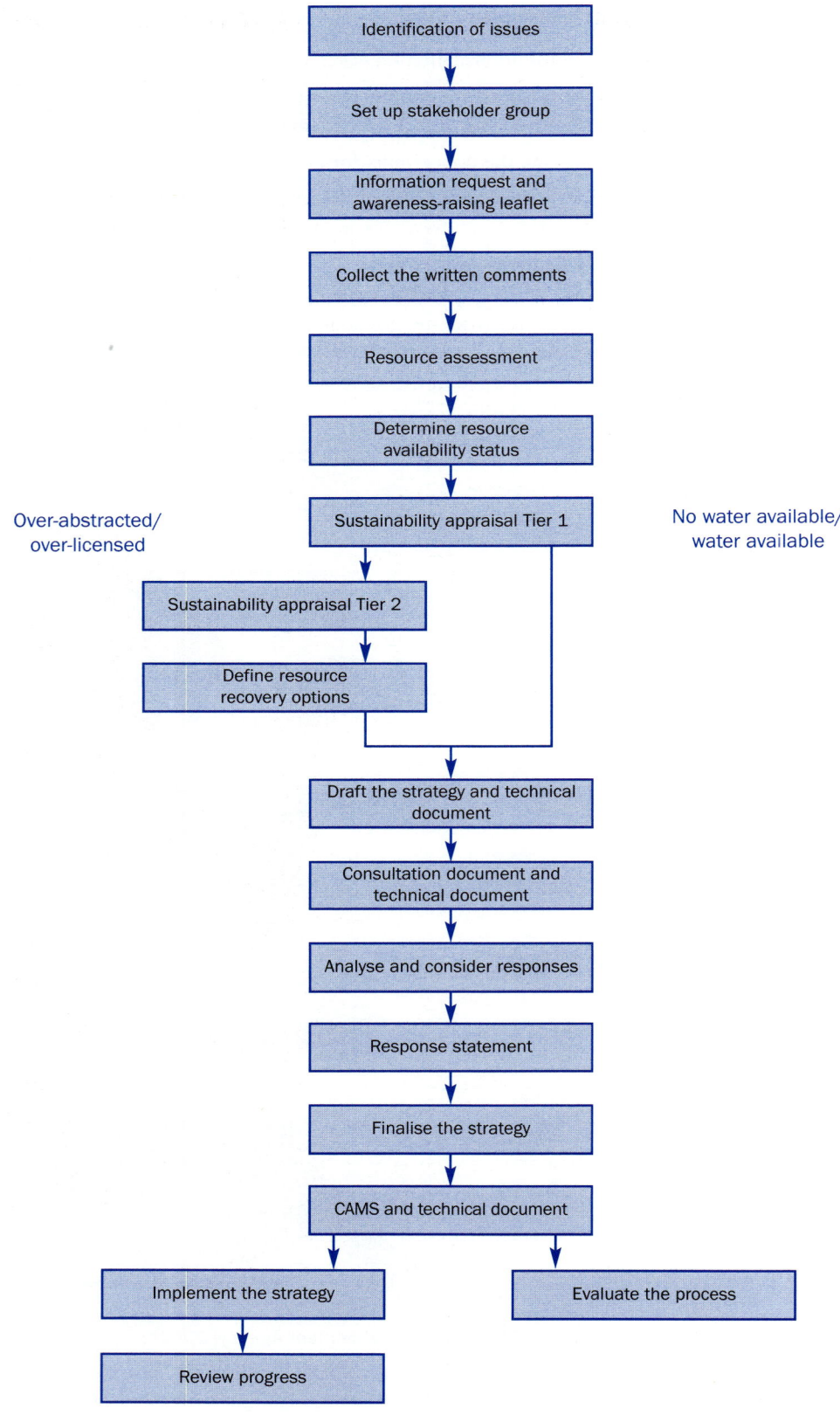

Figure 3.6 *CAMS process (Environment Agency, 2001b)*

3.2.4 Water supply stakeholders, regulation and legislation

Most water users obtain treated water from their local water company, with only a small proportion of wholesome water being taken from private supplies, and the regulatory system is configured to ensure that this system is fair for customers. Ofwat uses comparative competition and price setting to ensure that water companies cannot abuse their position in the market. "Inset appointments" allow a new supplier to supply large users of water that were previously serviced by a different water company, but very few of these have been brought into effect. Potentially, a water company could be forced to surrender abstraction licences to allow another company to compete with it.

The Environment Agency develops its own water resources strategies following extensive consultation and paying particular regard to water companies' resource development plans. The Agency's 25-year strategy (Environment Agency, 2001a) is applicable to each of its eight regions. The strategy takes a view of predicted demand until the year 2025 and compares this with available resources. Figure 3.7 shows a national picture of summer surface water resource availability, taken from this document.

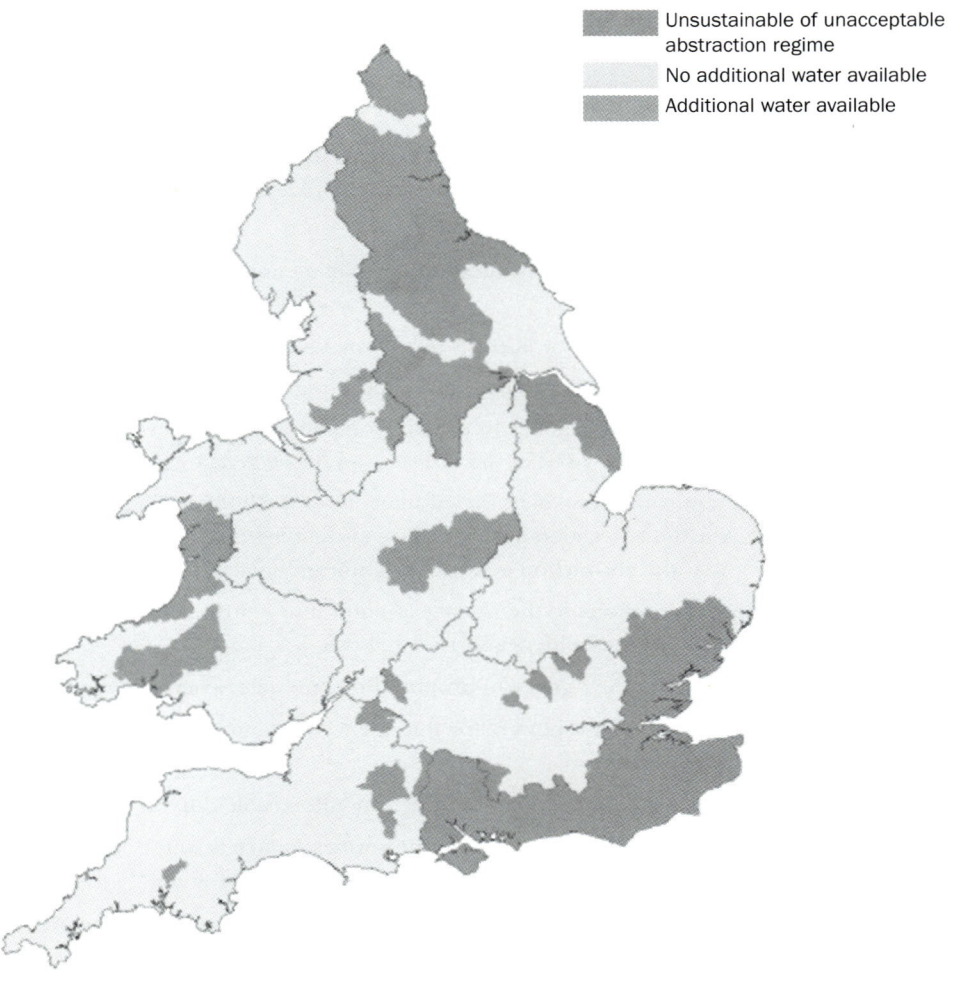

	Unsustainable of unacceptable abstraction regime
	No additional water available
	Additional water available

Figure 3.7 *Current indicative water resource availability: summer surface water (Environment Agency, 2001a)*

The system of abstraction licensing was introduced by the Water Resources Act 1963. After consolidation and amendment it is now contained in the Water Resources Act 1991, as amended by the Environment Act 1995. This also placed a new specific duty on water undertakers to promote water conservation to their customers. However, the principles remain fundamentally unchanged and the Environment Agency administers the abstraction licensing system. The Agency has duties and powers for granting new abstraction licences and amending and administering existing licences. In addition to its specific water resources powers and duties, there are also other requirements on the Environment Agency in licensing abstraction. These include taking account of costs and benefits, contributing to sustainable development and considering the needs of rural areas.

The European Water Framework Directive (2000/60/EC) (WFD) establishes a common framework for the protection and management of surface water and groundwater with an integrated approach. The WFD has significant implications for the Agency's management of water resources and, together with the CAM strategies, provides the consistent and structured strategy framework for resource assessment and licence determination. The CAMS initiative facilitates the management of water resources in a more sustainable way. Other European legislation affecting the management of water resources, eg Birds and Habitats Directive, has also been transposed into UK legislation, requiring the Agency to protect designated sites. This will influence the CAMS appraisal for catchments with designated sites, as more water may be required for the natural environment in these areas. Further discussion of European directives is given in Section 3.3.4.

The Water Act 2003 includes provisions to give effect to those parts of *Taking water responsibly* (DETR and WO, 1999) that required new legislation, including the following changes to the licensing systems:

- limiting the pre-qualification for making an application for an abstraction licence to a right of access only
- requiring all new licences to be time-limited
- allowing licences to be transferred by agreement between the parties concerned
- enabling the Agency to recover compensation costs in defined circumstances when a licence is revoked at the direction of the secretary of state
- removing from 2012 the entitlement of the holder of a permanent licence to compensation for the revocation of that licence at the direction of the secretary of state on the grounds that the abstraction is causing significant environmental damage
- giving powers to the Agency to enter into enforceable water management arrangements with licence-holders and recover costs
- allowing the Agency to propose that one water company seeks a bulk supply from another
- providing new powers for the Agency to require information from abstractors on how water is used
- placing water companies under an enforceable duty to further water conservation
- placing a duty on all public authorities to take account of water conservation both in conducting their affairs and in their own use of water
- placing a duty on the secretary of state (in England) and the Welsh Assembly Government to take steps to encourage the conservation of water and to report on progress and future plans (on a three-yearly basis in England, timing to be decided in Wales).

3.2.5　Sustainability issues in water resource planning

The water companies' traditional approach to water resource management was to predict the future demand and to provide sufficient resource, often a new reservoir, to meet it. The current approach is to assess the sustainability of options and determine the most cost-effective one through assigning values to their costs and benefits. The costs might be the investment and operational expenditure associated with the scheme, together with the value of any detrimental environmental impacts. Conversely, the benefits would typically be the value of water to the user, any additional recreational opportunities and any environmental enhancements.

Both surface and groundwater sources have a finite sustainable yield, beyond which there may be depletion of the resource in the long term and significant impacts on river systems. River flows and groundwater regimes need to be maintained to protect river and wetland ecosystems, fisheries, recreation, navigation and licensed abstraction. Planning to meet rising demand levels may, therefore, conflict with the role of water in maintaining and improving biodiversity – a vital sustainability indicator. For example, the Environment Agency's water resources strategy identifies large areas, especially in the south-east of England, where no further water is available during summer, or where damage to the environment is already occurring as a result of existing abstractions (Figure 3.7). The strategy indicates that further reductions in abstraction beyond those already planned will amount to 700 Ml/d by 2025. However, the Agency also recommends the development of new resources that total some 1800 Ml/d by 2025 and identifies that much of this can be achieved by the enhancement of existing systems alongside some new large schemes (including the raising of some existing reservoirs in East Anglia and the South East). There may also be a need to consider additional reservoir storage within the Thames catchment and water-transfer schemes in some areas. Such schemes will need more work to demonstrate that their environmental impacts are acceptable.

The preparation of CAMS will contribute to sustainable development through holistic and effective management of the water environment at the catchment scale. A sustainability appraisal is required as part of each strategy, which uses a largely qualitative approach to develop plans for the development of local water resources, by taking into account the implications of different options on all aspects of sustainability. Options are screened and refined to identify those that will achieve the greatest environmental benefits with the lowest social and economic impacts. Where it is clear that a qualitative approach is inadequate, for example, where it is proposed that licences need to be varied or revoked, some quantification of costs to abstractors will be included in the appraisal.

3.3　Wastewater planning

3.3.1　Introduction

There are two components to wastewater planning:

- wastewater disposal (foul sewerage) and treatment
- surface water drainage (storm sewerage).

The normal requirement for new developments is the provision of separate drainage systems for the foul and surface water flows. Foul water systems deal with sanitary and wastewater discharges from buildings and other flows from a site that cannot be discharged to watercourses or groundwater without prior treatment. Surface water systems deal with surface runoff (usually, but not exclusively, produced by rainfall) from roofs of buildings, paved surfaces, car parks and sometimes contributing natural areas.

3.3.2   Wastewater disposal

The appropriate treatment and disposal of wastewater from consumers and industry is fundamental to the overall health and welfare of society. It is also an integral part of sustainable water management. The quality of water in a river can help determine riparian land use. In a residential development, wastewater comprises water from sinks, baths, showers, WCs, washing machines and other water-using appliances. It is mostly of poor quality and is normally unsuitable for reuse or recycling and requires treatment before disposal.

Under Section 104 of the Water Industry Act 1991, the sewerage undertaker may agree (after paying appropriate fees) to "adopt" some or all of the foul water sewers within a new scheme as part of the public sewerage system, provided the system meets the sewerage undertaker's technical requirements. In most cases, only lengths of sewer in public roads or in areas where the sewerage undertaker has rights of access will be adopted; other parts normally remain the responsibility of the site owner or of the purchasers of individual properties. Pumping stations within a site may be adopted provided access rights and ownership of the land they occupy are transferred to the sewerage undertaker. If no local sewer exists, a sewer can be requisitioned. A developer who requests such a sewer has to pay an annual charge for up to 12 years for the provision of the sewer, though a single commuted sum is often agreed to. The basis of this charge is defined under Section 98 of the Water Industry Act 1991.

The public sewerage system conveys the wastewater flows to wastewater treatment works from where the treated effluent is then, typically, discharged to surface water bodies. Consents for these discharges require approval from the Environment Agency. For surface waters, the Agency sets river quality objectives that are use-related and consist of target chemical and biological classes, together with a date by which the objective should be achieved. The Agency regulates discharge consents and ensures that they meet strict criteria for maintaining, and wherever possible improving, water quality.

As with water supply planning, planning for future wastewater discharges (Figure 3.8) requires long-term strategic appraisal. At a regional scale, requirements for future wastewater treatment infrastructure need to be evaluated, together with the impacts of additional discharges on the water environment.

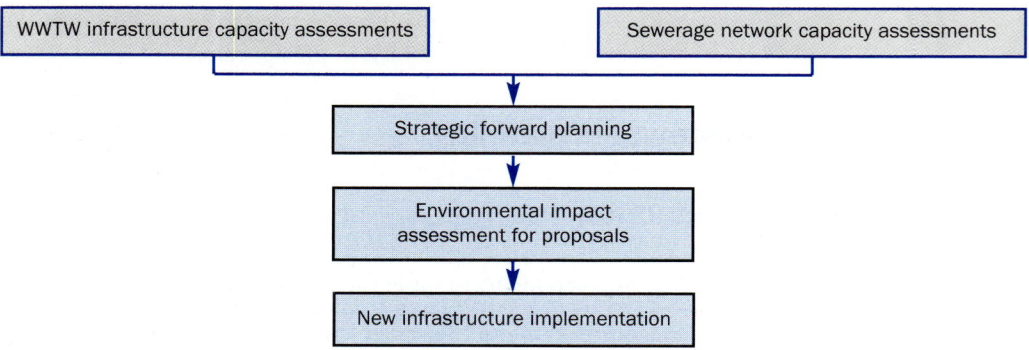

Figure 3.8   *Wastewater planning*

A further option may also be available as a result of developing sewage technology, which has improved the feasibility and potential economic and water resource benefits of relatively small-scale local (perhaps site-specific) sewage treatment. The developer may choose to carry out a feasibility study for consideration by the sewerage undertaker and Environment Agency or to opt for inset provision (see Section 5.5.3).

3.3.3 Stakeholders in wastewater disposal

The main parties involved in the wastewater disposal system are the:

- builder or developer
- local planning authority
- Buildings Regulations enforcement authority
- sewerage undertaker
- Environment Agency.

The district council is the local planning authority and the Building Regulations enforcement authority, although the Building Act 1984 also provides for private-sector bodies to become approved inspectors as an alternative to local authority control. The authority co-ordinates its own responses and those of other agencies for the drainage aspects of any planning proposal.

The sewerage undertaker assesses the foul sewer connection for the quantity and characteristics of the sewage effluent to establish whether the development can be served by the existing system. A financial contribution may be required to improve the receiving network in taking the increased load, and charges may also be levied for treatment of trade wastes if on-site pre-treatment is not carried out.

The Environment Agency exercises its responsibilities for the protection and improvement of both ground and surface water quality by regulating and monitoring polluters, issuing consents and, when necessary, taking enforcement action.

3.3.4 Legislation and controls on wastewater disposal

Several parliamentary Acts and European directives provide mechanisms to protect and enhance the quality of both groundwater and surface waters. The Water Act 1989 established private water undertakers and sewerage undertakers, which collectively are known as the water service companies. The Act split between two organisations the responsibility for provision of services (by the water service companies) and regulation (by the Environment Agency) of the water environment. The Act effectively established the discharge consent process, which requires sewerage undertakers to apply to a "higher" authority for permission to discharge treated and untreated wastewater into streams, rivers and coastal waters. The Environmental Protection Act 1990 brought in similar discharge consent requirements for other (industrial) discharges to the environment. The Pollution Prevention and Control Act 1999 allows provision for integrated pollution prevention and control measures (IPPC), which the Environment Agency regulates through discharge consents. For wastewater treatment works serving populations of more than 150 000, an EIA is required under the Town and Country Planning (Environmental Impact Assessment) (England and Wales) Regulations 1999. All significant continuous discharges of treated wastewater have numeric consents that limit the volume and concentration of key pollutants permitted to be discharged. These discharges are monitored regularly; if found to be non-compliant the discharger can be prosecuted. Intermittent discharges of stormwater from combined sewer systems are also becoming liable to discharge consents, typically with criteria for volume or frequency of discharge.

The nature of the consents is determined in compliance with the previously mentioned Acts, the Water Resources Act 1991, the Salmon and Freshwater Fisheries Act 1975 and a range of regulations. The Water Act 2003 also brings in further controls to protect habitats affected by poor water quality and lack of water.

This UK legislation transposes many European directives, including:

- Bathing Water Quality Directive (76/160/EEC)
- Shellfish Waters Directive (79/923/EEC)
- Surface Waters (Dangerous Substances) (Classification) Directive (76/464/EEC)
- Urban Wastewater Treatment Directive (91/271/EEC)
- Nitrates Directive (91/676/EEC)
- Habitats Directive (92/43/EEC).

The Water Framework Directive (2000/60/EC), transposed into UK legislation in the Water Environment (Water Framework Directive) (England and Wales) Regulations 2003, adds further requirements for whole-catchment water quality assessments and reporting, together with consideration of ecological impacts of, for example, wastewater discharges. In particular, the WFD requires river basin management plans (RBMPs) to be drawn up (in draft by 2008 and finalised by 2009) and implemented to achieve "good water quality" status of surface and groundwater. Where water quality is already "high" or "good" there will be a requirement to maintain this status; improvement will be required in those water bodies failing to achieve "good" status. These plans will need to include a full economic analysis of water use, investments and forecasts, plus information on water abstraction and distribution. It is expected that the WFD may have a fundamental impact on planning and land-use policy in the future. The Environment Agency is the competent authority charged with implementing the WFD. The objectives of the RBMPs will be statutory, as will the requirement to achieve "good ecological status" and prevent deterioration. The WFD also requires public participation and the dissemination of data upon which decisions have been based. Therefore some of the good practice discussed in this guide may become statutory for water management.

3.3.5 Surface water drainage

Development alters the hydrological processes of an area, as impermeable surfaces, roofs and roads direct surface water from a site differently compared with its original greenfield state. The rate of surface water runoff increases, particularly during storms or periods of heavy and prolonged rainfall. The greater flow rates and volumes may increase the risk of flooding downstream. The options available to developers for surface water drainage of a development site include:

- sustainable drainage, including soakaway or other on-site infiltration
- public sewers and highway drains
- main or non-main river.

There is legal requirement of the sewerage undertaker to accept drainage of properties to a public sewer, if it exists. However, if the capacity of the sewer is insufficient, on-site storage may be required. The reduction of surface water runoff from new developments can be encouraged by surface water storage areas, flow-limiting devices in conjunction with surface or sub-surface storage or, where ground conditions permit, the use of infiltration areas or soakaways. PPG25 *Development and flood risk* (DLTR, 2001a) encourages the use of sustainable drainage systems (SUDS) where appropriate as a sub-catchment-scale measure to mitigate the influence of development on flood risks elsewhere. SUDS aim to mimic natural drainage patterns by attenuating total and peak flows of runoff and encouraging natural groundwater recharge; they also have potential to improve water quality and contribute to good design in improving the amenity and wildlife interest of developments. Rapid rates of surface water runoff and the type of material it transports can lead to increased pollution. The installation of oil interceptors and silt traps on surface water systems serving all types of development are essential in many locations and SUDS may reduce pollution problems further, particularly those from diffuse pollution, further. Several recent CIRIA publications – Martin *et al*, 2000, 2001; Pratt *et al*, 2002; and Wilson *et al*, 2004 – provide detailed guidance on the implementation of SUDS. More information is available at <www.ciria.org/suds>. Some issues remain on the "adoption" of SUDS, however. These are being addressed by Defra and the National SUDS Working Group, which has produced the *Interim code of practice for sustainable drainage systems* (NSWG, 2004), and by CIRIA, which has developed model agreements for the adoption and maintenance of sustainable water management systems (Shaffer *et al*, 2004).

3.3.6 Stakeholders in surface water drainage

County councils have two drainage roles: as a highway authority and a land drainage authority. This does not include trunk road drainage, which is the responsibility of the Department of Transport via the Highways Agency and the Welsh Assembly Government via its Transport Directorate. Local authorities retain the responsibility of drainage of non-main rivers, although the county council may have an interest if significant flows are diverted to non-main river watercourses from a proposed development.

The Environment Agency, when consulted, provides guidance on conditions to be attached to planning consents and may require the developer to obtain a discharge consent. The internal drainage boards (IDBs) have similar responsibilities to the Environment Agency in their areas. The IDB may levy contributions on a developer to fund enhancement of the drainage system or to cover additional operational costs to handle additional runoff.

Sewerage undertakers have a responsibility to provide a drainage service and need to assess planning proposals in the light of the impact on the system downstream. The undertaker may object to the proposal; the local authority will usually take note of the objection and agree suitable changes with the developer.

3.3.7 Legislation and controls on surface water drainage

Drainage works are normally covered by the Building Regulations 2000, which are written to meet the requirements of the Building Act 1984. The Building (Amendment) Regulations (2001) in England and Wales require rainwater drainage from roofs and paved areas around buildings to "be adequate" and to discharge to a hierarchy that gives precedence to infiltration systems followed by watercourses and sewers. Guidance on what is considered to be adequate is given in Approved Document H (DTLR, 2001c), which, as well as giving advice for domestic dwellings, also refers to the British Standards on the subject. Together with approved inspectors, local authorities are responsible for administering these regulations.

The 1991 and 1994 Land Drainage Acts define the land drainage authority role of the local authority. The Acts allow the authority to ensure that riparian owners carry out maintenance on watercourses and to execute land drainage schemes. Under the Highways Act 1980, the county council has the responsibility to prevent roads from flooding and has powers:

- to adopt a highway drain
- to prevent water flowing on to or from a highway
- to require developers to obtain consent for any works or use of a watercourse for highway drainage.

Under the Water Industry Act 1991, sewerage undertakers have duties to provide a system of public sewerage including stormwater drainage. A highway authority can enter into an agreement with the sewerage undertaker for its sewers to be used for conveying surface water from roads repairable by the authority. Similarly, the sewerage undertaker can enter into an agreement with the highway authority to use the authority's drains to carry surface water from premises or streets. The Act prohibits either party from refusing to enter into or consenting to such agreements on unreasonable grounds.

The Environment Agency has "permissive" powers for all watercourses that are designated as main rivers, under the Water Resources Act 1991. Permissive powers provide statutory authority allowing the Agency to carry out necessary maintenance and improvement works. Although they are excluded from this role for non-main rivers, under PPG25 planning authorities are advised to consult the Agency on all matters related to runoff into watercourses and proposed development liable to flood. In addition, local and highway authorities need to consult the Agency before exercising their responsibilities under their general drainage powers. The Town and Country Planning Act 1990 allows the imposition of conditions on a planning permission with regard to drainage proposals, and the Agency will provide advice and recommendations to the local authority in this regard.

3.3.8   Sustainability issues for wastewater planning

The water resource in England and Wales is intensively used, with river water often being abstracted and discharged, generally after treatment, several times during its path from source to sea. Any reductions in water quality at a particular location, either in the short term or the long term, could have serious implications for downstream users as well as for the environment and the riparian land use.

Where development is proposed in a catchment close to its capacity for accepting effluents, the treatment and discharge of the additional wastewater will be a concern. If development proceeds ahead of the sewerage system capacity and the ability of receiving sewage treatment works to process increased flows, inadequate foul drainage may result in pollution of the water environment. To overcome this, the sewerage undertaker could transfer flows to another catchment for discharge, or treat the effluent to a quality that is close to natural river quality and so limit impact on the water environment. Both solutions would require a sustainability assessment. The first solution may involve the transfer of large volumes of water between catchments, potentially disturbing the natural water balance for those catchments and consequently creating environmental risks. The second solution needs intensive industrial processes using substantial quantities of energy to treat the water; the treatment also produces contaminated waste that requires disposal to landfill.

Section 3.3.5 discusses the use of SUDS as a sustainable alternative to traditional piped surface water drainage, allowing attenuation of flow from the development, infiltration and environmental opportunities. Surface water drainage measures will need careful design for proposed developments over aquifers that are, or could be, used for public supply and thus are vulnerable to pollution. In these instances, options such as the introduction of permeable pavements and source-control measures may not be appropriate, or will require careful design to prevent infiltration of possibly polluted surface water.

4   Process interactions

4.1   Interaction between Environment Agency planning and land-use/ spatial planning processes

Although the Environment Agency was not a statutory consultee for regional planning guidance (RPG), PPG11 (DETR, 2000c) advised regional planning bodies (RPBs) to involve regional stakeholders, including the Agency, in preparing RPG. The inclusion of the Agency as a specific consultation body (SCB) for the preparation of RSS revision will increase its potential influence on sustainable water management issues in regional planning.

A protocol entitled *Working better together in town and country planning* (EA and LGA, 1999) has been agreed between the Environment Agency and the Local Government Association. PPG12 (DETR, 2000b) advised on the need for local planning authority (LPA) consultation with both water utilities and the Agency at an early stage in preparation of development plans. In the case of structure plans, the Environment Agency was a statutory consultee. For local and unitary plans there were no statutory consultees, although district councils were advised to consult with appropriate bodies (including the Agency) on a discretionary basis. Again, the inclusion of the Agency as a SCB for local development documents (LDDs) will further the consideration of sustainable water management in local development planning.

Under the Town and Country Planning (General Development Procedure) Order 1995, LPAs are required to consult the Agency on certain planning applications (including all applications requiring environmental impact assessment) and the Agency is often consulted on others. At the planning application stage, the Environment Agency development control teams liaise with local planning authorities in order to:

- advise on where proposed development may pose a risk from pollution or flooding
- ensure that the environment is protected from adverse effects of proposed development
- ensure that, wherever possible, the environment is enhanced in conjunction with development proposals
- identify demands on their duties and responsibilities, including flood defence, water resource and quality management, conservation and recreation
- avoid unnecessary conflict or overlap between the use of planning conditions and any possible consents or licences required from the Agency.

Where problems are foreseen, the Environment Agency may object to the development in principle or it may recommend specific controls, usually by the use of planning conditions and development plan policies. However, the LPA can still grant planning permission for development proposals against the advice of the Agency, and without the inclusion of recommended planning conditions. This is because it is the LPA's task to take account of all material considerations, which may require a balance between potentially conflicting interests and advice. However, PPG25 (DTLR, 2001a) advises LPAs to inform the Agency if they are likely to overrule its advice on flood risk.

The Agency's planning teams meet regularly with local authorities on a number of activities, including state-of-the-environment reporting, local Agenda 21 planning and strategic environmental assessments. In the south-east of England the Agency is also working together with the South East England Regional Assembly (SEERA) to overcome challenges when planning for new homes. A concordat agreement has been developed to find practical solutions to development issues in the South East, including building in areas at risk of flooding and drinking water supply.

The implementation of the Water Framework Directive in the UK will require closer collaborative working between the Agency and land use planners. The overarching aim of the directive is that most water bodies, such as rivers, lakes, groundwaters, estuarine and coastal waters, should achieve good ecological status by the end of 2015. The Directive requires that the water environment be managed on the basis of meaningful environmental boundaries, ie river basins. Accordingly, the Environment Agency will prepare by 2009 strategic river basin management plans (RBMPs). Each RBMP will set out the issues arising in the basin and indicate what needs to be done (the programme of measures) by 2015 to meet the defined objectives to achieve good status. The WFD requires that the impacts of development should be managed through spatial restrictions or mitigating measures to ensure that the environmental objectives for water are achieved. It also provides a statutory framework for water to be considered as a critical factor in spatial planning. There may be situations where an extended deadline, or a less stringent objective, is justified, eg where the resolution of an issue is technically unfeasible, disproportionately costly or there is an overriding public interest, but this is dependent on there being no deterioration in water quality. Accordingly, the RBMPs will be based on a detailed analysis of the pressures from human activities on the water bodies within the river basins and an assessment of their impacts. The aims of the directive are compatible with existing land-use planning objectives, but their successful delivery will mean earlier and more iterative working between the Agency and planning authorities. A joint SEERA/Agency project, "Preparing for Growth in the South East", is already acknowledging the requirements of WFD and promoting such collaborative work.

Figure 4.1 shows the current state of interaction between the Environment Agency and land use planning processes, for the purposes of environmental management and regulation.

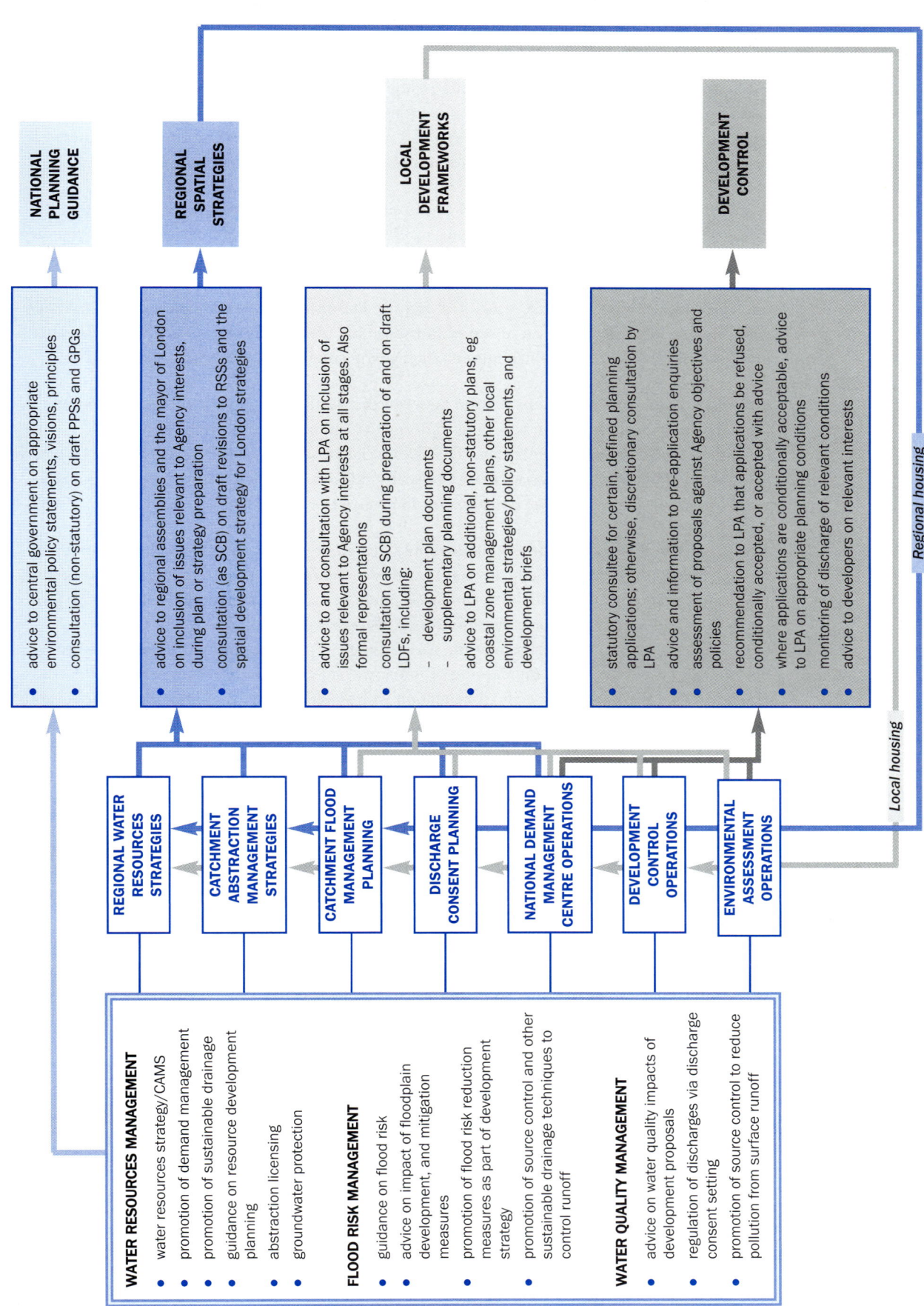

Figure 4.1 *Interaction between Environment Agency and land-use/spatial planning processes*

4.2 Interaction between water company planning and land-use/spatial planning processes

The interests of water companies are increasingly being represented within select committees and other advisory groups, to which the government responds on specific issues. Thus, the water industry, including Ofwat and DWI, will normally be consulted on the development of any government policy (including planning policy) that affects its operations.

Until 2004, land-use planners were not required by law to consult with water companies. However, PPG11 advised that, in drawing up draft RPG, RPBs should elicit the participation of regional stakeholders. Utility companies, eg water companies, were listed as examples of such stakeholders. In addition, PPG12 advised on the need to ensure that critical resources and infrastructure are in place, which will require liaison with water companies and sewerage undertakers. The identification of water and sewerage undertakers as SCBs for both regional and local development plans strengthens their involvement in development planning.

Overall, nothing precludes consultation between the parties early in the planning process. Similarly, water companies or sewerage undertakers can respond to public notices or invitations issued by planning bodies. This is especially useful for large developments or where the sustainability of water management is already difficult and the issues arising are going to need due (potentially iterative) consultation to ensure they are taken into account.

PPG12 indicated that development plans should give utility companies essential inputs to their own planning. LPAs were initially advised to consider the utilities' requirements for land both in their own and other authorities' areas to enable them to meet the demands resulting from future plans. The additional need for basic resources is also part of the consideration of wider environmental effects. Consultation at the earliest stage of plan preparation is considered to be essential and is confirmed by the naming of water and sewerage undertakers as SCBs. PPG12 also addressed the need for specific consultation with water companies on the plan's implications for their infrastructure. Early consultation with the water companies on the availability of water resources was advised at the regional planning level to "help local authorities ensure that new developments will minimise or eliminate the environmental impact of additional demand for water and sewerage services, thereby contributing to a more sustainable development process".

The majority of water companies will have had some input into emerging policies at the strategic planning level as voluntary consultees. Evidence suggests that in recent years it has become more common for such organisations to be invited to the EIP for RPG and structure plans. It is less common for the water companies to be involved at local plan inquiry level, although they may sometimes make objections to specific proposals.

While they are not statutory consultees, the water companies are often consulted by LPAs on major planning applications. Both PPG25 and PPS23 (DTLR, 2001a); ODPM, 2004g) advise on the need to consult water and sewerage undertakers, as well as the Environment Agency, in respect of wastewater disposal issues, particularly SUDS, relevant to flood risk and water quality issues. Detailed negotiations with developers about water supply and wastewater disposal infrastructure also take place at the pre-application stage as a part of the commercial negotiation process rather than in a formal consultation. Such negotiations will seek agreement on the developer's contribution to the costs of upgrades required to the infrastructure needed to make full provision for the needs of the development. This negotiation on the developer's contribution lies outside the planning process and the local planning authority will not become involved.

Figures 4.2 and 4.3 show the interaction between the water companies and land use planning processes, for water supply and sewerage provision respectively (see also Section 5.6.3).

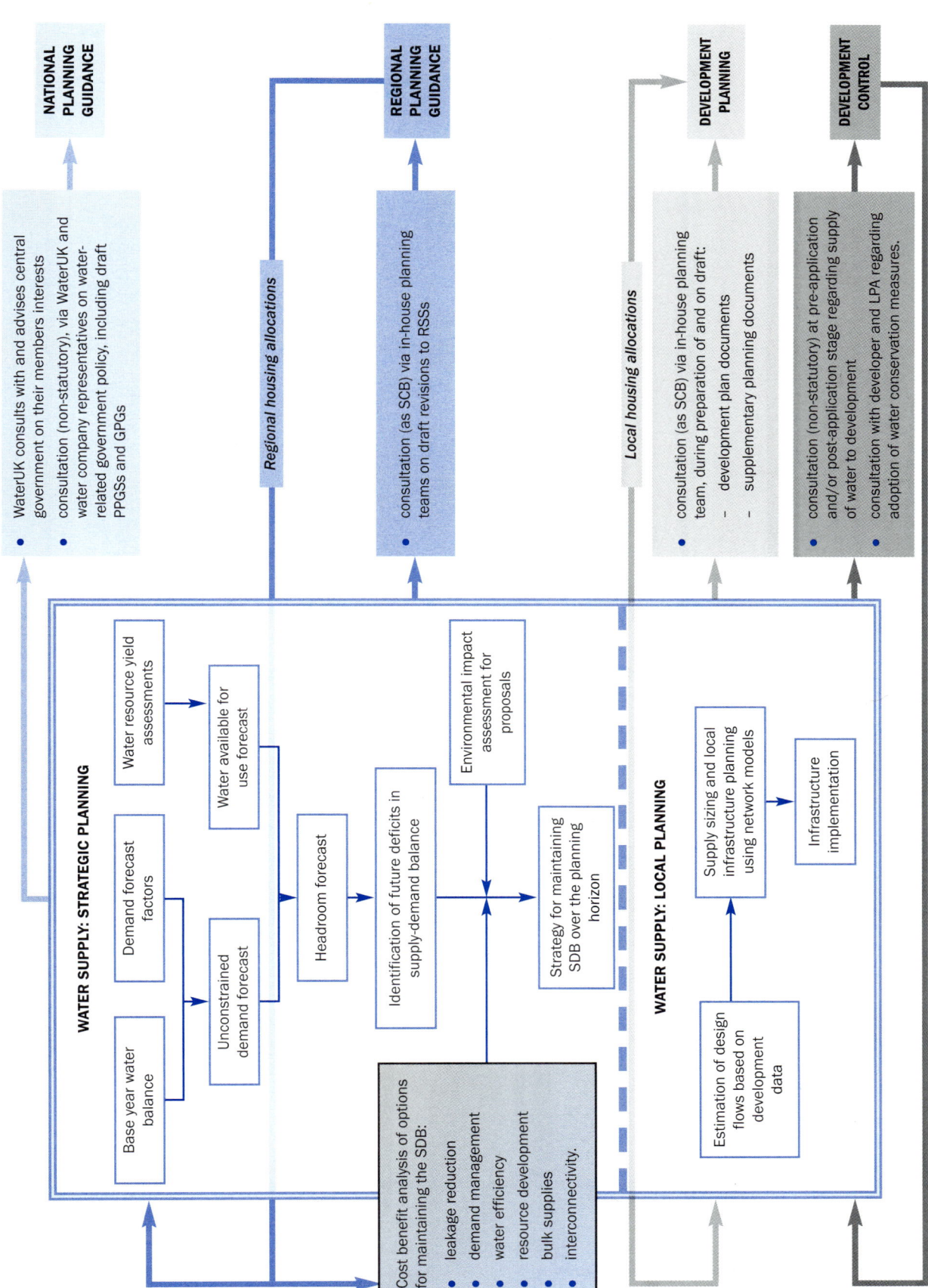

NATIONAL PLANNING GUIDANCE

- WaterUK consults with and advises central government on their members interests
- consultation (non-statutory), via WaterUK and water company representatives on water-related government policy, including draft PPGSs and GPGs

REGIONAL PLANNING GUIDANCE

Regional housing allocations

- consultation (as SCB) via in-house planning teams on draft revisions to RSSs

DEVELOPMENT PLANNING

Local housing allocations

- consultation (as SCB) via in-house planning team, during preparation of and on draft:
  - development plan documents
  - supplementary planning documents

DEVELOPMENT CONTROL

- consultation (non-statutory) at pre-application and/or post-application stage regarding supply of water to development
- consultation with developer and LPA regarding adoption of water conservation measures.

WATER SUPPLY: STRATEGIC PLANNING

- Water resource yield assessments
- Demand forecast factors
- Base year water balance
- Water available for use forecast
- Unconstrained demand forecast
- Headroom forecast
- Identification of future deficits in supply-demand balance
- Environmental impact assessment for proposals
- Strategy for maintaining SDB over the planning horizon

Cost benefit analysis of options for maintaining the SDB:
- leakage reduction
- demand management
- water efficiency
- resource development
- bulk supplies
- interconnectivity.

WATER SUPPLY: LOCAL PLANNING

- Supply sizing and local infrastructure planning using network models
- Infrastructure implementation
- Estimation of design flows based on development data

Figure 4.2   *Interaction between water supply and land-use/spatial planning processes*

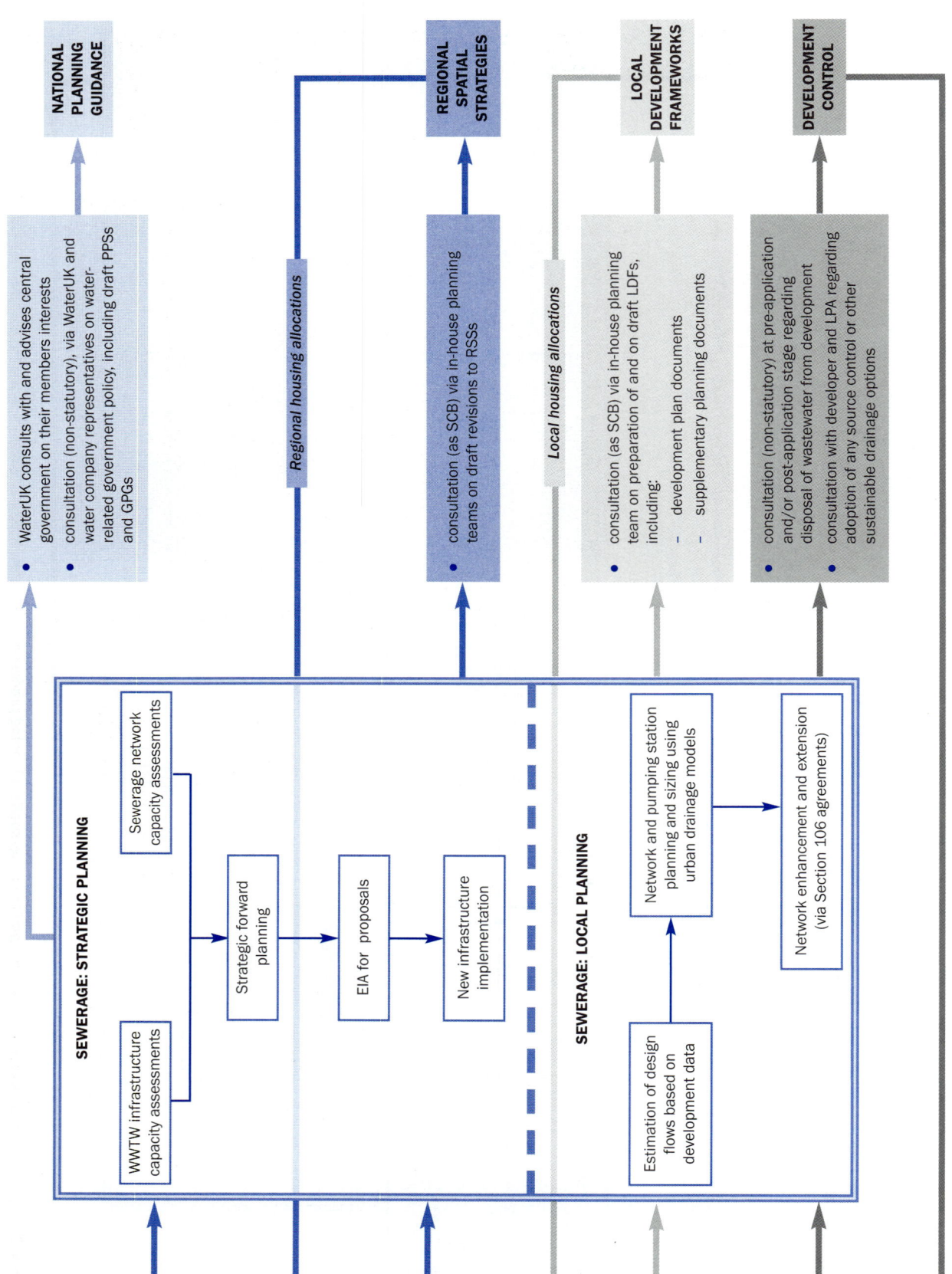

Figure 4.3 *Interaction between sewerage and land-use/spatial planning processes*

4.3 Interaction between developers' planning and land-use/spatial planning processes

The House Builders Federation (HBF) is the trade federation for private house-builders in England and Wales, and this national body actively represents the interests of its members at all levels in the development planning process. The HBF's planning team works on behalf of the industry on regional and local development plan preparation and revision, and on supplementary planning guidance and advice. HBF is primarily interested in the overall quantity of development, but it is also involved in issues that affect development across the board, such as costs.

All major housing developers, and many developers in the retail, leisure, industrial and other sectors, also have in-house planning teams, and many get involved individually in regional and local planning. This is generally to promote the development of their own sites (which HBF cannot do because of potential conflicts between members) and sometimes to object to specific policies. Developers will also obviously be involved in submitting planning applications and appeals – the most contentious applications often being those for housing.

Both house-builders and the HBF therefore engage with local authorities at all stages in the planning process from the setting of regional housing targets to the submission of planning applications for new development. They also respond to suggestions made by local authorities regarding potential development sites, as well as actively identifying new sites themselves. Their engagement is facilitated by and undertaken via the development planning process (and submission of planning applications) and supporting exercises such as the carrying out of land availability studies and urban housing capacity studies.

Figure 4.4 shows the current state of interaction between the planning processes of house-builders and developers and the land use planning process.

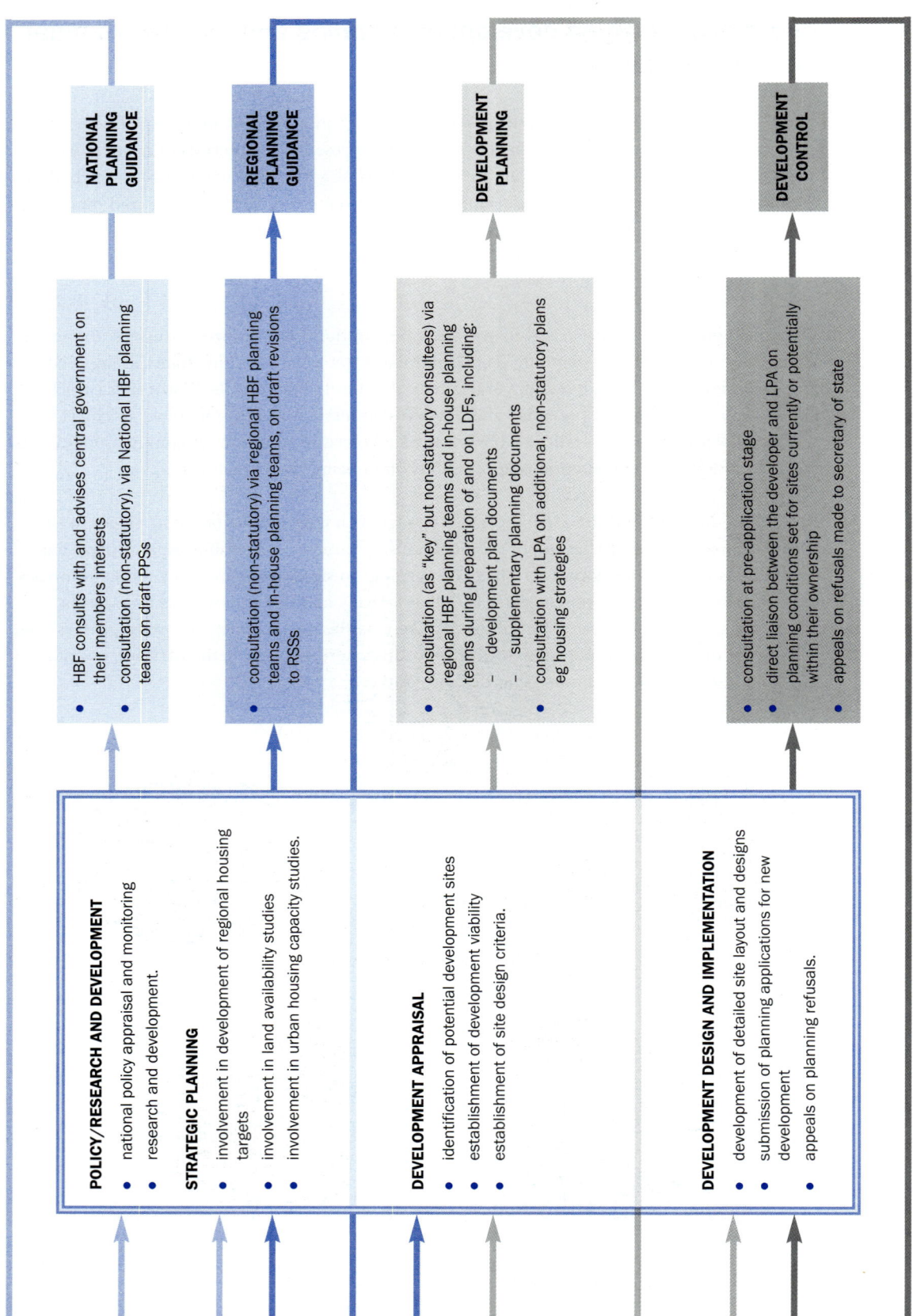

POLICY/RESEARCH AND DEVELOPMENT

- national policy appraisal and monitoring
- research and development.

STRATEGIC PLANNING

- involvement in development of regional housing targets
- involvement in land availability studies
- involvement in urban housing capacity studies.

DEVELOPMENT APPRAISAL

- identification of potential development sites
- establishment of development viability
- establishment of site design criteria.

DEVELOPMENT DESIGN AND IMPLEMENTATION

- development of detailed site layout and designs
- submission of planning applications for new development
- appeals on planning refusals.

NATIONAL PLANNING GUIDANCE

- HBF consults with and advises central government on their members interests
- consultation (non-statutory), via National HBF planning teams on draft PPSs

REGIONAL PLANNING GUIDANCE

- consultation (non-statutory) via regional HBF planning teams and in-house planning teams, on draft revisions to RSSs

DEVELOPMENT PLANNING

- consultation (as "key" but non-statutory consultees) via regional HBF planning teams and in-house planning teams during preparation of and on LDFs, including:
  - development plan documents
  - supplementary planning documents
- consultation with LPA on additional, non-statutory plans eg housing strategies

DEVELOPMENT CONTROL

- consultation at pre-application stage
- direct liaison between the developer and LPA on planning conditions set for sites currently or potentially within their ownership
- appeals on refusals made to secretary of state

Figure 4.4 *Interaction between developers and land-use/spatial planning processes*

5 Planning issues

5.1 Introduction

The implementation of sustainable water management within the land-use/spatial planning system is complex, because the processes have grown up almost independently of each other and the environment itself has only been specified as a priority for about 30 years. Regulation of the environment, water supply and disposal is constantly evolving, as are the planning processes and indeed the environment itself. This chapter sets out the range of issues that present challenges today; guidance on addressing these issues is set out in Chapter 6. In order to explain the main barriers to the incorporation of sustainable water management within the land use planning system they have been grouped under five topics, as illustrated in Figure 5.1. The remainder of this chapter discusses each of these topics in turn. The priority attached to different issues and the order in which they are considered will depend on individual circumstances, so the order in which they are discussed below is not significant.

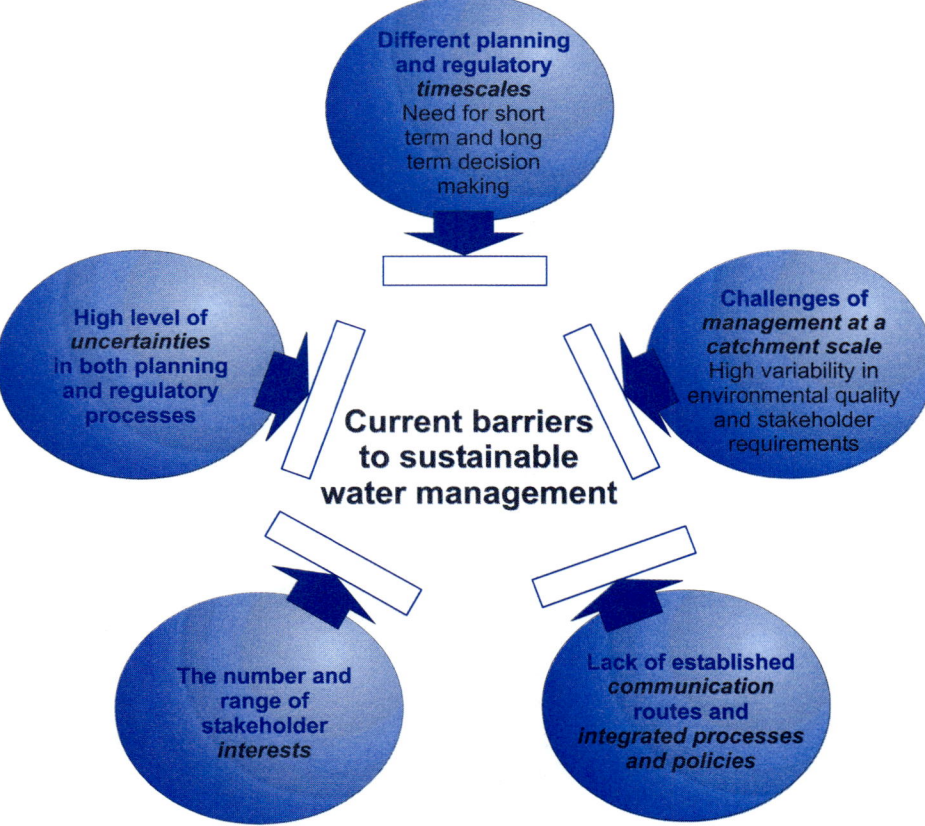

Figure 5.1   *Barriers to sustainable water management*

Challenge 1: meeting all stakeholder interests

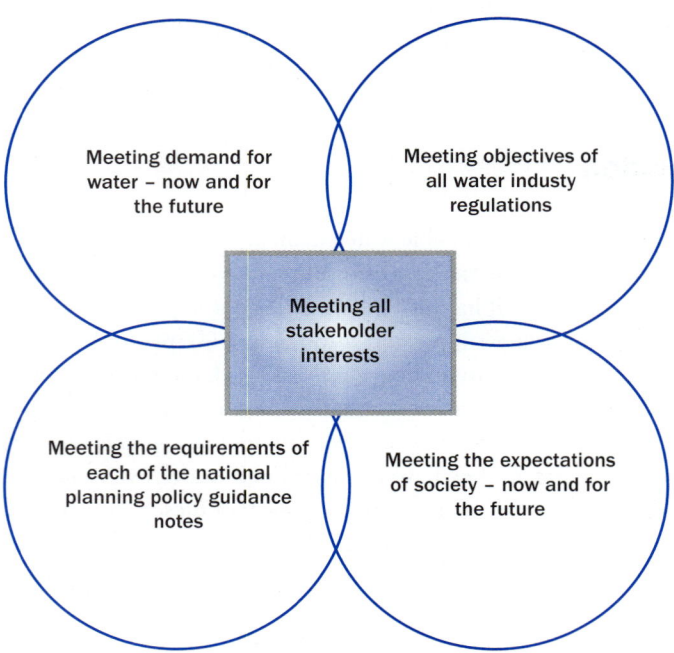

Figure 5.2   *Key stakeholder interests*

5.2.1   Competing demands for water

At certain locations and times the many competing demands for water are putting a strain on the sustainable, long-term availability of water resources, as shown in Figures 5.2 and 5.3. As well as having to satisfy human requirements, the water resource has to fulfil environmental functions. It is important to ensure that both ecological and amenity needs are met so that the environment is preserved and enhanced for the future. The concern is not just the quantity of available water, but the quantity available at a quality appropriate for the intended use. Water resources serve as both sources and sinks: ie a balance must be struck so that the residual flows following abstraction can provide the dilution required for effluents disposed to it without placing the environment at risk.

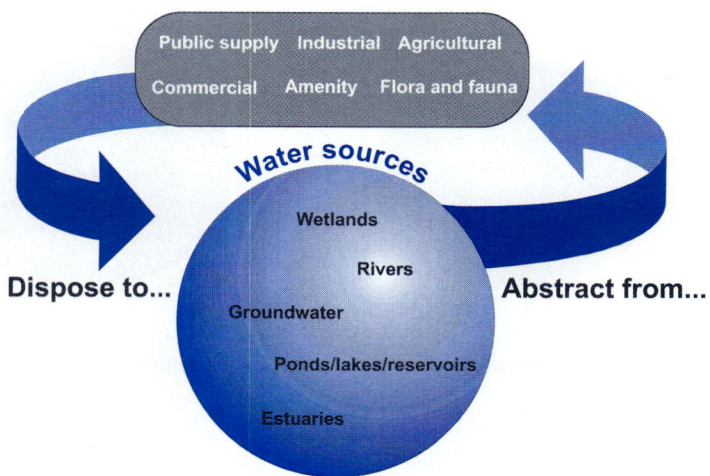

Figure 5.3   *Water resources and water users*

Where water resources are limited, the creation of additional demands for water supply and wastewater treatment from new development can pose practical and economic problems for both the water supplier and sewerage undertaker. To protect the environment, the Environment Agency may apply "load-standstill" to the discharge consent conditions of a sewage treatment works. Where these conditions are already stringent and are approaching the limits of available treatment technology, alternative solutions may have to be sought. Additional resources may need to be secured and this often creates a challenge for infrastructure to keep pace with land-use development.

Under current planning legislation there is no requirement for developers to contribute to the cost of upgrading sewage treatment works or of new water resource schemes and it can be problematic to secure upgraded infrastructure in advance of development. There are several ways of allowing developers to finance other network infrastructure (such as network extensions), but new infrastructure, such as works upgrades, will be financed from general customer tariffs, unless the developer and the statutory undertaker reach a bilateral agreement that accelerates the process. If the financial burden becomes prohibitive or the environmental regulation becomes restrictive, the only remaining option for the sewerage undertaker may be to transport wastewater to distant treatment works with additional capacity. The sustainability of this option would have to be determined, given that the transfers would require additional power, and potentially significant volumes of water might be diverted from its natural catchment.

5.2.2 Different regulatory objectives

The regulatory regime separates the economic and environmental regulators. In general, the roles of the Environment Agency, DWI and Ofwat (see Figure 5.4) are complementary, and the water companies and sewage undertakers are able to meet the challenges of managing their business while meeting the full complement of regulatory requirements. However, some issues do arise regarding the funding of environmental improvements by private water company customers.

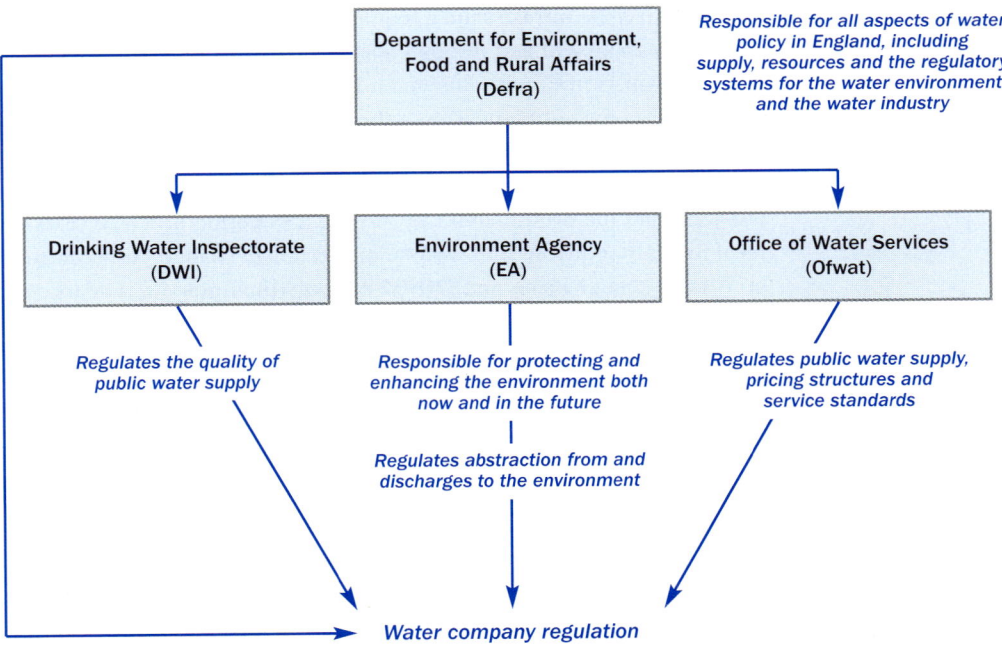

Figure 5.4   *Regulators in the water industry in England and Wales*

Water companies take account of current land-use plans in their water resource plans (WRPs) and asset management plans (AMPs). The timings of revisions to regional spatial strategies (RSSs) and local development frameworks (LDFs) and the WRPs and AMPs may increase the risks associated with funding timely infrastructure investment. This high-level planning within the water companies may influence their response to both land-use plans and individual development applications and apparent differences in decision-making at different locations.

The earlier that realistic development proposals are submitted to water companies, then the earlier can these proposals be incorporated into water company and Environment Agency assessment, planning and capital works programmes.

5.2.3 Water management aspects of planning policy guidance

Historically, the general principle underlying water management for developments in England and Wales has been that it would be technically possible for water supply, sewerage and sewage treatment to be made available anywhere. This principle does not account for the real and potentially significant environmental, economic, timing and sustainability constraints discussed in Section 5.2.1.

Water issues are distributed across several PPGs and PPSs, as indicated in Sections 3.1.3 to 3.1.5 of this guide, with water sustainability issues being highlighted in Section 2 of PPG11 (DETR, 2000c) and Sections 4 and 6 of PPG12 (DETR, 2000b), as well as the recommendation of SUDS in PPG25 (DTLR, 2001a) and PPS23 (ODPM, 2004g). The new PPS11 (ODPM, 2004a) and PPS12 (ODPM, 2004c) effectively restate these principles, particularly in Annex B of PPS12. This is reinforced by the emphasis on sustainable development as the underpinning principle of planning in PPS1 (ODPM, 2005a). This might indicate that other aspects of water management are not often perceived as critical issues in determining policies and distribution of development within spatial planning. However, PPG11 and PPG12 were clear that water availability, the timescale for its provision and the land-use and environmental consequences of any resource development needed are all factors that must influence the timing and distribution of development between different authority areas. Likewise, Section 6 of PPG12 indicated that the infrastructure requirements and potential environmental consequences of wastewater treatment and disposal need also to be considered. Section 2 of PPG11 stated that the potential impact of climate change on natural and human resources is an important consideration for testing policies at the regional scale. Paragraph 13(ii) of PPS1 identifies as a key principle the need for RPBs and LPAs to ensure that RSSs and LDFs contribute to global sustainability by addressing the causes and impacts of climate change. Paragraph 1.3 of PPS11 also identifies the need to look beyond the RSS period of 15–20 years, because of the longer-term forecasting involved in adaptation to climate change. Annex B to PPS12 specifically advises on climate change issues and ODPM has published practice guidance on planning and climate change (ODPM, 2004d). In addition, a planning toolkit for adaptation to climate change in water management is being produced for the Environment Agency and SEERA under the European Spatial Planning Adaptation to Climate Effects (ESPACE) project (Land Use Consultants, 2005).

PPS23 *Planning and pollution control* (ODPM, 2004g) advises on the relationship between controls over development under planning law, on the one hand, and under pollution control legislation on the other. It also provides explanation as to where responsibilities lie with respect to water quality, regulation of effluent and pollution prevention. Infrastructure development is tackled in Annex B of PPS12, which recommends early consultation with water companies and the Environment Agency to help LPAs ensure that new developments are located in ways that will minimise or eliminate the environmental impact of additional demand for water and sewerage services.

While PPS11 and PPS12 emphasise the need for consistency between the regional and local development plans and other regional and sub-regional strategies, neither they nor PPS23 provides specific guidance on:

- how the water company and Environment Agency planning processes integrate with land-use planning

- the questions that planners need to ask to gain an understanding of the sustainability of the solutions proposed

- to what extent planning conditions can be used to ensure appropriate mitigation measures are implemented.

There has been less emphasis on including water issues in a sustainability appraisal than, for example, on transport or energy, perhaps because the consequences of water sustainability are less immediately apparent. This has led to limited awareness and understanding among local authority planners of water management issues. Water companies are not statutory consultees, whereas, for certain policy development and development control issues, the Environment Agency is a statutory consultee, so there may be a perception that the status of the various water management stakeholders differs within the land-use planning system. This is likely to raise barriers rather than facilitate dialogue, although the identification of water and sewerage undertakers as SCBs for RSSs and LDFs will help to overcome this problem.

There are also potential conflicts to resolve between the requirements of different PPGs regarding water and other issues. For example, the priority in PPG3 (DETR, 2000e) for high-density housing on previously developed land might conflict with PPG25 on floodplain development in urban areas and with flood risk management. However, the sequential, risk-based test in Paragraph 30 of PPG25 does identify that, if provided with appropriate flood defences, such areas can be allocated for certain types of development. Likewise, PPG25 recommends that implementation of SUDS be considered for all new developments. This might appear to be at odds with the requirement for higher net density of development, because SUDS are often perceived (incorrectly) always to be a high-land-take drainage solution.

5.2.4 Meeting expectations of society, now and in the future

Household demand is rising significantly as a consequence of changes in *per capita* needs, driven by changing lifestyle patterns. Demand is also being concentrated into particular regions of the country where growth levels are highest. The latest prediction for new households is 3.3 million in England and Wales between 1996 and 2016, of which 1 million are expected to be in the South East – an area of limited water resource availability. Household size continues to decline, resulting in higher demand: for example, water consumption for gardening is independent of the level of occupancy. Furthermore, society increasingly demands appliances and fittings that deliver high performance. Power-showers and large baths are more readily associated with new homes than water-efficient devices. Conversely, the drive towards more energy-efficient washing machines has also contributed to water efficiency.

Water is undervalued in the developed world, so society is unconcerned about its inefficient use. The price of water does not reflect the reality that fresh water is a limited resource, and unless metering becomes widespread domestic customers are likely to have little incentive to use water efficiently. There is a simplistic perception that high rainfall reduces or removes the need to use water wisely, which is exacerbated by a failure to appreciate that water resources are not always available when and where they are needed. The fact that there is an environmental cost to treating and transporting water and wastewater is also not well understood.

Challenge 2: addressing the uncertainties

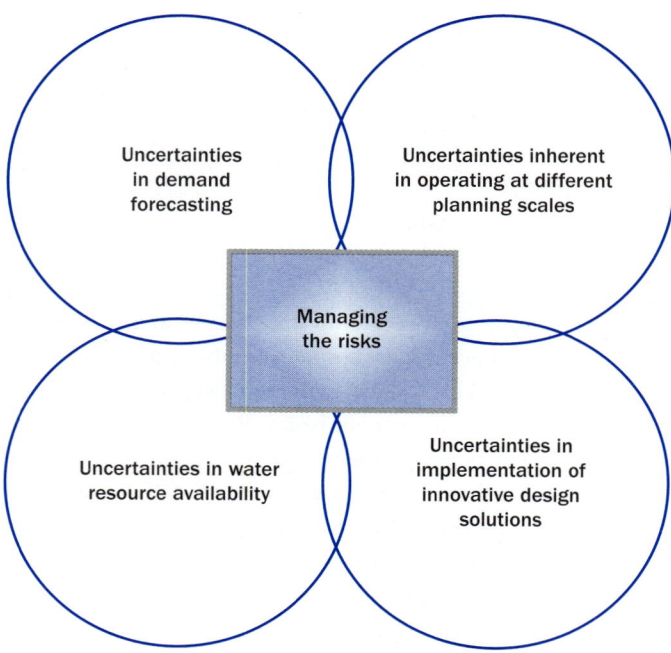

Figure 5.5   *Uncertainties in water management*

5.3.1   Uncertainties in demand forecasting

Increased demands arise from new developments (needed as a result of population relocation, lower-occupancy households or regional industrial expansion) and changes in water use driven by shifts in lifestyle. The size of these challenges will depend on both the scale and the timing of a development and the rate of change in people's lifestyles. Water companies have an obligation to supply water and a developer has a right to connect to an adjacent sewer, but there is no obligation to check the viability of the water supply and wastewater disposal (see Sections 4.2 and 5.6.3) when planning consent is given. This situation could lead to significant challenges and potential conflicts at a time when provision of such services is required, and could certainly cause delays amounting to several years.

Water companies are required to try to predict such changes in demand, but such estimates are inherently highly uncertain. When calculating water demand, companies use a combination of population figures from the Office of National Statistics (ONS) and estimates of household demand made for the water company area, usually in consultation with the LPA. The ONS produces estimates of existing population biennially and projections of future populations every three to five years. These statistics are routinely produced for sub-national areas, including local authority districts and unitary authorities. The level of uncertainty within these predictions is likely to increase at smaller, local scales, where fluctuations are less predictable. A key issue is that the forecasts are based on recent trend extrapolation and do not reflect any assumptions about future drivers changing the birth/mortality rates or population movement. Such uncertainties can present significant challenges to both land use and sustainable water management planning at the local scale in their influence on decision-making. ONS figures are (at the time of publication) still based on 1990 census figures, although 2001 census figures are available in summary form for local authority areas and equivalents.

As approximately 80 per cent of households (in 2001) still receive unmeasured supplies, estimates of both current and future household demand are also uncertain.

5.3.2 Uncertainties in water resource availability

As with prediction of demand, there are uncertainties associated with the calculation of water resource availability and these are compounded by the uncertainty in scenarios for future climate change. The uncertainties associated with both demand forecasting and water resource availability have to be built into water company planning. Effective planning can often be achieved if the timescales of changes in water-use patterns are reasonably predictable. Challenges may arise if the pace of development is such that the increase in demand exceeds current or planned resources.

5.3.3 Uncertainties in operating at different planning scales

Wholesome water supply, wastewater and sewerage treatment planning occur on a macro-scale (company-wide), initially without detailed consideration of local, micro-scale (resource zone) constraints or opportunities associated with the water environment. More detailed planning of water management at the local scale cannot be carried out until detailed development proposals are made available to water utilities and sewerage undertakers. Thus, if new development took place rapidly in a local authority area where the existing water infrastructure is at or near capacity, the water supply and sewerage undertakers may face problems in meeting this increased demand. This may be the case even if the regional water management systems have been sized to accommodate the increase. Conversely, planners are unable to identify sustainable locations for development (in terms of water) without knowledge of specific supply or disposal constraints. Knowledge sharing, although an obvious solution, may not always be possible, as much of such detailed information held by the water companies will be commercially sensitive.

5.3.4 Uncertainties in implementing alternative design solutions

A range of design options can help to minimise the water demand and effluent disposal requirements of new developments, but challenges to their widespread uptake need to be addressed (see Figure 5.6).

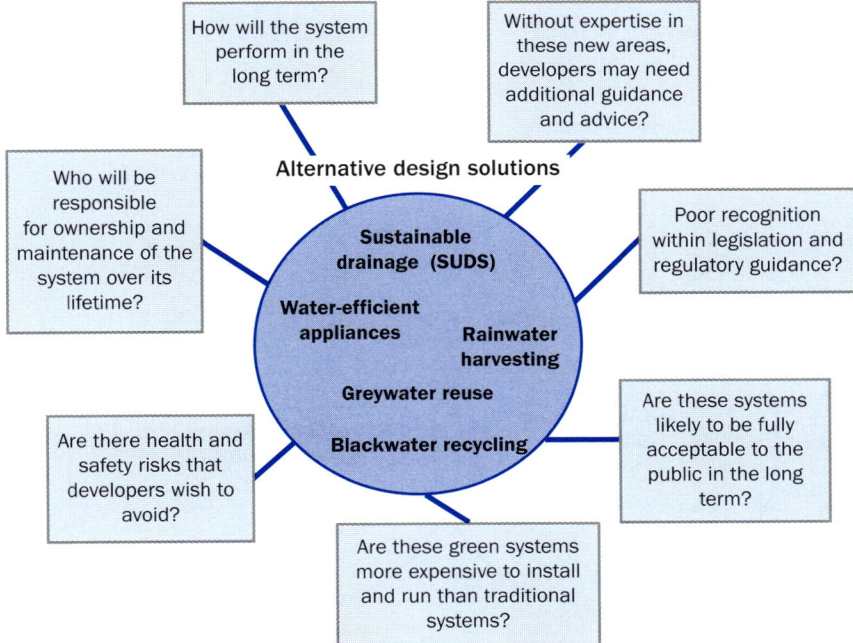

Figure 5.6   *Issues relating to alternative design solutions*

The Water Supply (Water Fittings) Regulations 1999 set minimum standards, eg maximum toilet flush volume, that manage the quantity of water used by domestic appliances. Developed through public consultation, the Regulations represent the UK consensus on reasonable regulation for water conservation within all buildings nationwide. Where there are difficulties in meeting water demands, current technology (as described in Section 3.2.2) could allow significant additional water savings, but the cost of the systems may be an issue. Other factors, such as those described in Section 3.2.2, may mean that potential water savings are reduced. However, a developer may voluntarily agree to adopt such technology to improve the sustainability of a development.

Developers also encounter problems in gaining the acceptance of NHBC and local authority building control officers for sustainable water design options. This is because, for example, the Building Regulations 2000 and Water Supply (Water Fittings) Regulations 1999 do not yet fully incorporate all these technologies.

Although this lack of representation of SUDS has been partly addressed in the new Approved Document of the Building Regulations Part H (DTLR, 2001c), the fifth edition of *Sewers for adoption* (WRc, 2001) makes little direct reference to such systems and states they are outside the document's scope. (SUDS are being considered for inclusion in the next edition of *Sewers for adoption*, however.) *The interim code of practice for SUDS* (National SUDS Working Group, 2004) was developed to facilitate the implementation of SUDS in developments in England and Wales by providing a framework for addressing them in planning and model agreements (Shaffer *et al*, 2004) and advice on their use.

Several new treatment technologies are able to treat water of poorer quality to supply standards than could be achieved in the past. Wastewater can also be processed to much higher effluent quality standards than was previously possible, but the overall sustainability of the technologies used may be an issue (see Section 3.3.8).

5.4 Challenge 3: timing issues

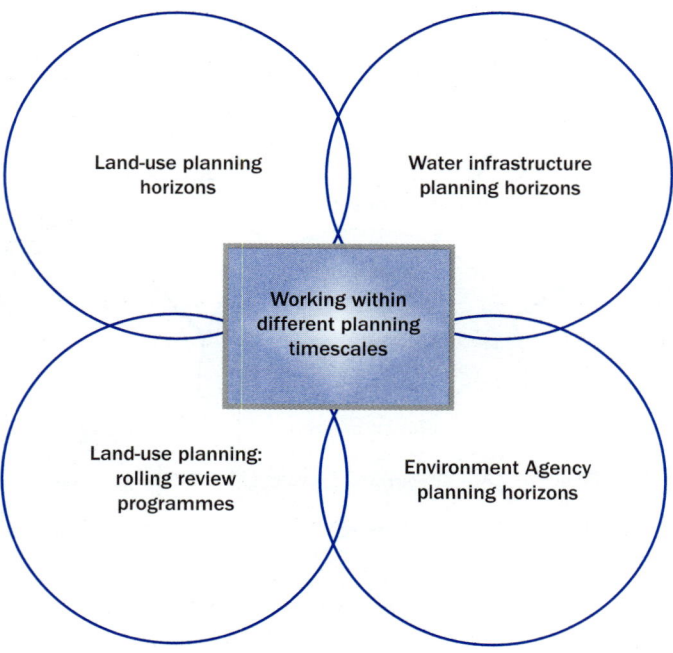

Figure 5.7   *Variability of planning programmes*

5.4.1 Land-use/spatial planning horizons and process duration

The development and revision of national planning guidance is not subject to any given timescale. It is undertaken in response to government policy objectives and government office timescales, and follows consultation with advisory bodies (see Chapter 3). RPG was generally issued to cover a 20-year period and, before 2001, the documents were revised and updated every 5–10 years. PPG11 established a continuous review process for RPG and this is to be continued: revisions to RSSs will be triggered when necessary, eg by the annual monitoring returns. Structure and local plans, covering a 10-year period, were to be reviewed every five years, although in practice this was often not met (see Section 3.5.1). The adoption of a portfolio of documents in the LDF combined with annual monitoring is expected to speed the process of continual review of local development plans. In addition, both PPS11 and PPS12 emphasise the need to look beyond the RSS/LDF timescale in some cases because some relevant forecasting horizons, eg for climate change, are longer-term.

The timing of revisions has varied markedly across the country, and even within regions. There is, therefore, a risk that lower-level plans may be based on higher-level plans that are due for revision. If the revision is imminent, this lack of fit could delay the publication of new plans right through the system, finally causing problems at the development control level. Ensuring the rapid national implementation of new approaches to land-use management (or sustainable water management) via changes in development plan policy could be a significant challenge. Indeed it was partly to address this challenge that the legislative changes in the Planning and Compulsory Purchase Act 2004 were introduced, along with a programme for culture change in planning as part of the Government's Sustainable Communities Plan.

Variations in the rate of implementation of planning guidance and policy can also present challenges for developers, who are best able to make efficiency and cost savings in developments when the procedures and policies adopted in local land use plans are consistent. Figure 5.8 shows an example of the timing of a regional land-use planning process, where a local plan was adopted before the structure plan and the structure plan was only fully adopted after the regional planning guidance was finalised for the subsequent plan period.

	90	91	92	93	94	95	96	97	98	99	00	01	02	03	04
PLANNING FOR THE SOUTH EAST															
REGIONAL (RPG9)															
Previous guidance (to 2011)					■										
Draft									■						
Public examination										■					
Final (to 2016)											■				
OXFORDSHIRE STRUCTURE PLAN (to 2011)															
Deposit draft						■									
Examination in public								■							
Adopted									■						
Amended													■		
WEST OXFORDSHIRE LOCAL PLAN															
Deposit draft					■										
Local plan inquiry						■									
Adopted								■							

Figure 5.8 *Planning process timescales in Oxfordshire*

5.4.2   Environment Agency planning horizons

Environment Agency water resources planning is developed over the medium to long term and is generally implemented regionally. There are several levels at which Agency planning is relevant to land-use planning and sustainable water management, including, for example, water resources strategies and catchment abstraction management strategies (CAMS) as well as the newly developing catchment flood management plans and river basin management plans. The Agency also provides environmental data that can be used in the planning process to inform decision-making. Environment Agency plans are developed and reviewed regularly over timescales no greater than 5–10 years (see also Section 3.2).

The CAMS represent a significant development in policy in sustainable water management by the Agency and could present challenges for water utilities in making longer-term plans for water supply infrastructure. CAMS strategies are likely to be reviewed over a 5–10-year period and could involve the greater use of time-limited abstraction licences in areas where there are doubts about the sustainability of an abstraction licence. Part of the process is to review the sustainability of abstractions within a catchment. This might lead to a reduction in, or loss of, abstraction licences, which in turn could necessitate a review of the water resource supply-demand balance and necessitate consideration of alternative sustainable options. The results of these reviews may not be compatible with proposed land-use development (depending on when this is identified).

The major challenge is to develop consistent and appropriate programmes for both land-use planning and environmental management planning that recognise the differences in planning horizons between the implementation of Agency strategies and the land-use planning horizons.

5.4.3   Water infrastructure planning horizons

Water supply and sewerage undertakers produce strategic plans designed to help them meet the requirements of Ofwat's five-year cycle of pricing reviews. The asset management planning process (AMP) identifies necessary infrastructure improvements over the short and medium term. The plans look up to 10 years ahead, but place the emphasis on the first five years. In addition, the water industry also makes long-term plans for its own asset development and replacement programmes, commensurate with the long life of many of its assets and the long lead-in time that may be required to carry out major new infrastructure developments. This level of planning may have a horizon of 25 years or more and, together with the Environment Agency requirements for long-term water resource plans, drives the water company long-term demand forecasts, which currently have 2024/25 as the planning horizon.

Again, the challenges lie in attempting to reconcile the lack of fit between water company long-term demand forecasts and the land-use planning horizons. There is a danger of inconsistencies where timescales are discordant.

5.5 Challenge 4: management at a catchment scale

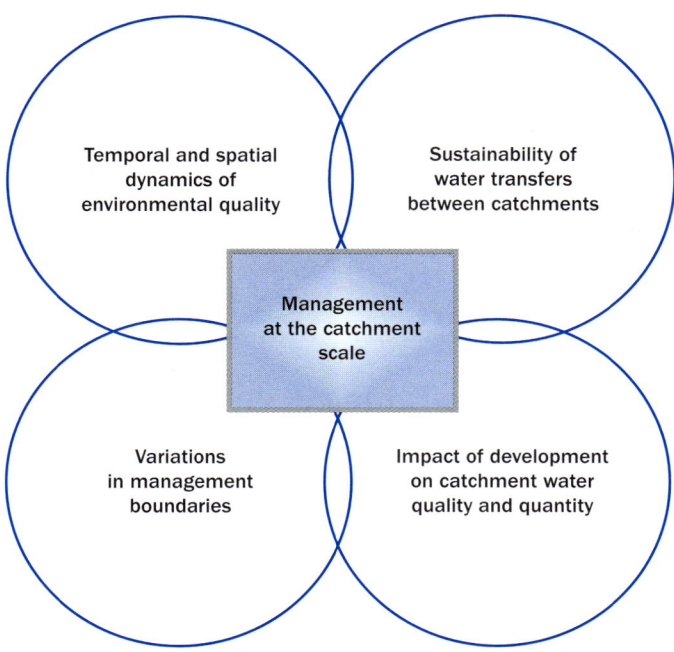

Figure 5.9   *Issues associated with catchment-scale management*

5.5.1 Variation in management boundaries

The management boundaries of the water companies and sewerage undertakers, the Environment Agency regions and land-use planning areas are not aligned. Where developments straddle these different boundaries, this can hinder sustainable water management within the land-use planning process and communication can be complicated because of the number of organisations involved. For example, the resource assessments and policies contained in the Agency's published water resources strategy, and similarly water company water resources plans, may not necessarily be applicable to the local authority area because their boundaries may be different.

While large developments on such boundaries are relatively rare, such issues may increase when the planning requirements within the Water Framework Directive are implemented. The WFD directs the development of management policies at the river "basin" scale; these management basins are large and their boundaries do not align with either regional or local authority boundaries. This will increase on the complexity of environmental assessments of proposed developments and affect the definition of appropriate mitigation measures. Decision-making at a catchment scale, as required by the WFD, may point to the adoption of, for example, demand management policies within such a boundary. Water charges will, however, be applied equally across a water company supply area.

5.5.2   Temporal and spatial dynamics of environmental quality

Spatial variability of environmental processes and quality is likely to lead to different policy objectives, different approaches to environmental management, and different requirements of land-use planning for developments in adjoining areas as well as for those in separate parts of the country. The variability of environmental conditions with time may also be high, and also unpredictable because of the uncertainty associated with the diverse processes operating at both macro and micro scales. Rapid changes in river water quality, for example, may lead to shifts in water quality objectives in some areas and, under the new CAMS, might nessitate revisions to authorised abstraction regimes. There is a danger that developers working at a national scale or across environmentally diverse areas may perceive as inconsistent a valid or justified variation in Environment Agency responses and policy.

5.5.3   Sustainability of water transfers between catchments and new treatment technology

As discussed in Section 3.2.5, the Environment Agency's water resources strategy (EA, 2001a) shows large areas, especially in the south-east of England, where no further water is available during summer, or where damage to the environment is already occurring as a result of existing abstractions. The strategy also identifies the potential need to develop further water-transfer schemes in some areas to help overcome these problems. Alternatively, there may be locally available water resources that are of a lower quality than would be appropriate for public water supply. Possible measures for such areas include:

- inset appointments (for water provision or wastewater treatment) that allow companies to provide services beyond their established infrastructure areas

- water-transfer agreements from high-resource areas to areas most at need

- new technology or innovative techniques that are able to provide additional capability to treat locally available poor-quality water to the required standards for public water supply.

There is a lack of guidance and practical experience on competition/inset appointments and how water trading might be implemented in practice. Provision of such guidance would promote awareness and understanding by planners and developers, and so facilitate application of these approaches.

Water transfers between two water company areas, or even between resource zones within the same supply area, depend on the network infrastructure being available or planned and of sufficient capacity. Practical limitations may therefore restrict the applicability of such solutions. The environmental impact of such solutions also has to be appraised in detail. Raw water transfers between either groundwater or surface water catchments will affect natural flow regimes and quality, and may have be detrimental to the environment in the catchments.

Options for the provision of water will also always be appraised in terms of their economic viability, and it will generally be the least-cost solution that is taken forward. Unless the environmental impacts can be fully quantified, the environment may not be represented sufficiently within the decision-making process.

5.5.4 Impact of development on environmental quality

Development has the potential to degrade the quality of both surface and groundwater systems. Unless mitigation measures are adopted covering the full range of potential impacts, the water environment can be placed at risk through:

- additional demands for water resources
- the enhanced volumes and reduced quality of the surface water runoff
- the increased wastewater treatment and dilution requirements
- the reductions in percolation and groundwater recharge.

However, the impact of land-use on water resources is extremely complex, so quantifying the effects of individual developments on this can be difficult. If these potential effects are to be identified and avoided or mitigated, it is essential that the Environment Agency and, where appropriate, water utilities are involved as early as possible in the planning process. Also, many parties share the responsibility for the existing environmental status and future pressures. There is a need for fuller understanding of the interaction of these cross-sectoral issues.

5.6 Challenge 5: education, communication and integrated planning

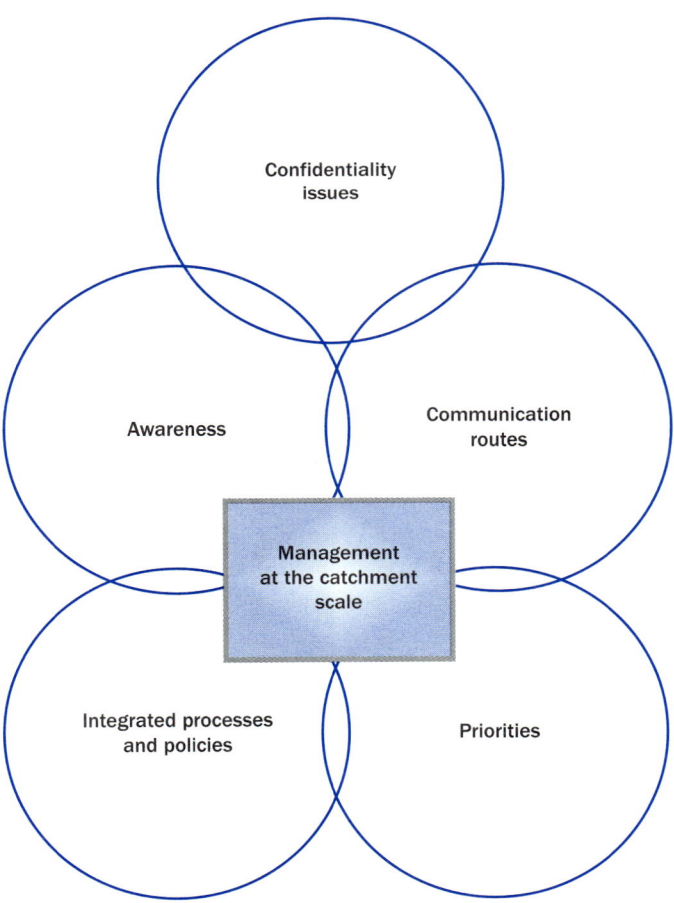

Figure 5.10   *Issues of communication and understanding*

5.6.1 Routes of communication

Historically, the routes of communication between land use planners, water utilities, sewerage undertakers and the Environment Agency may have been informal. This is changing, not least because of the requirement for spatial planning, which needs to be consistent with and supportive of other strategies and policies that affect land use and development but are not delivered through the planning system. Although communication may in the past have been effective, it relied on *ad hoc* personal knowledge and contacts between individuals within the respective organisations. Without clear lines of communication, maintaining a network of contacts between organisations is difficult, given the number of organisations and local offices involved. This is compounded by potential communications difficulties in finding the appropriate language with which to discuss and understand the wide variety of technical and other issues.

Strategic liaison between the Environment Agency and local authorities appears to be best at national and regional level; direct contact between individual local authorities and the Agency area offices is more variable. Consultation on development plans may involve some meetings, but liaison on planning applications is usually by correspondence only. There is the perception that LA planning teams view the consultation responses they receive as fulfilling a requirement without having a full understanding of the issues involved.

A lack of formal communication routes can create difficulties in ensuring that all of the correct stakeholders in a development have been contacted at the appropriate time and at the appropriate level, leading to land-use plans evolving independently from water resource or environmental management strategies. Lack of knowledge-transfer has in the past led to environment-related objections being raised at, for example, local plan or planning application stage, at which time only minor revisions are possible. The statement of community involvement (SCI) that is now required under the Planning and Compulsory Purchase Act 2004 provides the opportunity to identify all stakeholders and how they are to be involved by LPAs in both development planning and planning applications and to monitor that involvement and take action to remedy any deficiencies.

5.6.2 Awareness and training

In some areas, local authority planners have low levels of awareness of the water environment, relevant stakeholders, and Environment Agency and water company planning and management processes. Without both awareness and understanding of water management and the associated regulatory structure, sustainable decision-making and guidance driven by the land-use planning process is likely to be compromised. The need for more rapid decisions, particularly to meet LPA targets for decision times, is likely to require adapting current processes and priorities to avoid exacerbating this problem

Several factors in the stakeholder organisations may lead to poor communication and inconsistent responses including:

- the volume and complexity of information
- the speed at which regulation, policy and guidance need to respond to change
- staff turnover and mobility
- the size of the organisations.

5.6.3　Integrated processes and policies

Land-use planners develop long-range plans for the community's future growth and development, and for ensuring that development does not occur in the absence of critical resources or infrastructure. They rely on the water industry to keep them informed about water availability. Planning authorities therefore have the primary responsibility for determining future development-related growth levels, and water companies have the primary responsibility for delivery of essential water supply and sewerage services.

From a planner's point of view, if the water supply and sewerage undertakers have a duty to provide services wherever they are needed, if the costs will be borne by private companies and if the impacts can be mitigated by conditions, then there is no problem to resolve. There is no information on comparative environmental costs of alternative options or mechanisms through which to undertake an appraisal. Historically, the land-use planning and water management functions have been poorly integrated.

In addition to the communication issues detailed in Section 5.6.1, incomplete awareness or understanding of the processes and policies for guiding water supply development, wastewater provision and land-use planning may have contributed to this poor integration. This is manifested in variability of representation of sustainable water management policies within development plans. Although appropriate policies are gradually emerging as plans are updated or revised, there is a lack of consistent, rigorous approaches to identifying relevant issues in individual areas and balancing water issues with other sustainability issues (see also Sections 4.2 and 5.3.1).

5.6.4　Confidentiality issues

Several of the water management stakeholders, eg water companies and developers, are commercial organisations. As a result of commercial sensitivity issues, some of their information may not be available at all stages in the planning process. This could lead to a lack of transparency and openness during dialogue.

5.6.5　Priorities

Environmental protection will often have to be balanced against economic benefits during appraisal of the decision as to whether a particular development should go ahead or not. Without mechanisms in place for full consideration of such issues within the land-use planning system, there is a danger that the sustainability of the proposals in water management terms may not be given as high a priority as it deserves. Placing sustainable development as the core principle underpinning planning, and the incorporation of community involvement and sustainability appraisal, will go some way towards providing appropriate mechanisms.

6 Guidance

6.1 Introduction

Chapter 5 identified the issues in Box 6.1 for achieving sustainable water management when planning new development.

Box 6.1 *Issues in achieving sustainable water management in new development*

Meeting all stakeholder interests

- competing demands for water
- different regulatory objectives
- water management aspects of national planning policies
- meeting expectations of society now and in the future.

Addressing the uncertainties

- uncertainties in demand forecasting
- uncertainties in water resource availability
- uncertainties in implementing innovative design solutions.

Timing issues

- land-use planning horizons
- Environment Agency planning horizons
- water infrastructure planning horizons.

Management at a catchment scale

- variation in management boundaries
- temporal and spatial dynamics of environmental quality
- sustainability of water transfers between catchments and new treatment technology
- impact of development on environmental quality.

Education communication and integrated planning

- routes of communication
- awareness and training
- integrated processes and policies
- confidentiality issues
- priorities.

The guidance developed in this chapter is presented for the key stakeholders and recommendations are made in Chapter 7.

Stakeholder	Section
Land-use/spatial planners, eg in local authorities, regional assemblies	6.2
Environment Agency	6.3
Water companies and sewerage undertakers	6.4
House-builders and developers	6.5

The interactions between the processes of interest to these professional groups are summarised in Figures 4.1 to 4.4. This chapter contains three checklists to help land-use/spatial planners implement the guidance in regional planning, local development planning and development control. A key theme of the guidance is to improve the communication between the various stakeholders so that issues, constraints and solutions are identified as early as possible and effective actions can be taken. Box 6.2 summarises the steps for integrating water issues in spatial planning.

Box 6.2   *Key steps for integrating water issues in spatial planning*

- Raise planning professionals' awareness of water management issues, the water planning processes and its timescales.

- Consult with the water industry and EA as early as possible at key decision points in the spatial planning process to improve input of land-use planning information into sustainable water management and *vice versa*.

- Ensure wide availability of this CIRIA guide to all stakeholders.

- Prepare documents on regional water management issues by stakeholders to inform spatial planners. These should be web-based, so they can be updated easily, with hard copies sent out after each update.

- Prepare standard checklists for each planning tier, so that spatial planners ask water stakeholders the right questions at the right time.

- Convene regional stakeholder forums (with identified stakeholder representatives) to discuss regional issues and to improve understanding and dialogue when RSS revisions are prepared. These may also help identify water managers' concerns and constraints earlier in the process. Annex D of PPS11 advises on partnership working and community involvement in the RSS process.

- Convene forums dedicated to the local authority planning levels (again, with identified stakeholder representatives), with discussion and modification of pre-consultation draft plans. Chapter 3 of PPS12 outlines the requirements for community involvement in local development planning.

- Prepare guidance on appropriate planning policy and conditions where water resources are under pressure.

This book not give specific designs for sustainable water infrastructure, but Appendix 2 provides extracts from plan policies that exemplify good practice for:

- supply and sewerage
- flood risk management
- general environmental protection
- biodiversity.

Appendix 3 presents five case studies covering aspects of water management in planning and Appendix 4 gives the web addresses for some useful sites identified during the drafting of this guidance. CIRIA has published guidance on aspects of sustainable water management; see Box 6.3 below. Figure 6.1 provides a summary of the issues in the guidance, which follows in the remainder of this chapter. Figures 6.3 to 6.5 are example checklists that highlight the main routes for the communication of water-related issues at various stages in the planning process. While aimed principally at planners, it is hoped they will also prove a valuable starting point for dialogue between all stakeholders on water-related issues.

Box 6.3   *CIRIA guidance on technology for water sustainability*

C522	*Sustainable urban drainage systems – design manual for England and Wales* (Martin *et al*, 2000)	C609	*Sustainable drainage systems. Hydraulic, structural and water quality advice* (Wilson *et al*, 2004)
C523	*Sustainable urban drainage systems – best practice manual for England, Scotland, Wales and Northern Ireland* (Martin *et al*, 2001)	C625	*Model agreements for sustainable water management systems. Model agreements for SUDS* (Shaffer *et al*, 2004)
C539	*Rainwater and greywater use in buildings. Best practice guidance* (Leggett *et al*, 2001)	C626	*Model agreements for sustainable water management systems. Model agreement for rainwater and greywater use systems*
C582	*Source control using constructed pervious surfaces. Hydraulic, structural and water quality performance issues* (Pratt *et al*, 2002)	PR80	*Rainwater and greywater use in buildings. Decision-making for water conservation*

Land-use/spatial planners

- initiate and organise regional stakeholder forum and local committees
- co-ordinate formal stakeholder participant lists and contact details
- commit staff to training in water management issues
- use issues documents and stakeholder consultation to develop planning policies that promote sustainable water management
- ensure consistent interpretation of national guidance within regional plans
- use planning checklists to ensure effective consultation
- ensure land allocation fully considers water issues. Consider constraining development or existing demand in areas of water stress, together with appropriate mitigation for necessary development
- commit to public/developer awareness-raising and education campaigns, in association with the water industry
- commit to facilitating long-term operation and maintenance solutions for water conservation/sustainable drainage solutions.

Housebuilders/developers

- participate in regional stakeholder forum and local committees to ensure maximum understanding of relevant water management issues
- commit to pre-application discussions for major developments with regulators and water managers
- commit to development of high-quality proposals taking account of sustainable water management planning policy
- commit to inclusion of water conservation and sustainable drainage solutions for new development
- support public awareness-raising and education campaigns.

Actions to address water sustainability issues

Regulators

- fund R&D into innovative water conservation, drainage, resource and treatment options
- fund R&D into consistent methods for valuing the water environment
- work with water industry on use of multi-criteria tools to give the water management appropriate weight in decision-making
- raise awareness among land-use planners of water management processes and industry regulation
- integrate regulatory and land-use planning via formalised regional stakeholder forum and local committees
- develop regional issues documents and commit to ongoing consultation and plan reviews
- set up working group to ensure compatible regulation.

Water industry

- consider innovative water conservation, drainage, resource and treatment options
- include environmental costs and benefits within option appraisal processes
- raise awareness among land-use planners of water management processes and industry regulation
- integrate water industry and land-use planning through regional stakeholder forum and local committees
- develop regional issues documents and commit to ongoing consultation and plan reviews
- commit to ongoing customer awareness-raising and education campaigns
- implement water-efficiency measures on own sites.

Figure 6.1   *Guidance to stakeholder on actions to address water sustainability issues*

6.2   Guidance for land-use/spatial planners

This section gives guidance on how spatial planners and the land-use planning system can steer sustainable development in the context of water management.

A successful planning system promotes economic prosperity by delivering land for development in the right place, at the right time and at an acceptable cost. However, the government commitment to sustainable development implies this must not be at the expense of the natural environment, which includes the water environment. The decision-making processes must include structured and transparent appraisal methodologies to minimise long-term risks to:

- the security of the public water supply
- maintaining environmental quality
- the capacity to sustain agricultural and industrial demands for water.

PPS1 (ODPM, 2005a) identifies sustainable development as the core principle underpinning planning, which should facilitate and promote sustainable, inclusive patterns of development by making suitable land available for development in line with economic, social and environmental objectives to improve people's quality of life. The planning system could also be used to improve understanding, awareness and management of our water environment. Apart from flood risk, and to some degree protection of water resources and water quality, water supply and drainage issues have not been as prominent in planning as they might be.

A good starting point is for local authorities to address sustainable water use and implement good practice within their own sites and new developments. Important issues include water management in council-owned swimming pools, water use in public parks and other open spaces and water use, drainage and sewerage on their own sites. Locally based initiatives of this kind should be checked for consistency or conflict with objectives of neighbouring areas and validated against national policies. A good example of this is the Water in Hampshire Project (see Appendix 3.5) and the subsequent publishing of Hampshire CC's Corporate Water Action Plan (HCC, 2001 and 2002). This includes a list of specific actions with measurable targets and performance indicators. Other authorities could implement such changes through their in-house environmental management systems.

6.2.1   National planning policies

PPGs, which are in the process of being replaced by PPSs, are the way the government sets out its objectives for housing, transport, urban regeneration and a whole range of policy areas. regional planning bodies (RPBs) and local planning authorities (LPAs) must take national policy into account when preparing regional or local development plans. This helps to ensure consistency in the application of planning policies and enables the government to implement the land-use aspects of international obligations and European directives.

The impact of development on our water resources must be integrated with the land use planning process, where appropriate, and a full consideration of all the issues undertaken at each level of decision-making. Significant improvements could be achieved through addressing water issues consistently using the existing policy guidance (see Figure 6.2). This will require local authorities to interpret the current PPGs and PPSs, recognising the central importance of water in achieving sustainable development.

PPG3 Housing → *Creating sustainable residential environments* →

Objective
- Housing that has no detrimental impact on the long-term sustainability of national, regional or local water resources.

Mechanism
- Development proposals accompanied by a water resource assessment, prepared in consultation with water companies and Environment Agency.

PPS11 Regional spatial strategies →

Covering
Economic development
Housing
Transport
Retail and leisure use
Cultural
Rural development
Biodiversity and nature
Conservation
The coast
Minerals
Waste
Energy
Other: air quality, health

→

Objective
- Regional plans that promote development that does not have a detrimental impact on the long-term sustainability of national, regional or local water resources.

Mechanism
- Regional plans establish characteristics of water resources of regional and sub-regional significance, the pressures associated with those resources, potential conflicts with development pressures and opportunities for environmental improvement.
- Regional plans map water resources issues from EA water resource strategies, highlighting resources at risk of over-abstraction or pollution.
- Regional plans set a vision for integration of sustainable and environmental land-use planning with water resource planning; identify regional and sub-regional priorities; highlight areas where water efficiencies can be implemented, eg agriculture. Proposals for implementing such efficiencies.
- Regional plans should list all water issues that require appropriate local planning policies.
- Regional plans should identify "border" issues requiring close working with agencies in other English regions, Wales and Scotland.

PPS12 Local development frameworks →

4
Sustainable development

→

Objective
- Development plans that take environmental considerations comprehensively and consistently into account.

Mechanism
- Clear identification of all water management issues that require comprehensive consultation.
- Clear identification of consultees for each issue.
- Timescale and issues for consultation to ensure effective integration of water resource and environmental planning.
- Identify opportunities for mitigation through planning conditions.

PPS23 Planning and pollution control →

Annex 1
Pollution control, air and water quality
Annex 2
Development on land affected by contamination

→

Objective
- Prevent environmental pollution, eg from industrial development and redevelopment of contaminated land.

Mechanism
- Close consultation between relevant parties.
- Sewerage undertaker to regulate trade effluents.
- Environment Agency to grant discharge consents.
- LPA to refuse planning permission if it is not satisfied about adequacy of sewerage infrastructure.
- Undertake a risk assessment.

PPG25 Development and flood risk →

Objective
- To control and reduce the exposure of people and property to flood hazard and risk.

Mechanism
- Sequential risk-based test for development (para 30).
- Undertake flood risk assessments.
- Use SUDS where appropriate.

Figure 6.2   *Incorporating water issues in development plans using existing guidance*

6.2.2   Development planning

Development plans have an important role in setting out both opportunities and constraints to development, and in covering the full suite of topics that require consideration before decisions on development size, location and characteristics can be made in a sustainable way, particularly in a plan-led system. Water management issues must form an integral component of these required considerations, as discussed in the following sections. If it becomes apparent that sustainable water management is impossible to achieve in certain parts of the UK, the government may need to review its policy and legislation and consider revising the current demand-led approach to water supply to an approach based on the capacity of water resources.

Regional planning

The RSS provides a spatial framework to inform the preparation of local development plans, local transport plans and other relevant regional and sub-regional strategies and programmes. Water company water resources plans, Environment Agency LEAPs and CFMPs would benefit if they were developed in conjunction with the development of regional plans via a regional stakeholder forum at pre-consultation stage of the draft revisions to the RSS.

Once regional planners have identified potential strategic development areas, these draft proposals could be submitted to the water industry and Environment Agency for review and comment. Through discussions, the planners will already be aware of information on where there is likely to be spare capacity in current water resource (including supply and sewerage) infrastructure and where environmental pressures may mean that further development of water resources could pose additional sustainability concerns. The draft proposal review would enable more detailed confirmation that the level of development is appropriate in terms of water sustainability; it would also provide an opportunity to receive comments on any concerns and discussion of possible mitigation.

A checklist (Figure 6.3) is provided at the end of this book, which acts as a tool by which planners can identify the questions, consultation and actions necessary to include water sustainability in regional planning.

Local development planning

Until 2004, county structure planning formed the strategic framework within which policies were applied in line with the overall regional planning guidance (now the RSS). This strategic planning element of the development plan system has been incorporated in the RSS. Where new sub-regional spatial strategies are developed in support of the RSS, sub-regional water management issues, such as those identified in the previous section, can be considered fully.

Spatial strategies and local development plans ought to include appropriate environmental policies, with water issues specifically being recognised and incorporated. The latest Hampshire County Structure Plan (HCC, 2000a; see Appendix 3) shows how this can be done, although even this example could be taken further. The plan states that "development will not be permitted where it is likely to lead to the deterioration of the quality of groundwater or surface water". This could be strengthened with a policy that "gives preference to development where it is likely to lead to improvements in the quality of groundwater or surface water". Together the policies would act as both stick and carrot for future sustainable development. Appendix 2 gives further examples of planning policies relevant to sustainable water management. While the debate on the relative merits of urban, brownfield and new greenfield sites will not primarily be driven by water issues, water can still be an important component. Consideration should be given to the timing of new developments so they can integrate better with existing and future water supply and sewerage infrastructure.

Local authorities have a duty to prepare community strategies, which they are to develop in conjunction with other public, private and community sector organisations. Community strategies should promote the economic, social and environmental well-being of their areas and contribute to the achievement of sustainable development. While they are not an appropriate mechanism for the consideration of technical water resource issues, they could be a useful means of introducing the concepts and needs for demand management and other water conservation measures, eg rainwater harvesting, water-efficient appliances and sustainable drainage systems, into water-stressed areas. Research by the ODPM (2003b) identified the benefits to be obtained from linking community strategies and local development frameworks (LDFs) in terms of achieving an integrated approach towards future development within a local authority area based upon sustainable development objectives.

A checklist (Figure 6.4) is presented at the end of the book, which provides planners and others with the basis of a tool to identify questions, consultation and actions by which they may include water sustainability in development planning.

Supplementary planning documents

SPDs are prepared to expand policy or provide further detail to policies in DPDs. SPDs may include design guides, area development briefs, master plans or issue-based documents. They are designed to respond to issues that are locally important but do not merit the statutory status of the development plan. For example, an SPD might expand upon the approach to be taken in assessing and mitigating the impacts of any development on environmental quality in an area where there are concerns about surface water quality or residual flows in a river catchment.

The development of major sites can be successfully promoted by the preparation of development briefs and master plans that elaborate DPD policies as they should apply to a particular site. They could identify land to be used for SUDS within the development, areas of land at flood risk that should be devoted to public open space, or specify water efficiency measures to be considered for use within the new buildings. Further information on planning briefs can be found within GPG13 *Development plans: a good practice guide* (DoE, 1992c).

6.2.3   Development control

The pre-application discussions between developers, local authorities, the Environment Agency and water management stakeholders are an important means of:

- ensuring high-quality, sustainable development
- reducing the chances of presenting applications that are not viable
- speeding up the planning application process.

The water issues in these discussions could be based around the development control checklist provided at the end of this chapter. Alternatively, water supply and sewerage issues could be included in a revision of the planning application forms. The inclusion in appropriate LDFs of detailed explanation of particular environmental constraints and opportunities for planning in the area should also help raise developers' awareness, identify opportunities for planning obligations, and indicate the types of planning condition likely to be imposed.

For development that may result in polluting emissions, such as waste management facilities and some industrial plants, separate consents are currently required from the planning authority on land-use matters and from the Environment Agency on pollution control matters. The Environment Agency has recently been working with the Local Government Association (LGA) and the Confederation of British Industry to produce a concordat, aimed at synchronising the two processes and reducing delays and uncertainty. While this approach has not managed to achieve consensus, it is supported in PPS23 (ODPM, 2004g) as an important move to further integrate the land-use planning and environmental regulation processes.

A checklist (Figure 6.5) is provided at the end of the book that planners and others can use as a tool to identify questions, consultation and actions related to conditions and planning obligations by which water sustainability can be included in development control.

6.3 Guidance for the Environment Agency

Within the existing planning framework, the greatest long-term impact of the Environment Agency's interactions with the planning system will arise from operating at a national and regional level, to influence PPSs and RSSs. This requires the Agency to present consistent policy objectives and approaches at a national level, based upon sound science and analysis, while representing adequately and appropriately the key differences in water management issues between regions.

Under the current system, the Agency's most effective role at the more detailed planning levels (local development plans and development control) is in:

- identifying development proposals that raise potential issues for environmental protection
- providing examples of good practice for water management in the design of homes, gardens, open spaces, public, commercial and industrial buildings
- identifying appropriate planning conditions to mitigate for potential environmental impacts.

6.3.1 National planning policies

At a national level, the Environment Agency should continue to argue for water to be treated as a key sustainability criterion consistent with its overall vision. This may be achieved through direct communication with government policy-makers, responses to consultation exercises and effective consultation on all new planning and policy initiatives. Additional measures that could be undertaken by the Environment Agency at a national level are given in Box 6.4.

Box 6.4   *National measures for the Environment Agency*

- Revise national water resource strategies in conjunction with water companies and water users. This is being developed at a water resource unit level and will be consistent with the CAMS process.

- The EU Water Framework Directive requires the EA to carry out catchment-based water management planning with the objectives of identifying and maintaining "good" ecological status in surface waters and providing some of the information required to assess the "cost" of water within particular regions. Co-ordination of these assessments at a national level is needed to ensure that they are carried out objectively and consistently, as part of the Common Implementation Strategy, and are appropriately publicised to the planning development forum.

- Sponsor and facilitate research on climate change impacts to provide a sound basis for national forward planning and to help reduce uncertainties in managing the water supply-demand balance.

- Promoting efficient use of water within agriculture and agri-environment schemes to protect and enhance the water environment.

- Continue to encourage demand management within domestic and commercial sectors, providing a lead in promoting trials that measure and demonstrate the benefits of demand management to the environment and the consumer.

- Continue to promote research to further understanding of the public health and environmental issues involved in non-wholesome water reuse.

- Promote new technologies including the installation of water meters wherever possible, in line with government policy.

- Link highway drainage to consistent planning policies on stormwater management/reuse.

6.3.2   Development planning

Regional planning

There are many opportunities within the existing planning system for the Environment Agency to contribute to the planning process at a regional level. The Agency has been proactive in recent years in seeking to ensure that environmental issues are given appropriate weight within regional planning guidance, eg *Regional planning guidance for the South East, Environment Agency users' manual* (The Planning Co-operative, 2001). Appendix 2 provides some examples of regional policies, from current RPG documents.

For the South East Region, RPG9 (GO-SE, 2001) includes many policies containing water sustainability issues; examples are given below.

Policy E2

The Region's biodiversity should be maintained and enhanced with positive action to achieve the targets set in national and local biodiversity action plans through planning decisions and other measures.

Policy INF1

Development should be guided away from areas at risk or likely to be at risk in future from flooding, or where it would increase the risk of flood damage elsewhere. Existing flood defences should be protected where they continue to be relevant.

Policy INF2

New development should be located and its implementation planned in such a way as to allow for sustainable provision of water services and enable timely investment in sewage treatment and discharge systems to maintain the appropriate standard of water quality. Techniques that improve water efficiency and minimise adverse impacts on water resources, on the quality, regime and ecology of rivers, and on groundwater, should be encouraged. Redevelopment should identify and make provision for rectification of any legacy of contamination and drainage problems.

Regional initiatives

A good way for the Environment Agency to set out water management objectives and requirements at a regional level would be to develop a regional issues document, possibly modelled on the *Thames environment 21* document produced by Thames Region of the Agency (EA, 1998). Other regional initiatives to promote sustainable use and reuse of water have been made, but such documents are currently not available on a consistent national basis and do not have any statutory status. This material might be generated from the future WFD river basin management plans and could be presented on a planning portal on the Environment Agency and/or government office website. This would give planners a clear path to important, up-to-date regional information. Such a document could be discussed, together with pre-consultation drafts of RSS revisions by means of a regional stakeholders' forum, as is encouraged in PPS11. This forum would allow further opportunities for the Agency to:

- raise other stakeholders' awareness of the significance of water issues
- promote the inclusion of strong environmental policies in land-use plans
- promote water-sensitive policies as part of the drive to sustainability
- extend liaison and discussion with water companies within a land-use planning framework.

Local development planning

Existing structure and local plans have offered, and the new LDFs will continue to offer, the Agency the opportunity to advise on and promote appropriate water management policies for local areas. This can be done most effectively by strengthening and formalising consistent dialogue with planners and water companies. This approach (encouraged in PPS12) has greatest potential impact on policies delivered into LDFs and carried through to detailed proposals, eg in the choice of sites for development. The Environment Agency should use this forum to promote the water management objectives and aims it has developed in its various spatial plans:

- catchment abstraction management strategies (CAMS)
- catchment flood management plans (CFMP)
- the forthcoming river basin management plans (required by the WFD)
- the national and regional water resources strategies, *Water resources for the future* (EA, 2001a).

The Environment Agency also has a role in promoting the consideration of cross-cutting themes in LDFs, such as:

- including water issues as part of the "sustainability appraisal" of LDDs
- addressing the implications of additional sewerage loads from development in catchment headwaters on discharge consent criteria and water quality objectives
- making appropriate comparison of brownfield sites on floodplains with greenfield sites for housing development (as implied by PPG25)
- use of sustainable drainage systems to meet biodiversity objectives in particular areas.

To overcome the specific problems of differing boundaries for planning and water resource management, the Agency already identifies at a local level the boundary differences in areas where they may have significant impact on the policies to be pursued. If this were carried out at a national level, it would enable the Agency to develop consistent policies for responding to development plans in such situations.

Within LDFs, the Environment Agency is well placed to:

- advocate the inclusion of strong area-specific environmental policies in local plans
- promote the benefits of better management of water for long-term environmental and social gains
- assist planners in developing planning policies to protect wetlands and sensitive groundwater zones, river flows, water quality, fisheries, amenity or nature conservation
- promote storm drainage source control measures wherever possible to contribute to flood risk mitigation or reduction in the future
- protect functional floodplains and washlands from inappropriate development
- establish the critical water sustainability indicators against which planning applications can be assessed.

6.3.3   Development control

Traditionally the Agency has provided water management expertise in development control through responses to consultation on planning applications and requesting certain design approaches by conditions on planning consents. Although this needs to continue, the Agency can also implement water management at this level through influencing the content of the plans in the plan-led system. Initiatives in this respect are already established, eg the Agency's Water Demand Management (WDM) Team, which provides expertise in water conservation, water efficiency and demand management. The WDM Team provides technical support and policy advice to all levels of the Agency on topics such as leakage, demand forecasting, water-saving technologies, water reuse, metering, tariffs and economic incentives. It has published useful information on these issues on the Agency website.

It is recommended that such efforts should be continued and publicity broadened, focusing particularly on local authority planners and on all developers. A planning section is under preparation for the Agency website. This will be of most value if it provides both national and regionally specific information for planners, including downloadable copies of:

- planning contacts within the Agency
- current water resource maps showing areas of limited water resource
- maps of groundwater vulnerability, water quality objectives and other environmental designations
- decision-support checklists to help with water sustainability appraisals.

Continued pursuit of efficient and innovative water management strategies in all aspects of the Agency's operations will strengthen its guidance and demonstrate to developers and local authorities the effectiveness of water management measures . This would be enhanced by specifying water efficiency measures when renovating Agency buildings or taking on new premises and monitoring and publicising the effectiveness of these activities at a corporate level.

In a partnering approach the Agency could provide developers with "in-principle" agreement to some design aspects of the plans before they are submitted to the planning authorities. The voluntary adoption of water demand management measures by developers could then be promoted legitimately as environmental gain. For economic reasons, some developers will not wish to pursue opportunities, even with partnering from water companies, so more formal planning conditions may be necessary if progress is to be made. The Environment Agency should take an active role in pre-application discussions for major developments, such as by helping prepare those development planning briefs that will have a major impact on the sustainable use of water. As a starting point, the Southern Region of the Environment Agency provides a general guidance leaflet on water efficiency in construction, *Sustainable water management – promoting water efficiency* (EA, 2001c). This (and similar) guidance could be distributed nationally.

6.4 Guidance for water and wastewater service providers

Water companies possess a wealth of information, most of which is already disseminated to the Environment Agency. After taking issues of confidentiality into account, this information should be provided to other stakeholders in the planning process. The challenge is to integrate water issues with the land-use planning process, for example to dovetail the planning of development with the five-year asset management planning (AMP) process.

6.4.1 National level

Defra, Ofwat and the water companies are already participating in several national initiatives. Participation should be continued, enhanced and in some cases extended. Examples of such initiatives and future developments are outlined in Box 6.5.

WaterUK, representing the water industry, meets regularly with Ofwat, Defra and the Environment Agency. This quadripartite group could steer the involvement of its members in dealing with water in the planning arena and encourage the uptake of this guidance.

Box 6.5   *National initiatives in sustainable water management*

Watermark	
The Watermark project aims to provide a benchmark for water use in the public sector and establish targets for water conservation, reduce consumption and costs for the public sector. See <www.watermark.gov.uk>.	Co-operating with this programme and promoting it will help the water industry to identify with national benchmarks for water efficiency and use this to manage supply demands, with the eventual aim of reducing variability in demand between similar operations. This in turn will allow improved demand predictions.
Water Efficiency Awards	
The Water Efficiency Awards are funded jointly by the Environment Agency and Water UK. They aim to publicise and promote examples of good water management.	Ofwat, Defra and Water UK should continue to support this and similar initiatives and promote them, particularly within the public sector – especially where they link to new buildings/housing. This will raise the awareness of water efficiency achievements within local authorities and with public-sector planners. This may provide an incentive for house-builders to embrace sustainable water management.
Climate change assessments	
UKWIR already commissions research to assess the impacts of climate change on aspects of water company operations.	This research should be continued to study the implications of the UKCIP02 climate change scenarios (Hulme *et al*, 2002) on the future sustainability of water. The findings need to be made available and accessible to planners and other stakeholders.

In addition, every water company has projects on distribution network modelling, leakage reduction, promotion of the efficient use of water, implementing water legislation. Information on some of these projects has already been publicised and could be made available to other planning stakeholders, after allowance has been made for confidentiality issues.

6.4.2   Development planning

Regional planning

Water companies have an important regional planning role, as they operate over large areas, often covering significant sections of the regions used for planning. The lack of an exact spatial match between planning regions and water company boundaries means that water companies should ensure a co-ordinated approach to working within the planning system at this level. RPBs and LPAs also need to understand that sustainable water management within and across catchments does not neatly match administrative boundaries.

To support this collaborative approach, it is suggested that, where they do not exist at present, water companies should develop the role of a regional planning liaison representative. This function would collate information for the various water planning functions, eg resource planning, supply and sewerage, within the company and use this to support the discussions with the Environment Agency, other water companies (where appropriate) and RPBs and LPAs. This information could be presented in a regional issues document, which could be made available and readily updatable via a planning portal on the water company, GO and/or RDA websites. There is a need for commitment to regular discussion via the regional planning forum where the water companies can have early involvement with draft RSS revisions.

It is recommended that water companies actively participate in the whole of the RSS revision process via the regional planning representative.

Local development planning

At the local level, water companies should make inputs to the planning system (development plan process and major development applications). Foremost this would be by identifying the constraints on, and opportunities for, future water supply and wastewater disposal within local authority areas. This will offer a real opportunity to guide future development more sustainably and cost-effectively. Issues of timing and location can be understood from the early stages of planning for new development. RPG9, the regional guidance for the South East (now the RSS), already espouses this approach.

Within the planning process at this stage there exists an opportunity for water companies to invest time in directing core policies towards key water sustainability issues. These should remain in place for some time to guide future and more detailed plans. Water and wastewater treatment is already regarded as an issue in sustainable development, but it may not always be given the prominence it deserves. Early involvement in the development plan process would also allow water companies to pursue the inclusion of policies that promote cost-effective water efficiency projects, as well as providing for the necessary infrastructure to support sustainable development within the region.

Investment in water infrastructure at the local level requires an understanding of the patterns and pace of growth across the catchment. Continuing liaison at district and borough level will improve the exchange of information and enable investment to take place when and where it is needed. Detailed data on future growth is often required, eg population projections at the parish level, to enable proper appreciation of the impact on infrastructure. Water companies and sewerage undertakers should be proactive in making responses to consultations on LDDs.

The implementation of sustainable drainage systems is seen as a key aspect of achieving sustainable development in England and Wales. The incorporation of SUDS needs to be considered early on in the site evaluation and planning process, as well as at the detailed design stage. The National SUDS Working Group has produced the *Interim code of practice for sustainable drainage systems* (NSWG, 2004) to facilitate the wider use of SUDS and to make the adoption and allocation of maintenance more straightforward. There remain some difficulties for water and sewerage companies in adopting these systems, even though most companies recognise the benefits they can deliver. *Model agreements for SUDS* (Shaffer *et al*, 2004), used with the *Interim code of practice*, will help to ease, if not totally overcome, these difficulties.

6.4.3 Development control

Where there has been good consultation up to this stage in the planning process, the involvement of the water companies in development control will be less onerous. Water companies will be primarily concerned with water delivery and sewage removal. This scenario assumes that appropriate and effective policies have been put in place and implemented further up the "planning tree", such that the development is being proposed in a sustainable location and scale and within a time-frame that facilitates the development of the most sustainable infrastructure options.

Water companies should:

- provide information to developers so they are able to satisfy planning checklists
- encourage voluntary water demand management measures from developers as environmental gain, as this encourages their remit to encourage water efficiency.

While water companies and sewerage undertakers are not statutory consultees in the planning process, there are significant benefits in being involved in development control and third-party applications. Ongoing consultation as appropriate is to be encouraged. Water companies can, for example, assist local planning authorities by identifying the time required to meet potential additional demands on the water infrastructure in the most sustainable way, for example by preparing briefing notes for local planning authorities. This will help reduce the burden on both the local planning authorities in issuing consultations and on the water companies in administering and focusing their responses.

6.5 Guidance for house-builders and developers

6.5.1 National level

The House Builders Federation generally represents house-builders nationally so it has an important role in national consultation. The HBF is responsible for raising concerns of developers with respect to new or existing national policy, and conversely for assisting the transfer of new knowledge and policy to their members. Several sustainable water management initiatives for new homes already exist at a national level and support from the house-building industry is vital to ensure that research and development is disseminated and incorporated within new developments across the country (see Box 6.6).

Box 6.6 *Recent water management initiatives*

- Established with EPSRC funding, the Watersave network <www.watersave.net.uk> works to identify how water can be used more efficiently in the home. It is supported by the Environment Agency, several water companies, Ofwat, CIRIA, several universities and others.

- The designation and testing of water fittings on the basis of their water efficiency (equivalent to an energy efficiency rating). This is already being addressed in part through the Market Transformation programme <www.mtprog.com>, which aims to increase the market penetration of water-efficient and energy-efficient products.

- Research and use of the latest techniques that allow low-water-use construction.

- Research and development into sustainable drainage systems, including initiatives to develop standard adoption agreements <www.ciria.org/suds> likely to be acceptable on a national basis (with regional variations) and potential economic, amenity and ecological benefits.

- The Sustainable Construction Client Award Scheme <www.ciria.org/environment_rp642.htm> aims to increase the implementation of best practice (including water management and pollution control) in the construction supply chain.

From 2001–02, all 10 sewerage service providers in England and Wales have offered surface water drainage rebates for customers who are not connected to public sewers for surface water drainage. Customers must be able to demonstrate that the property concerned does not benefit from a surface water drainage service. The rebates vary by company in terms of both the amount of the reduced charge and how it is applied (standing charge or variable element). If house-builders and developers recognise this potential for long-term cost savings for their customers, the benefits could be used to enhance the attractiveness of the property.

House-builders already demonstrate their commitment to the environment through the use of "green" construction methods and their contribution to the development of the Sustainable Buildings Code initiated under the Government's Sustainable Communities Plan. Some developers, including housing associations, have a continued involvement in the development after construction and take a long-term view on sustainability. A commitment to sustainable water management would form another component of a comprehensive environmental policy.

House-builders are closest to the general public in the planning system, so are well placed to raise awareness of water issues.

For industrial and commercial developments, water efficiency can deliver significant reductions in cost for the owner or tenant of the premises, as has been demonstrated in several trials (EA, 2001c and d, 2002a). Developers can promote such savings to assist in selling such developments.

6.5.2   Development planning

Regional planning

Developers need to be able to distinguish between those areas where planning permission is likely to be granted or granted subject to certain constraints, and those locations where planning permission may be refused or restricted for reasons relating to the water environment. While this distinction can only be made on a site-specific basis at the local planning level, the RSS provides the framework, eg in terms of the scale and distribution by district of housing needs, for site-specific allocations by LPAs. There needs to be early consultation between planners, major house-builders, developers, the Environment Agency and water companies at the regional planning stage to identify and evaluate broad areas for development and levels of growth. Evaluation of the constraints and opportunities for water supply and wastewater disposal will enable sustainable solutions to be progressed and unsustainable options to be revised at an early stage. Developers who are involved in long-term strategic development planning need access to information on water-related constraints and water infrastructure planning proposals at regional level, and to take account of these in identifying and promoting strategic areas for development. Major developers, as well as umbrella organisations like the HBF should consider being represented at the new regional stakeholder forums.

Local development planning

With more comprehensive LDF policies relating to water, and with better access to information relating to the local water environment, developers will be better equipped to develop and bring forward more sustainable development proposals. They will also find that this helps to avoid abortive costs on promoting developments where water sustainability issues are likely to make applications unacceptable. Developers need to engage in the local planning forum, to keep abreast of water issues relevant to their local areas. At local planning level, where site layouts and infrastructure planning are being agreed, developers should dedicate resources to consult with the Environment Agency and water companies via planning checklists, to identify likely risks and appropriate mitigation measures.

In developers' strategies for local development, there needs to be better understanding of the potential benefits to the community and the local environment of incorporating sustainable water management solutions, eg SUDS, rainwater harvesting and reuse techniques, low water-use appliances. Also the strategies will need to consider how these could be designed and marketed to maximum effect. In undertaking such promotion, they will need to engage the public in taking responsibility for the water environment. Throughout the world there have been many innovative schemes in which greater water efficiency has benefited both developers and consumers (see the Californian case study in Appendix 3).

Professional development for developers' staff will raise awareness of water management principles, so that maximum value is gained from consultation and knowledge-transfer processes. For house-builders, NHBC and HBF should be responsible for promoting this to their members, with advice from the Environment Agency and water companies. Raised awareness levels, improved communication and more structured direction of development design criteria are likely to reduce confrontation and smooth the passage of development proposals through the subsequent planning application process.

6.5.3   Development control

For large developments, pre-application consultation with relevant water management stakeholders is vital to ensure that all water issues have been addressed at final application stage. Water conservation is a novel sustainability concept for the public to address, whereas there is a much higher level of commitment to energy conservation principles. Developers need to consider combined water and energy conservation developments on the basis of lower running costs and long-term environmental benefits. A development that embodies these principles is Beddington Zero Energy Development (BedZED, <www.bedzed.org.uk>), in Sutton, Surrey. Every aspect of BedZED has been designed to conserve finite natural resources and to have minimal impact on the environment, and the development has integrated plans for transport, energy efficiency and water conservation. This is an example of what might ultimately be achievable rather than what can easily be incorporated into existing designs.

Wherever appropriate, the solutions shown in Box 6.7 should be considered for all new developments, especially those in identified water-stressed areas.

Box 6.7   *Practical water conservation and management solutions*

- drainage source control measures and SUDS
- water-efficient appliances (including dual-flush toilets, low-flow showers and taps)
- rainwater harvesting, rainwater and greywater reuse techniques
- environmental blackwater treatment.

Developers currently have to meet the Water Supply (Water Fittings) Regulations 1999, but there is no legal requirement to go further, though the Code for Sustainable Building may set a more aspirational standard. In water-stressed areas discussions between developers, water companies and the Environment Agency regarding the specifications for water appliances and fixtures may help to identify mitigation measures – such as more water-efficient devices (Environment Agency, 2002a) – that allow more sustainable development. It is also important that housing corporations and housing associations that draw up their own specifications also consult the Agency and the water companies at the formulative stage of their proposals.

The following checklists can be found as pull-out pages at the back of this book.

Figure 6.3   Regional planning checklist

Figure 6.4   Local planning checklist

Figure 6.5   Development control checklist

7   Recommendations

This chapter highlights the recommendations that could help further integrate sustainable water management issues into spatial planning. These recommendations could form a background to the consolidation and redrafting of the planning policy guidance notes as planning policy statements (PPSs). Some of the recommendations are not necessarily issues that need to be addressed today; rather they are possible steps that could be taken if achieving sustainable water management becomes more difficult in the future. As a result, these recommendations will need to be reviewed in the future through further research, consultation and evaluation to ensure that they are appropriate to be taken forward.

Recommendations to further integrate sustainable water management within the current land-use/spatial planning process.

1   Land-use/spatial planners would benefit from improved access to guidance and advice to ensure that they are more aware of water (and other) sustainability issues and can be proactive in introducing them into relevant plans. This could be at several levels including better signposts to existing information, the provision of training (this could be via professional institutions linked with organisations with expertise on specific topics), and the identification and provision of sources of advice. In addition, improvements could be made to the available information that land-use planners can use, or point developers to, in fostering awareness of sustainable water management issues.

2   The land-use/spatial planning process may also benefit from the development of key indicators and decision support tools that enable the semi- or (if possible) fully quantitative assessment of the sustainability of the components of a development (including water management) to maximise the overall sustainability. This would help to improve the transparency of the planning process.

3   The Environment Agency should continue to monitor the sustainability of water management within England and Wales and, if necessary, highlight the requirements for further steps to increase the consideration of these issues within the land-use planning process.

4   The Building Regulations 2000 (as amended), and the Water Supply (Water Fittings) Regulations 1999 and associated reference documents (DLTR, 2001c; DETR, 1999c), should continue to be regularly reviewed (possibly on a five-yearly basis) as appropriate to take account of new technology, enhance sustainable water management and promote its implementation.

5   Environment Agency advice and guidance is, necessarily, region-specific. However, the Agency could undertake a national review and standardisation of its guidance documents related to the planning system to ensure there are no inconsistent messages.

6   The Environment Agency's advice will increasingly be focused by the integrated river basin management plans (RBMPs) it needs to develop to meet the WFD (Chapter 3). These are not due to be completed until 2009, but an initial assessment of the river basins and the anthropogenic factors will be undertaken. It is clear that the preparation and requirements of the RBMP need to be publicised to planners so that they can engage with the RBMPs as they develop in order to secure, as far as possible, the integration of these two separate statutory planning systems.

7   Developers require consistent advice from the planning process. They could develop a national forum to debate the consistency of planning advice and implementation of water supply and disposal and building regulations throughout the country. This would need to cover a wide range of issues, but should have special interest sections with one focusing on water sustainability issues. The same forum could be used to disseminate, discuss and promote new and emerging advice and guidance regarding water-efficient developments and sustainable drainage schemes.

8   Developers should discuss their proposed developments and associated water management issues with land-use planners, water service providers and regulators at the earliest juncture to facilitate the development of sustainable solutions.

9   Ofwat could also demonstrate its receptiveness to funding water company initiatives to subsidise water efficiency in new homes, eg rebate programmes, third-party funding.

10 Water companies could carry out more work with developers to provide impetus and direction in trialling the use of water-saving measures in new developments (and refurbishment programmes).

It is recommended that this guidance should be reviewed after three years to identify the need for further guidance/recommendations. The review should also recommend the date of the next review, which may be after a further five years. CIRIA also recommends that an industry forum could be held to monitor the influence and usefulness of this guidance and advise on the scope of any revision.

Potential steps that may be considered for future improvements in integrating sustainable water management within the land-use/spatial planning process.

There is scope to enhance sustainability planning policy guidance. For example, PPG3 *Housing* (DETR, 2000e) could include policies that cover sustainable water resource planning to a level of detail appropriate to the importance of the issue in each region.

Within regional spatial strategies, region-wide strategic water management policies could be included, which would have statutory status.

Greater involvement of stakeholders in all stages in the planning process may be required. Local development frameworks and the statement of community involvement should help to simplify this process.

A1 Stakeholders

A1.1 Water management

A1.1.1 Defra, central government

Function

The Water and Land Directorate of the Department for Environment, Food and Rural Affairs (Defra) is responsible for all aspects of water policy in England and Wales. Its remit covers water supply and resources, and the regulatory systems for the water environment and the water industry. Defra's areas of responsibilities cover:

- drinking water quality
- the quality of water in rivers, lakes and estuaries
- coastal and marine waters
- sewage treatment
- reservoir safety.

Aims and objectives

The overall aim of the department is that of "sustainable development", including:

- a better environment at home and internationally, and sustainable use of natural resources
- economic prosperity through sustainable farming, fishing, food, water and other industries that meet consumers' requirements
- thriving economies and communities in rural areas and a countryside for all to enjoy.

The department's objectives are to:

- protect and improve the rural, urban, marine and global environment and conserve and enhance biodiversity, and to lead integration of these with other policies across government and internationally
- enhance opportunity and tackle social exclusion through promoting sustainable rural areas with a dynamic and inclusive economy, strong rural communities and fair access to services
- promote a sustainable, competitive and safe food supply chain that meets consumers' requirements
- improve enjoyment of an attractive and well-managed countryside for all
- promote sustainable, diverse, modern and adaptable farming through domestic and international actions and further ambitious Common Agricultural Policy (CAP) reform
- promote sustainable management and prudent use of natural resources domestically and internationally
- protect the public's interest in relation to environmental impacts and health, including protection from diseases that can be transmitted through food or water.

Organisational structure

Overall responsibility for this department lies with the Secretary of State for Environment, Food and Rural Affairs, who has ministers of state leading departmental teams for:

- environment (covering sustainable development, climate change, environmental protection and water issues, wildlife and conservation, SSSIs, national parks and areas of outstanding natural beauty)
- rural affairs (covering rural affairs and countryside issues).

There also two parliamentary under-secretaries responsible for:

- animal health and welfare, forestry, floods and coastal management
- food and farming, inland waterways

Current interaction with the planning process

Defra will be involved in the development of PPSs in relation to environmental matters.

A1.1.2   Environment Agency

Function

The Environment Agency is an executive agency of the Department of Environment, Food and Rural Affairs (Defra). Its wide-ranging responsibilities include the management of water resources, control of pollution in inland, estuarial and coastal waters, and flood management including water level management. The principal duty of the Agency is to "contribute towards the achievement of sustainable development". In carrying out its functions, the Agency has general duties to protect and enhance the environment and promote recreation.

Aims and objectives

EA's vision is "a better environment in England and Wales for present and future generations". This is to be achieved by effective regulation and by working with and influencing others. The Agency is required to exercise its duties consistently, reasonably and in the public interest.

Aims relating to sustainable water management include:

- achieving a significant and continuous improvement in the quality of air, land and water
- maximising benefits of integrated pollution control and integrated river basin management
- providing effective defence for people and property against flooding from main rivers, and effecting a supervisory role with respect to all flooding issues
- managing water resources to achieve a proper balance between the needs of the environment and those of abstractors
- developing a better-informed public through open debate, providing soundly based information and rigorous research
- setting priorities and proposing solutions that do not pose excessive costs on society.

Although the Agency operates within an extensive regulatory framework, it has very limited legal powers to prevent and control pollution and flooding arising from development.

In contributing to the development plan process, the Agency aims to:

- consider the impact of development on the wider environment and natural resources
- adopt the precautionary principle in evaluating the impact of the development
- promote the "polluter pays" principle
- make recommendations that ensure adequate protection of the environmental resources necessary for sustaining life
- promote the design of development that minimises the impact on the environment
- promote practices that work with, not against, nature and natural processes.

Organisational structure

Staff at the Agency's head office include policy and process teams that produce policies and provide advice and procedural guidance to the operational staff in the area offices. Water resource planning is carried out at a strategic level and a regional strategic unit deals with other region-wide issues. Land-use planning issues are relevant at all levels and the structure should ensure that the Agency efforts are prioritised and focused on those planning proposals where the environmental consequences are the greatest. The Agency also operates a Water Demand Management Team (formerly the National Water Demand Management Centre) (see below).

Current interaction with the planning process.

See Chapter 4.

A1.1.3   Environment Agency Water Demand Management Team

The WDM Team provides four main services.

1   **The promotion of publications, seminars and media events** to disseminate efficient water use by companies, consumers and manufacturers. The provision of information and education on all aspects of water conservation in the home, business and industry. The production of a free bi-monthly publication, *The Bulletin*, which provides up-to-date information on demand management and water conservation.

2   **The provision of advice to Agency and government policy-makers** on water conservation and demand management issues, including leakage, metering, demand forecasting, water-saving technology, recycling water, tariffs and economic incentives.

3   **The implementation of technical assessments** and the development of demand management methodologies (assessing leakage levels and reviewing demand forecasts, for example) and the provision of *ad hoc* and structured technical support to Agency staff.

4   **The direction of the Agency's research and development programme** on water conservation and demand management, securing project managers from water resources staff and providing co-ordination with external research programmes. The team often works in partnership with UK Water Industry Research Ltd (UKWIR) on jointly sponsored projects.

The topics covered by the one-stop-shop service of the WDM Team include:

- demand forecasting
- leakage from customer and company pipes
- tariffs and economic incentives
- education on efficient water use
- domestic and non-domestic metering
- industrial and agricultural demand
- levels of service
- water-saving technology and management
- water use restrictions.

With the support of the WDM Team, the Agency:

- demands a more efficient use of water by the water companies and by industry
- encourages a more efficient use of water by the public and a change in public attitude towards water usage
- promotes low-water-usage domestic appliances, supported by legislative changes if necessary
- demands reductions in leakage before considering any cases for investment in new reservoirs
- supports compulsory metering where water supplies are under stress and where meters are economically sensible to install
- supports the voluntary acceptance of water-meters when accompanied by other water-saving incentives for the customer.

A1.1.4 Internal drainage boards

Function

Internal drainage boards are the operating authorities that look after ordinary watercourses in areas known as internal drainage districts. They fund their activities through a direct charge on agricultural land occupiers within their internal drainage district and from special levies on local authorities.

The 235 internal drainage boards of England and Wales operate in low-lying areas where flood protection and land drainage are necessary to sustain agricultural and developed land use. This often requires pumped drainage to evacuate water. Although their powers are permissive in practice, most boards designate certain watercourses in their area upon which to carry out regular maintenance. Initially, internal drainage boards concentrated on agricultural drainage, but in recent years substantial development has taken place in many districts. For many boards a significant part of the work is to provide adequate standards of flood protection to urbanised areas, including major industrial complexes, by means of pumping stations and channel systems.

Aims and objectives

Internal drainage boards have a duty to exercise general supervision over all matters relating to land drainage within their districts. The Land Drainage Acts 1991 and 1994 provide for:

- general supervision over all aspects of land drainage within the district
- improving and maintaining the drainage system, including the operation of pumping stations
- regulating activities in and alongside the drainage system, other than on those waterways designated as main rivers and those under the Environment Agency's control
- duties to conservation
- raising income to support land drainage works.

Organisational structure

Board members, who must be owners or occupiers of land within the district, are elected by agricultural rate-payers for a three-year term. Local authorities may contribute to a board's costs and are then able to nominate members. Internal drainage districts vary in size from a few hundred hectares to tens of thousands of hectares, which influences the arrangements in place for their administration. Large boards engage full-time administrative and technical staff, while the smaller boards contract work out or belong to a group of boards managed as a consortium.

Current interaction with the planning process

Internal drainage boards are not statutory consultees, but will generally be consulted, on a non-statutory basis, on local plans and planning applications within their defined area of interest. They are unlikely to be involved further up the planning process.

A1.1.5   Local authorities

Function

Local authority drainage departments look after those ordinary watercourses that are not in an internal drainage district. Local authorities fund flood defence activities through the council tax and from central government through the standard spending assessment mechanism.

Aims and objectives

Local authorities have similar powers to internal drainage boards. Their level of involvement on flood defence and land drainage matters varies considerably, dependent upon the nature of the council's area and particularly whether any drainage districts are established. The Land Drainage Acts 1991 and 1994 provide for:

- works to alleviate flooding
- regulating activities in and alongside waterways, other than the main rivers and within a drainage district
- duties to conservation
- raising income through general charging arrangements to cover the costs of flood alleviation schemes and other land drainage work.

Organisational structure

Where the councils are responsible for drainage, this remit is likely to fall within the technical services department. Usually it is the larger district and unitary authorities (mainly in urban areas) who have these departments. Smaller councils may not have the capability and may look to their parent authorities to fill the role.

Current interaction with the planning process

Local authority technical services departments may be consulted on surface and foul drainage at planning application stage for specific sites. They will not usually be involved within the development planning process. Again, these departments are found mainly in the larger urban district or unitary authorities, which traditionally had "agency powers" – ie a remit to act on behalf of the old water authorities, before these were transferred to the water companies.

A1.1.6   Highways Agency

Function

The Highways Agency (HA) is an executive agency of the Department for Transport (DfT). This department is responsible for overall government policy on motorways and trunk roads in England and for determining the strategic framework and the financial resources within which it operates. The HA is then responsible for maintaining, operating and improving the network of trunk roads and motorways in England on behalf of the Secretary of State for Transport. The assemblies of Wales, Scotland and Northern Ireland are responsible for their own highway networks.

Aims and objectives

Responsibility for the maintenance and improvement of the Highways Agency network is divided between 19 maintaining agencies. These agencies generally comprise a consortium of consultants and contractors employed on term contracts let by competitive tender. In total the Highways Agency is responsible for some 20 000 km of highway drainage.

The HA's overall aim is to deliver reliable trunk roads and motorways as part of an integrated transport system, and to support sustainable development. Specifically relating to water management, the HA has an objective to "minimise the impact of the trunk road network on both the natural and built environment". In pursuing this and other objectives, the HA works in partnership with local highway authorities, sharing both information and expertise.

Organisational structure

The Highways Agency is the national body with responsibility for motorways and trunk roads, on behalf of the Secretary of State for Transport. County councils and unitary authorities have agency powers to act on behalf of the Highways Agency on trunk roads (not motorways), as well as being the highways authority in their own right for "county" roads (all other roads). This remit will lie within technical services departments.

Current interaction with the planning process

The Highways Agency was a statutory consultee for structure plans, and would normally be consulted on local plans where there is a trunk road or motorway. It is now a specific consultation body for development plan documents. It is often also consulted at strategic level for regional planning and will be involved in the preparation of the regional transport strategy, which is now incorporated in the RSS, though it does not appear to be an SCB for the RSS.

At planning application level, the Highways Agency is involved only with trunk roads and motorways, but retains powers of "direction" on any planning application. The highways authorities are statutory consultees on non-trunk roads, but have no powers of direction.

See Section A1.1.17, Storm water drainage, on the following page.

A1.1.7 Water supply/sewage disposal companies

Function

There are 25 water and sewerage companies across in England and Wales. The 10 largest of these are both water undertakers (ie suppliers) and sewerage undertakers (ie responsible for removing wastewater). In some parts of England and Wales, however, water and sewage are dealt with separately by different organisations.

Water companies encompass a wide range of environmental policy, through which they seek to minimise the environmental impact and maximise the sustainability of their core activities. The industry is committed to habitat creation and restoration and the protection of endangered species. It is also working to understand the impact of wider environmental changes such as global warming on water supply. The water industry works with many environmental and countryside groups to build on its environmental policy.

Aims and objectives

Water supply

Under the Water Industry Act 1991 (WIA), the general duties of water undertakers are to:

- develop and maintain an efficient and economical system of water supply within its area
- ensure that all such arrangements have been made for providing supplies of water to premises in that area and for making supplies available to persons who demand them
- ensure that such arrangements have been made for maintaining, improving and extending the water undertakers' water mains and other pipes.

The Act includes specific duties to:

- make connections to the water mains for domestic and non-domestic purposes within its area (Sections 41–57) if served a notice by the owner or the occupier of the premises and/or the local authority and/or a development board or corporation, eg the Commission for New Towns. In this context, the premises concerned can be those on which buildings already exist or those for which there are proposals to erect buildings. This process is referred to as requisitioning
- ensure a constant supply and adequate mains pressure (Section 65–66)
- supply only water that is wholesome at the time of supply (for domestic purposes) (Sections 71–75)
- provide a supply of water for fire-fighting (fire hydrants) (Section 58)
- supply water for other public purposes, eg for cleansing sewers and drains, for cleansing and watering highways or for supplying public pumps, baths or wash-houses (Section 59), if required by the appropriate authorities.

Sections 60–65 of the Act relate to disconnection of supply.

The Environment Act 1995 amended the WIA by including a new part on water efficiency (Part IIIA). Under this amendment, it is the duty of a water undertaker to promote the efficient use of water. However, this duty does not give the undertaker the authority to impose on its customers any requirement regarding water efficiency. The Water Supply (Water Fittings) Regulations 1999 seek to minimise wastage and to promote water efficiency. For example, maximum flush volume of WC cisterns is now limited to 6 litres. These new regulations do not impose any additional duties on water undertakers.

Sewerage services

Under the WIA, sewerage undertakers' general duties (from Section 94 of the Act) are:

- to provide, improve and extend such a system of public sewers (whether inside its area or elsewhere), and so to cleanse and maintain those sewers as to ensure that that area is and continues to be effectively drained

- to make provision for the emptying of those sewers and further provision for effectively dealing, by means of sewage disposal or otherwise, with the contents of those sewers

- in performing these duties, to have regard to its existing and future obligations, to allow for the discharge of trade effluent into its public sewers and the need to provide for the disposal of that trade effluent.

The main duty of a sewerage undertaker under the Act is to provide a public sewer connection to be used for drainage for domestic purposes of premises in its area (if served a notice by the owner or the occupier of the premise, and/or the local authority, and/or a development board or corporation, eg the Commission for New Towns. This process is known as requisitioning. However, unless the undertaker had been made fully aware of the requirements at an early stage in the planning process, it is unlikely that the requisitioned capacity could be provided immediately.

The WIA also lays down the powers of a sewerage undertaker in regard to the adoption of sewers and sewage disposal systems. These powers cannot be used in contravention of the pollution prevention sections of the Water Resources Act 1991.

Sewerage undertakers have the duty to ensure that collecting systems (ie sewerage systems) satisfy the requirements laid down in the Urban Wastewater Treatment (England and Wales) Regulations 1994. The latter stipulate that treatment plants must operate efficiently under all local conditions, effluent and sludge must be reused wherever appropriate and the impact on the environment of the disposal routes for treated wastewater and sewage sludge must be minimised. The collection systems must be designed to take into account treatment requirements and be designed according to BATNEEC, taking into account the volume and characteristics of urban wastewater and the prevention of leaks and the limitation of pollution of receiving waters due to stormwater overflows. The Regulations also laid down the timetable for the improvement of wastewater treatment levels. "Urban waste water" is defined in the Regulations as domestic wastewater or the mixture of domestic wastewater with industrial wastewater and/or runoff rainwater. These Regulations transpose the EU Urban Wastewater Treatment Directive (91/271/EEC) for England and Wales.

The Environment Act 1995 amended the WIA to impose an additional duty on sewerage undertakers (Schedule 22, para 103 of the Environment Act 1995). They now have "the duty to provide a public sewer for domestic sewerage purposes of premises that are not connected with a public sewer where there are adverse effects, eg smells and nuisance to the environment or amenity from the existing system and where the connection of the first time connection of the premises to mains sewerage is the most cost-effective solution" (Section 101A of the WIA). Essentially, this means that the sewerage undertaker has the duty to connect premises to the public sewer on environmental grounds rather than being requisitioned to do so by the owner or local authority.

Stormwater drainage

The duties of the sewerage undertakers in relation to stormwater drainage are covered under their general duties under the WIA. Historically, surface and foul water have been conveyed together in a combined sewer, but separate systems are now more common. This reduces the risk of treatment works being overwhelmed by high discharges. The concept of sustainable drainage, which incorporates a range of source control systems, is being strongly promoted to try to minimise the impact of development on the environment. These systems encourage the attenuation, infiltration and treatment of stormwater before discharge to local watercourses.

A highway authority can enter into an agreement with the sewerage undertaker to use its sewers to convey surface water from roads repairable by the authority. Similarly, the sewerage undertaker can enter into an agreement with the highway authority to use the authority's drains to carry surface water from premises or streets (Section 115). The Act prohibits either party from refusing to enter into or consenting to such agreements on unreasonable grounds.

Organisational structure

Water companies are commonly structured to reflect their activities and their geographical area. Day-to-day operations can be managed from regional centres with management, planning and support functions being provided from central departments. The large capital investment by the companies has meant that they have had large engineering departments designing new works and systems. Some companies have outsourced functions such as engineering, procurement and customer service and billing to specialist service providers.

Plans to meet the future demands of customers require inputs from engineers, hydrologists and other specialists within the company. Such plans are produced within guidance and timescales set by the regulators; consequently, central responsibility for their production and acquisition of the associated data usually rests with the water company's regulation department.

Requests for supplies to new developments are managed by a dedicated team that oversees the entire process of new connections from application, through design to pipe laying.

Current interaction with the planning process.

See Chapter 4.

A1.1.8   Office of Water Services (Ofwat)

Function

Ofwat is the economic regulator of the water industry in England and Wales. Its function is to:

- regulate customer charging
- ensure that companies carry out their responsibilities under the Water Industry Act 1991
- protect the standards of service
- encourage companies to be more efficient
- work to encourage competition where appropriate.

It also compares and publishes the activities of all the companies. This helps poor performers to rise to the standards of the best.

Aims and objectives

Ofwat is responsible for making sure that the water and sewerage companies in England and Wales give their customers a good-quality, efficient service at a fair price.

It has powers to set price limits, to approve companies' codes of practice and to check that their services are performing to a set of "guaranteed standards" with which the companies are legally bound to comply. Ofwat also provides guidelines to help the companies deliver a better service to customers.

Organisational structure

Ofwat is an independent economic regulator led by the Director General of Water Services.

Current interaction with the planning process

Ofwat will be consulted on the development of any government policy (including planning policy) that affects its operations and those of the water industry.

A1.1.9 Drinking Water Inspectorate (DWI)

Function

The DWI regulates public water supplies in England and Wales. It is responsible for assessing the quality of drinking water, taking enforcement action if standards set in the Water Supply (Water Quality) Regulations 2000 are not being met and taking appropriate action when water is unfit for human consumption.

Inspectors carry out technical audits of each water company. These have two main parts:

- an annual assessment of the quality of drinking water supplied by the companies
- inspections of individual companies.

The assessment of water quality is based on information received regularly from the water companies. This information includes the results of the millions of tests made each year to see if the water meets the standards. Inspections are also undertaken to be sure that the results are reliable and give a true picture of the quality of the water supplied.

Aims and objectives

The DWI aims to ensure that all drinking water is delivered to customers to a standard that exceeds that set by the government. It funds research into water quality issues and water quality treatment technologies and disseminates information across the industry. The Committee on Products and Processes for Use in Public Water Supply (CPP) provides expert advice to government authorities in England and Wales on approvals of water supply appliances, and the DWI provides this committee with administrative and technical support services. The DWI publishes a full list of "substances, products and processes approved under Regulations 25 and 26 for use in connection with the supply of water for drinking, washing, cooking and food production purposes" (DWI, 2001).

Organisational structure

The DWI comprises a team of professionals with a wide range of expert knowledge in all aspects of water supply, including chemistry, microbiology and engineering. The government's chief medical officer advises the DWI on health matters.

Current interaction with the planning process

The DWI will be consulted on the development of any government policy (including planning policy) that impacts on its operations and those of the water industry.

A1.1.10   English Nature

Function

English Nature is the government body that promotes the conservation of England's wildlife and natural features. It achieves this by taking action itself and by working through and enabling others. The organisation was set up by the Environmental Protection Act 1990, and it is a statutory body. EN was formerly funded by the Department for Environment, Transport and the Regions (DETR) and now by the Department for Environment, Food and Rural Affairs (Defra). It works closely with the Joint Nature Conservation Committee, Scottish Natural Heritage and the Countryside Council for Wales (see below) for a consistent approach to nature conservation throughout Great Britain and towards fulfilling the country's international obligations.

Aims and objectives

Powers have been given to English Nature through several Acts of Parliament, including the National Parks and Access to the Countryside Act 1949, the Countryside Act 1968, the Nature Conservancy Council Act 1973, the Wildlife and Countryside Act 1981 (amended 1985), Environmental Protection Act 1990 and the Countryside and Rights of Way Act 2000.

Its duties are to:

- advise the government on nature conservation
- provide advice and information on nature conservation to organisations and individuals
- designate important areas for wildlife and natural features as sites of special scientific interest (SSSIs) and to secure the sustainable management of these sites
- issue licences to people working with protected animals and plants
- establish and manage national nature reserves and marine nature reserves
- support and carry out research
- implement, on behalf of government, international conventions and EC Directives on nature conservation including the Conservation (Natural Habitats &c.) Regulations 1994
- implement English Nature's share of the UK Biodiversity Action Plan in England and assist in the practical application of sustainable development
- help people experience and care for wildlife and natural features
- offer grants to help others carry out nature conservation.

English Nature works very closely with local wildlife trusts and leaves much of the detailed planning liaison work to them.

Organisational structure

English Nature is governed by a council, whose chairman and members are appointed by the secretary of state for the environment. It also liaises with the Countryside Agency and the CCW.

Current interaction with the planning process

English Nature was a statutory consultee for the development of structure plans and an advised consultee on local plans. At this stage, areas are designated for development and nature conservation/environmental protection. Recently, it has also become involved in regional planning. English Nature is now a SCB for RSSs and DPDs and it is a statutory consultee on planning applications for development potentially affecting SSSIs or other nationally recognised sites of nature conservation importance.

A1.1.11   Campaign for the Protection of Rural England (CPRE)

Function

The CPRE is a registered charity with approximately 59 000 members and supporters. It operates as a network with more than 200 district groups, a branch in every county, regional groups and a national office. This enables the CPRE to campaign at a national level and to carry out local action. Founded in 1926, the CPRE is one of the longest-established and most respected environmental groups in the UK.

Aims and objectives

The CPRE campaigns to protect and enhance the countryside. It aims to highlight problems and threats to the countryside, carry out research, canvass opinion and advocate solutions. It seeks to influence decision-makers and opinion-formers and often works in partnership with other bodies locally and nationally. The work of the CPRE focuses on land-use planning, transport, natural resources, farming and food, the quality, character and diversity of the countryside, and rural economies, services and quality of life.

Through lobbying, advice, research, publicity and education, the CPRE works to stop:

- unnecessary building and development on greenfields
- massive road, airport and port developments destroying countryside
- degradation of landscapes and habitats caused by intensive farming
- pollution – including light and noise pollution – in rural areas

and works to encourage:

- regeneration of urban areas and better use of empty homes
- locally grown and marketed foods
- sustainable management of woods, forests and farmland.

Organisational structure

As well as being a registered charity, CPRE is a company limited by guarantee. It is managed and administered by trustees who sit on an executive committee. The organisation is directed and guided by means of a twice-yearly general meeting, which is attended by voting delegates from the county branches and regional groups. Policies and campaigns are guided by a policy committee composed of people with expertise in the fields with which CPRE is concerned and key volunteers from the organisation.

The national organisation is based in an office in central London directed by a chief executive. It has a small number of regionally based staff to service its nine regional groups, which are constitutionally part of the national organisation. The regional groups' boundaries mirror those of the government's regional offices. The majority of the organisation's income is derived from membership subscriptions, donations from supporters and legacies. Each of the local county branches is a separate, independent charity. CPRE operates as a partnership between these branches and the national organisation, sharing resources, information and aims. Membership income is shared between branches and the national organisation.

Current interaction with the planning process

The CPRE lobbies and campaigns at different levels within the planning process, seeking to influence both planning legislation and development plans on all scales.

A1.1.12   Countryside Agency/CCW

Function

The Countryside Agency was formed from the merger of the Countryside Commission and the Rural Development Commission.

The Agency is the statutory body working to:

- conserve and enhance the countryside
- promote social equity and economic opportunity for the people who live there
- help everyone, wherever they live, to enjoy this national asset.

It aims to:

- lead with research and advice
- influence others, especially central and local government
- demonstrate ways forward through practical projects.

Within Wales, the Countryside Council for Wales (CCW) not only undertakes these aims but also performs English Nature's functions, and it liaises with both bodies.

Aims and objectives

The Agency is charged with adopting an integrated approach in its duties to champion the English countryside and to be a centre of rural expertise. However, the body has no legislative powers or formal duties.

Organisational structure

The Countryside Agency has eight regions following standard government office regions. Regional staff promote the Agency's policies and programmes to organisations in the region, and advise the Agency on how to shape its work to respond to the problems and opportunities of the region.

Current interaction with the planning process

Land-use planning is one of its most important priorities. The Agency understands that a living countryside depends on exploiting economic opportunity and recognises the substantial pressure for development on greenfield sites. Through input to the planning system, the Agency aims to support a strategic way forward, providing for the needs of society in a manner that respects environmental and other objectives. The Agency appears to have rather more than just a consultative role in formulation of government policies relating to the countryside, eg the recent Rural White Paper, but this role is an informal one.

The Agency makes substantial contributions to development plans, and stands up for the interests of the countryside in individual planning cases of national importance. The Agency was a statutory consultee for structure plans and is an advisory consultee for local plans/UDPs. It is now a CSB for RSSs and DPDs.

A1.1.13   Royal Society for the Protection of Birds (RSPB)

Function

The RSPB champions the conservation of birds and other wildlife in the UK and worldwide, in the interests of wildlife, the natural environment and people. It promotes the diversity, populations and distribution of birds and other wildlife through the protection and re-creation of habitats.

Aims and objectives

The RSPB is a registered charity, so its funds are restricted to those raised from members and voluntary donations.

The RSPB's mission is to conserve, maintain and, where practicable, enhance:

- the populations and natural ranges of wild birds
- the extent and quality of important habitats
- the value of the wider countryside and the marine environment for birds and other wildlife.

Organisational structure

In England, the society is divided into six regions that focus on local needs of members and supporters and the regionally specific environmental demands. Each of the regional offices manages a variety of activities, ranging from working with local policy-makers, fund raising, protecting vulnerable sites and recruiting new members.

Current interaction with the planning process

The RSPB contributes, where possible, to development plans to help ensure that biodiversity and conservation issues are adequately addressed. The RSPB was represented at public examinations into the RPGs for the South East and Anglian regions, both in 1999. Where specific development proposals are likely to affect sites of interest to the RSPB, it takes an active role in the planning application process.

A1.1.14 Local wildlife trusts

Function

As well as running a network of nature reserves, local wildlife trusts provide support and expertise in wildlife and land management issues to external bodies and private landowners. The expertise of the trusts covers a broad spectrum, including land and marine management, surveying, policy formulation, education and sustainable development.

Aims and objectives

Although the trusts have no officially designated powers, they do have a powerful role in the designation of local wildlife sites. Unusually for charitable organisations, they are recognised in national planning guidance.

Organisational structure

The 47 local wildlife trusts are independent charities that employ more than 1200 staff, cover the UK and range in geographical size from Sheffield to Scotland. The trusts have regional and national structures, with a body called the Wildlife Trusts providing a single voice for issues in the UK.

Current interaction with the planning process

The trusts are advisory consultees. At the local level, they are important consultees for development with respect to wildlife issues. English Nature passes down much of the local consultation, leaving detailed work required for local plans and development control to the trusts. The organisations are known to be very active in the process.

A1.2   Land-use planning

A1.2.1   ODPM, central government

Function

ODPM was created as a central department in its own right in May 2002 and took over the work of the DTLR with respect to land-use planning. It is responsible for policy on housing, planning, devolution, regional and local government and the fire service. It also takes responsibility for the Social Exclusion Unit, the Neighbourhood Renewal Unit and the government offices for the regions. The ODPM's remit is to create a fair and efficient land use planning system representing regional differences and promoting development that is both of a high quality and sustainable. Its activities in this respect are undertaken through the provision of guidance and advice, and in making decisions on regional and local development plans, called in applications and appeals. At present a programme of planning reform is being implemented via the Planning and Compulsory Purchase Act 2004 and revision of PPGs to more concise and clearer PPSs.

Aims and objectives

The Secretaries of State for the Environment and for Wales are the highest decision-making authorities in the planning systems of England and Wales and have statutory powers to determine planning appeals, to call in or make directions on planning applications and development plans, and to issue RSSs and PPSs. Decisions can only be overturned by UK or EU courts, and then only if there is an error of law.

The ODPM's objectives promote the development of a sustainable planning framework that:

- provides for the nation's needs for commercial and industrial development, food production, minerals extraction, new homes and other buildings, while respecting environmental objectives
- uses already developed areas in the most efficient way, while making them more attractive places in which to live and work
- conserves both the cultural heritage and natural resources, including wildlife, landscape, water, soil and air quality, taking particular care to safeguard designations of national and international importance
- shapes new development patterns in a way that minimises the need to travel.

Organisational structure

The deputy prime minister leads all of the ODPM policies, in particular the delivery of the Sustainable Communities Plan. Within the ODPM ministers of state direct departmental teams covering:

- local and regional government
- housing and planning
- regeneration and regional development.

The teams are supported by two parliamentary under-secretaries of state, who hold additional responsibilities, in particular for the Building Regulations and the Ordnance Survey.

Permanent staff in the planning directorate are responsible for developing policy through PPSs etc. Government regional offices monitor development plans and call in contentious planning applications. The Planning Inspectorate, now a semi-autonomous government agency, deals with appeals and local plan inquiries and independent examinations of DPDs, inspectors also determine appeals transferred from the secretary of state.

Current interaction with the planning process

ODPM determines national planning policy, and approves and issues RSS revisions following EIP and consultation on proposed changes. GOs check submitted LDDs and make any necessary representations before the independent examination and binding report. The secretary of state has powers to intervene by a direction to modify or submit a DPD for approval, where there are issues of national or regional importance and to direct modification of a SPD. Central government is consulted, via government regional offices, on all development plans. Although planning applications are made to local planning authorities, planning appeals are directed to the secretary of state.

A1.2.2 Local government

Function

As local planning authorities, county and district councils are responsible for controlling the use of land and development in accordance with national government policy. This is undertaken through preparing development plans and deciding on individual planning applications.

Aims and objectives

County and district councils have duties to prepare development plans, now under the LDS, for their area and powers to determine planning applications. They have additional duties and powers under numerous Acts, eg a duty to protect listed buildings and conservation areas under the Planning (Listed Buildings and Conservation Areas) Act 1990 and a duty to protect wildlife under the Wildlife and Countryside Act 1981.

Organisational structure

County, unitary and district councils have evolved haphazardly from the many reorganisations of local government. The drive towards efficiency and streamlining of decision-making has led to further change in the past few years. Most councils have the following or similar departments:

- planning – including development control, policy-making/forward planning (local and structure plans), conservation, special projects/environmental improvements
- technical services – including drainage and highways.

The figure below shows the typical organisational structure of a local authority and its planning department. Water issues would generally be addressed by the forward planning function, and development control through the planning application consultation process.

As instigators of development plans and the regulators of the development control system, local government is at the heart of the planning process.

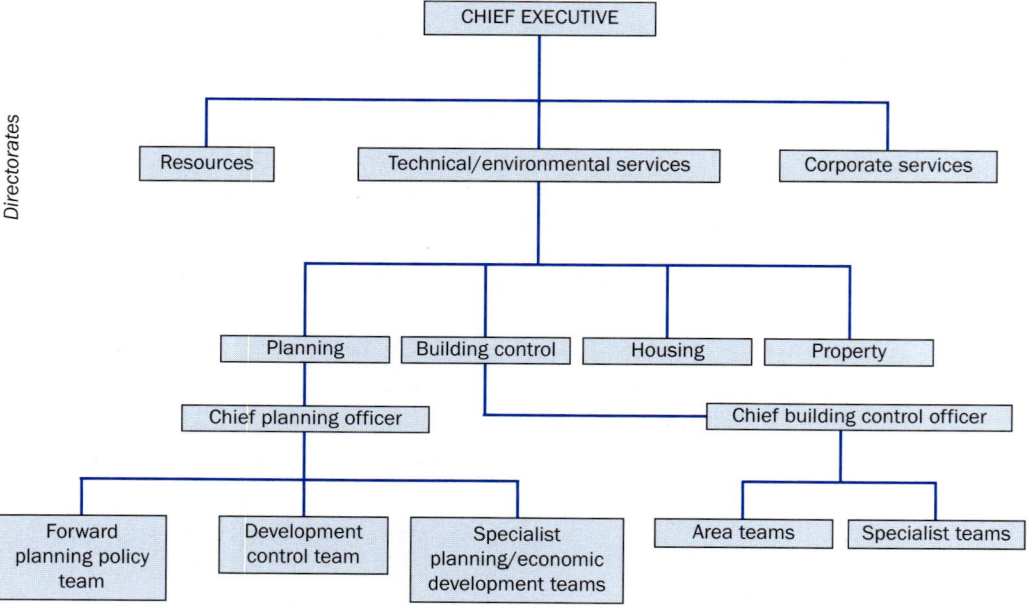

Figure A1.1   *Current interaction with the planning process*

A1.2.3   Developers/house-builders

Function

Many UK property and industrial developers are interested in both greenfield and brownfield development. Developers contribute towards the funding of essential infrastructure, eg water-supply/wastewater treatment infrastructure, that might be required as a result of the development via legally binding Section 106 Agreements (Town & County Planning Act 1990).

The House Builders Federation (HBF) is the trade body for private house-builders in England and Wales. It works with central and local government and many third parties, including non-governmental organisations and business communities on planning, housing, regeneration, design and economic and regional development. The HBF liaises closely with ODPM, BRE and the National House Building Council (NHBC) on technical matters pertinent to the industry. It scrutinises proposed changes to the Building Regulations to allow the industry to recommend amendments. The HBF communicates with the media, house-builders and the general public as well as politicians and organises media briefings to explain house-builders' perspectives on a wide variety of issues.

The NHBC is the independent regulator and standards-setter for the new homes industry and is an approved inspector under the Building Act 1984.

Aims and objectives

House-builders and developers are all commercial organisations with responsibilities to their shareholders to deliver development at a profit.

Neither developers nor the HBF or NHBC have legislative powers or responsibilities with respect to planning. The overall aim of the HBF is that this country should provide a decent home for all in an environmentally, economically and socially sustainable way. NHBC's aim is to help the house-building industry construct good-quality new homes that meet the reasonable expectations of home-buyers.

Organisational structure

Major house-builders throughout the UK will have the following sections.

1   **Strategic development teams** (at either national or regional level) that identify and secure options on land with long-term development potential. They then promote this land through the structure and local development plan processes.

2   **Local (area) development teams** identify short-term opportunities (often land for which planning permission has already been granted). The teams interact with the planning process mainly through the development control system.

3   **In-house technical departments**. Their responsibilities include evaluating water conservation and sustainable drainage issues (of individual development projects) alongside highway and other technical infrastructure matters.

In the HBF's London headquarters, permanent planning staff co-ordinate research and other functions on national planning issues from the members' viewpoint. Regional offices match the government planning regions and within each there are one or two planning advisers.

Current interaction with the planning process

See Chapter 4.

A2 Example planning policies that seek to promote water sustainability

A2.1   Sustainable, water use, supply and sewerage **128**

    A2.1.1   Policy guidance... 128

    A2.1.2   Example planning policies... 129

        Regional planning 129

        Structure planning.. 131

        Local planning 132

A2.2   Sustainable flood risk management **134**

    A2.2.1   Policy guidance... 134

    A2.2.2   Example planning policies... 134

        Regional planning 134

        Structure planning.. 136

        Local planning 136

A2.3   Environmental protection: general **138**

    A2.3.1   Policy guidance... 138

    A2.3.2   Example planning policies... 138

        Regional planning 138

        Structure planning.. 138

A2.4   Environmental protection: biodiversity **139**

    A2.4.1   Policy guidance... 139

    A2.4.2   Example planning policies... 139

        Regional planning 139

        Structure planning.. 140

A2.1 Sustainable water use, supply and sewerage

A2.1.1 Policy guidance

Guidelines on types of policies that should be considered.

General

Evaluate impacts of development proposals on water resources in full consultation with both the Agency and likely supply and sewerage providers. "Water-stressed" areas should be highlighted by incorporation of the Environment Agency water resource map(s) covering the plan area.

Adopt the precautionary principle with regard to the potential impact on groundwater resources. Groundwater-sensitive zones should be highlighted by incorporation of Environment Agency aquifer mapping and protection zones.

Require applicants to submit a statement demonstrating how their proposals address sustainability criteria relevant to water management.

Water supply and use

Only permit proposals for major new water resource developments if it can be proved that the need cannot be met through demand management and further leakage control measures.

Refuse development if it creates a requirement for water resources that will adversely affect water quality, amenity, fisheries, biodiversity or long-term security of supply to all stakeholders, including both existing and future customers.

Ensure that new development is phased to allow sufficient time for provision of new supply infrastructure. This new infrastructure must be sustainable and contribute zero risk or positive gain to both the local and the wider environment.

Ensure that development does not take place in areas without adequate sustainable water supplies.

Establish the requirement for water efficiency and water recycling measures in all types of new development

Use supplementary planning guidance to facilitate adoption of these water conservation measures.

Wastewater drainage

Ensure that development does not proceed in areas where the sewage treatment works and receiving watercourses do not have the capacity to cope with additional load without degradation of water quality.

Only allow development to proceed where the necessary drainage and sewerage can be provided without detrimental environmental impact and within the development timescale.

Use policies that promote the inclusion of water quality improvements within proposals, as a positive environmental criterion for development.

Surface water drainage

Sustainable drainage initiatives should be considered for all development sites and implemented wherever possible. Sustainable drainage solutions do not necessarily require high land-take or particular soil types. Recommend consultation with Agency for guidance on design and implementation.

Use supplementary planning documents to facilitate adoption of these sustainable drainage measures.

A2.1.2   Example planning policies

Regional planning

Regional Planning Guidance for the South East (RPG9)

> **Policy INF2 (Part A): The water cycle – supply and quality**
>
> New development should be located and its implementation planned in such a way as to allow for sustainable provision of water services and timely investment in sewage treatment and discharge systems to maintain the appropriate standard of water quality. Techniques which improve water efficiency and minimise adverse impacts on water resources, on the quality, regime, and ecology of rivers, and on groundwater, should be encouraged. Redevelopment should identify and make provision for rectification of any legacy of contamination and drainage problems.

Regional Planning Guidance for East Anglia (RPG6)

> **Policy 52: Liaison over water issues**
>
> To ensure that the issues relating to water supply are fully understood and debated, local planning authorities should hold regular discussions with the Environment Agency, water companies and conservation organisations when developing water-related policies and proposals. They should also work closely with the Environment Agency, water companies and conservation organisations on all other water-related issues.
>
> **Policy 53: Protection of water resources**
>
> In preparing development plans local planning authorities should take account of the Environment Agency's Regional Water Resource Strategy, Local Environment Agency Plans, Catchment Abstraction Management Strategies, groundwater vulnerability maps and groundwater source protection zone maps. The protection of water resources and provision for water abstraction should be given a high priority and rates of development should not exceed the capacities of existing or planned water supply systems, taking into account environmental constraints, to meet projected demand.
>
> **Policy 54: Inter-regional water issues**
>
> The regional planning body and the Environment Agency should work with the water industry and the regional planning body for the South East and the Greater London Authority to formulate a sustainable long-term policy relating to inter-regional water provision.
>
> **Policy 55: Water efficiency and recycling**
>
> Development plans should include policies to promote increased water efficiency and recycling in both existing and new developments. The provision of on-farm winter storage facilities for water should be encouraged subject to other planning policies.
>
> **Policy 56: Water quality**
>
> Local authorities should work closely with the Environment Agency, the water industry and other interested parties to ensure that water supplies are brought up to European standards and that all beaches in East Anglia reach and maintain compliance with the European Union Bathing Water Directive.

Regional Planning Guidance for the East Midlands (RPG8)

Policy 46: Water use and development

Development plans should include policies to promote the most efficient use of water and ensure large users of water will be located where abstraction will not put supplies to other users, or the environment, at risk. Development should proceed only if the necessary water supplies, drainage and sewerage are available and can be provided without significant environmental impact or economic costs within the development time-scale. Mitigating measures, funded by the developer, may be required in order to make development possible.

Development plan policies and the plans and programmes of the Environment Agency and water service providers should be co-ordinated to:

- protect or improve water quality and significantly reduce the risk of pollution, especially to vulnerable groundwater
- manage demand, conserve supply, reduce wastage and promote local recycling of water and the multiple use of water resources
- protect and enhance wetland species and habitats
- reduce unsustainable abstraction from watercourses and aquifers to sustainable levels
- reduce the effects of development on the water environment by incorporating sustainable drainage systems
- ensure that the timing and location of development takes account of potential economic and environmental constraints on water resources
- reduce the impacts of abstraction when river flows are low, especially by encouraging winter abstractions and storage reservoirs, particularly for agriculture.

Regional Planning Guidance for the South West (RPG10)

Policy RE 1: Water resources and water quality

To achieve the long-term sustainable use of water, water resources need to be used more efficiently. At the same time, water resources and water treatment infrastructure must be made available in the right location and at the right time to support development planned for the period covered by the regional guidance. The quality of inland and coastal water environments must be conserved and enhanced. Local authorities, the Environment Agency, water companies and other agencies should seek to:

- plan their water infrastructure and water treatment investment programmes in accordance with the regional spatial strategy
- aim to conserve water through demand management and efficient distribution
- protect groundwater resources
- protect and enhance river and coastal water quality.

In particular, development plans and other plans and programmes of bodies and agencies associated with future development and water issues, will need to:

- take water-related issues into account from an early stage in the process of identifying land for development and re-development and should co-ordinate the timing of new development with the provision of sustainable water supplies, sewage treatment and discharge systems in accordance with advice in PPG12 (Development Plans)
- seek to avoid sites where water supply and/or drainage provision is likely to be unsustainable
- encourage use of sites where past problems can be solved
- promote the use of sustainable urban drainage solutions and the production of detailed supplementary planning guidance to facilitate their adoption.

Structure planning

Staffordshire and Stoke-on-Trent Structure Plan (adopted 2001)

Policy NC9: Water resources

Groundwater resources and standing water bodies and river systems with their associated wetlands will be safeguarded whenever possible. Development or land use change which would lead to pollution or degradation of these resources will not be permitted unless, exceptionally, it can be demonstrated that adequate mitigation measures to counteract the effect of such adverse impacts can be satisfactorily implemented. Development will not be promoted or permitted in locations where adequate water resources do not exist, or where the provision of water to serve such development would cause detriment to the natural environment.

Surrey Structure Plan (adopted 2004)

Policy DN1: Infrastructure provision

The local planning authorities will ensure that the infrastructure requirements of a development are established when identifying proposals in local development frameworks and in determining planning applications.

Planning authorities will not permit development unless the infrastructure which is required to service the development is available or will be provided within a timescale determined by the local authorities.

In assessing infrastructure requirements, local planning authorities will have regard to the cumulative impact of development.

The developer will be expected to provide or contribute to infrastructure improvements related to new development including any requirements emerging out of local development frameworks.

Policy SE1 Natural resources and pollution control

Developments should be located and designed to promote the efficient use of energy and water. Development which requires the provision of new water supply or sewage treatment infrastructure should not prejudice existing water abstractions, river flows, water quality, wetland habitats or fisheries.

Policy LO4 the Countryside and green belt

Operational development associated with water supply and treatment, sewage treatment, flood defence purposes will be acceptable where need is justified and adverse impacts can be satisfactorily mitigated.

Oxfordshire Structure Plan Review (deposit draft 2003)

Policy EN10: Water resources

Proposals for major new reservoirs in Oxfordshire will be permitted only if there is a proven need for increased water resources which cannot be met in more economical and environmentally less intrusive ways, and all reasonable measures to manage demand from water, including controlling loss through water leakage, have been taken.

Policy EN9: Water Resources

Development will be permitted only where adequate resources for the development already exist or can readily be provided without risk to existing abstractions, water quality, the water environment or nature conservation.

Policy EN7: Water quality

Development that will lead to unacceptable deterioration in water quality will not be permitted.

Hampshire Structure Plan (adopted 2000)

Policy E1: Water

Development will not be permitted where it is likely to lead to the deterioration of the quality of groundwater or surface water.

Local planning

Welwyn Hatfield District Plan (revised deposit draft 2002)

Policy R9: Water supply and disposal

Permission will not be granted for proposals that:

- would be detrimental to existing water abstractions, fisheries, amenity or nature conservation
- would cause adverse changes on flows or levels in the groundwater, or any rivers, streams, ditches, springs, lakes or ponds in the vicinity.

Proposals should be consistent with the long term management of water and water services.

In addition, all development should include water conservation measures. The council accepts that some water conservation measures such as SUDS, reed beds and alternative water supplies can only be used on large-scale developments, but other measures should be incorporated in small-scale development proposals. These include:

- water butts
- rainwater recovery systems
- soft planting
- the use of permeable surfaces and minimal hard landscaping on areas such as driveways and patios to help reduce surface runoff.

Policy R9A: Water conservation measures

New development will be expected to incorporate water conservation measures wherever applicable, including SUDS, water butts, soft landscaping and permeable surfaces to help reduce surface water run-off.

Welwyn Hatfield District Plan (deposit draft)

Policy SD1: Sustainable development

All development proposals must be consistent and will be permitted where it can be demonstrated that the principles of sustainable development are satisfied and that they accord with the objectives and policies of this plan. To assist the council in determining this, applicants will be expected to submit a statement with their planning application demonstrating how their proposals address the sustainability criteria in the checklist at Appendix 1.

Management of water resources

4   Use local sources for the water supply and disposal of waste if possible.
5   Prevent pollution of ground and surface water and enhance water quality where possible, eg renew sewers, waterway maintenance, reed beds for waste water treatment.
6   Protect the hydrology of the site and the surrounding areas, eg use permeable surfaces for car parks, provide swales, and open water areas, minimise road length, avoid water run-off into water courses.
7   Minimise water consumption through the use of water efficient fixtures and fittings, reed bed systems, ponds, rainwater storage and recovery and grey water re-use.

South Cambridgeshire Local Plan (adopted 2004)

Policy EN45: The water environment

There is a general presumption against development which will have an adverse environmental impact on the water environment, nature conservation, fisheries and water-related recreation.

East Hertforshire Local Plan (revised deposit draft, 2004)

Policy SD16 Ground Water protection

Development which may cause the contamination of or otherwise prejudice the groundwater will not be permitted. Development proposals in areas of known groundwater importance will be required to submit a detailed assessment of the impact the development proposals will have on the groundwater resource, including measures to mitigate any potential threat to the groundwater.

Policy ENV25: Water environment

(I) The Council will seek to ensure, through consultation with the Environment Agency, British Waterways and other relevant bodies, the preservation and enhancement of the water environment. Support is given in principle to initiatives which lead to:

- improvements in surface water quality and the ecological value of watercourses and their margins
- deculverting and naturalisation of the river channel; which promotion of nature conservation centred on water habitats
- river corridor landscape enhancements
- enhanced sustainable improvements in public access and leisure use of water features.

Proposals, which would involve the culverting or diversion of any water course, will be resisted.

(II) With regard to watercourses, development of the following types would only be acceptable in exceptional circumstances: culverting, diversion, artificial reinforcement of beds/banks using 'hard' materials, buildings and hard surfaces in close proximity (within 10 metres). Such developments in close proximity to watercourses will also normally be expected to retain or re-establish open river corridors on one or both sides of river channels, with appropriate retention/planting of indigenous species.

South Bedfordshire Local Plan Review (adopted 2004)

Policy IS1: Water supply

Development which in the opinion of the district planning authority, after consultation with the Environment Agency, poses an unacceptable risk to the quality of ground or surface water will not be permitted.

Policy IS2: Water supply

Planning permission will not be granted for development needing to abstract water from a river, water table, aquifer or other groundwater source where in the opinion of the district council, after consultation with the Environment Agency, such abstraction is likely to have an adverse impact on water quality, the water environment and the flow of water to other uses.

Policy IS5: Sewerage and sewage disposal

New development will only be permitted in locations where mains, foul sewers, sewage treatment, surface water drainage and storm water discharges of adequate capacity and design are available or can be provided in time to serve the development.

Rother District Local Plan (revised deposit draft 2003)

Policy DS1 Development principles

In determining whether development is appropriate in a particular location, proposals should accord with the following principles

- best use is made of existing infrastructure, including transport, community facilities and mains drainage
- it avoids areas at risk of flooding, allowing a margin for future climate change

Policy GD2 Ensuring availability of infrastructure and services

Development will only be permitted when it is satisfactorily demonstrated that the infrastructure and facilities required to service the development are available, or will be provided.

Such provision may require funding contributions, off-site works or phasing, which will be secured by legal agreements.

Where a site, either defined in the Local Plan, or otherwise proposed for development, comprises land in separate ownerships, it must be demonstrated that proposals will secure the provision of necessary infrastructure to serve the whole site.

A2.2   SUSTAINABLE FLOOD RISK MANAGEMENT

A2.2.1   Policy guidance

Guidelines on types of policies that must be considered:

- require early consultation with the Environment Agency
- direct development away from flood risk areas and ensure protection of the floodplain. Highlight floodplain areas by incorporating Environment Agency's indicative floodplain maps covering plan area
- require application of PPG25 *Development and flood risk*
- use available redevelopment opportunities to gain restoration of "lost" floodplains
- seek consideration of managed retreat schemes where appropriate
- seek every opportunity to promote the use of sustainable drainage solutions to minimise or remove runoff from new development sites
- use Supplementary Planning Guidance to facilitate the adoption of these drainage measures.

A2.2.2   Example planning policies

Regional planning

Regional Planning Guidance for East Anglia (RPG6)

> **Policy 44: Development in areas at risk from flooding**
>
> Development proposals should be resisted in floodplains and in areas at risk from flooding or coastal erosion. In identifying such areas, local planning authorities should have regard to the flood plain maps provided by the Environment Agency and to guidance published by Defra. The flood return period and continuing advice on the potential impacts of climate change scenarios should also be considered. Development plans should also promote the use of sustainable urban drainage solutions (SUDS) and local planning authorities should produce detailed supplementary planning guidance to facilitate their adoption.

Regional Planning Guidance for the East Midlands (RPG8)

> **Policy 47: Development and flood risk**
>
> Development plans should include policies to prevent inappropriate development in coastal and fluvial floodplain areas. Development should not be permitted if, alone or in conjunction with other developments, it would:
>
> - be at unacceptable risk from flooding
> - inhibit the capacity of the floodplain to store water
> - impede the flow of floodwater
> - otherwise unacceptably increase flood risk
> - interfere with coastal processes.
>
> unless provision is made by way of conditions or agreements for adequate measures to mitigate the effects on the flooding regime, including provision for maintenance and, if appropriate, the enhancement of biodiversity.

Regional Planning Guidance for the South West (RPG10)

Policy RE2: Flood risk

Flooding causes risk to both property and life and protecting property and people in areas of flood risk is expensive. Local authorities, the Environment Agency, other agencies and developers should seek to:

- protect land liable to river and coastal flooding from new development, by directing development away from river and coastal floodplains;
- promote, recognise and adopt the use of sustainable drainage systems for surface water drainage;
- adopt a sequential approach to the allocation and development of sites, having regard to their flood risk potential in accordance with advice in PPG25 (*Development and Flood Risk*).

Development plans should:

- identify inland and coastal areas at risk from flooding based on the Environment Agency's indicative Maps and, supplemented where necessary by historical and modelled flood data and indications as to other areas which could be at risk in future
- provide criteria for redevelopment proposals in flood plains, in order to minimise their cumulative adverse impact and secure enhancement of the floodwater storage and ecological role of flood plains.

Regional Planning Guidance for Yorkshire and the Humber (RPG12)

Policy R2: Development and flood risk

Development Plans should adopt a sequential risk-based approach to development and flooding as defined in PPG25. To enable the risk from flooding to be appropriately managed in the region:

In functional floodplains* and washlands**, and in undeveloped floodplain areas where the risk from tidal and fluvial flooding is high, development should be avoided.

In previously developed areas, and areas of undeveloped floodplain where the risk from flooding is lower, development should be of an appropriate type and design and will require the availability or provision of an appropriate standard of flood defence and the incorporation of flood mitigation and/or flood warning measures.

Following application of the sequential approach, where other considerations in favour of the development, (for example the significant need for economic and social regeneration and the need to recycle previously developed land) outweigh the flooding issues in identified flood risk areas, development will only be permitted where it has been established, following consultation with the Environment Agency and other relevant organisations, that any necessary protection or management measures can and will be provided and are consistent with the emerging Catchment Flood Management Plans (CFMPs) and, where relevant, the Humber Estuary Shoreline Management Plan (SMP).

In liaison with the Environment Agency, local authorities should adopt a strategic approach to assessing the risk of flooding and the potential implications of development for flooding elsewhere.

Those proposing development in flood risk areas should carry out Flood Risk Assessments (FRAs). Where local authorities propose to allocate for development in the floodplain they will need to undertake FRA. The Environment Agency and other bodies should provide information and advice to assist in the preparation of these FRAs.

Local Authorities and the Environment Agency should take into account the latest information available from each other to ensure that their policies consistently deal with managing the risk from:

Tidal flooding around the Humber Estuary and along the coast

Fluvial flooding along river corridors and other significant watercourses resulting from catchments within and beyond the region.

[* *Functional floodplains are the unobstructed or active areas where water regularly flows in time of flood.*

** *Washlands are areas of floodplain where water is stored in time of flood.*]

Structure planning

Staffordshire and Stoke-on-Trent Structure Plan (adopted)

Policy NC10: Flood risk

Development will not be permitted which would:

- be located in the floodplain, unless acceptable mitigating measures are provided;
- be subject to an unacceptable risk of flooding, or increase the risk of flooding elsewhere;
- adversely affect the water environment as a result of an increase in surface water run-off;
- detrimentally affect existing or proposed flood defences, or prevent responsible bodies from carrying out flood control works and maintenance activities;
- necessitate additional public finances for flood defence works.

Oxfordshire Structure Plan Review (deposit draft 2001)

Policy EN8: Flood risk and surface water drainage

Development in undeveloped areas at high risk of flooding or in the functional flood plain will not be permitted. A flood risk assessment will be required for proposals for development except where there is little or no flood risk. Proposals for redevelopment of existing buildings and their cartilage within areas of high flood risk should aim to improve conditions locally and not worsen flood risk elsewhere.

New development should not lead to an increase in run-off, which would exacerbate flood risk elsewhere. The use of sustainable drainage systems to regulate run-off will be required as part of development proposals.

Hampshire Structure Plan (adopted 2000)

Policy E2: Water

Development other than change of use, which would be at direct risk of flooding or likely to increase flooding elsewhere, will not be permitted. Within defined flood risk areas, any development permitted should incorporate flood containment or public safety measures justified on that account.

New development or the extension or intensification of existing development along the coast must take into account areas identified as being at risk from coastal flooding or coastal erosion.

Local planning

Welwyn Hatfield District Plan (deposit draft)

Policy R8: Floodplains and Flood Prevention

Within the floodplains identified on the Proposal Map, planning permission for development will not be granted where proposals would:

- decrease the capacity of the floodplain to store flood water
- impede the flow of water
- increase the number of people and properties at risk from flooding.

Planning permission for new development outside floodplains will not be granted where the proposals would result in an increase in flooding downstream because of increased run-off.

The use of sustainable drainage systems will be encouraged, dependent on local site and underlying groundwater considerations.

Proposals for development necessary to prevent an increase in flooding will be considered in terms of their impact on biodiversity, the landscape and recreation.

South Gloucestershire Local Plan (revised deposit draft, 2002)

Policy EP2: Flood risk and development

Development, including the extension and intensification of existing uses or land raising, which generates surface water runoff or water discharge will not be permitted where the development could:

a. itself be at risk from flooding; or

b. require protection from flooding; or

c. reduce the capacity of the flood plain; or

d increase the risk of flooding elsewhere; or

e. impede the flow of flood waters; or

f. affect the integrity of tidal or fluvial defences; or

g. alter the water table; or

h increase river channel instability; or

i. cause unacceptable silt deposition; or

j. prevent maintenance of the watercourse; or

k. preclude the solution to existing flooding problems;

unless adequate environmentally acceptable measures are incorporated which provide suitable protection, attenuation or mitigation.

Policy L17: Water environment

Development which would have an unacceptable effect on the water environment, including surface water and groundwater quality and quantity, river corridors and associated wetlands, will not be permitted.

Policy L17a Water environment

Development proposals will be required to incorporate sustainable drainage systems (SUDS) for the disposal of surface waters. Where this is not practicable it must be demonstrated that an acceptable alternative means of surface water disposal is incorporated.

East Herts Local Plan second review (revised deposit draft, 2004)

Policy SD17: Surface water drainage

(i) Where appropriate and relevant, all development proposals will be expected to take into consideration Best Management Practices to surface water drainage, as advocated by the Environment Agency. Where applicable, planning obligations (or as subsequently revised) may be sought to ensure the on-going maintenance of such practices, including off-site provision.

(ii) Proposals that do not take sufficient account of such techniques and/or are detrimental to the effectiveness of existing schemes based on such techniques will be refused.

South Bedfordshire Local Plan Review (adopted 2004)

Policy IS3: Flooding

In areas of high flood risk, as indicated on the proposals map, new development, including the raising of land, will not be permitted.

The redevelopment of previously developed sites will be permitted providing a flood risk assessment demonstrates that:

- it would not be subject to an unacceptable flood risk
- flood protection or mitigation measures ensure that there is no risk of flooding elsewhere as a result of the development. Any such measures should be provided as part of the development or otherwise implemented prior to its commencement.

Policy IS4: Surface water runoff

New development that will generate surface water, which is likely to result in unacceptable adverse effects, such as an increased risk of flooding, will not be permitted.

Where proposals for new development are made, they must include appropriate attenuation measures. (Developers will be expected to cover the cost of assessing surface water drainage impacts and of any appropriate mitigation works, including long-term management.

A2.3 ENVIRONMENTAL PROTECTION: GENERAL

A2.3.1 Policy guidance

Guidelines on types of policies that must be considered:

- refuse development that may put the water environment, eg river corridors, inland waterways/lakes, wetlands – at risk

- require positive environmental enhancement as part of the development proposals

- target policies that contribute towards environmental objectives within the Environment Agency LEAP (local Environment Agency plan) documents covering the plan area; include relevant maps from this document, where appropriate.

A2.3.2 Example planning policies

Regional planning

Regional Planning Guidance for East Anglia (RPG6)

> **Policy 37: General management principles for conserving and enhancing the natural, built and historic environment**
>
> To conserve and enhance the important aspects of East Anglia's natural, built and historic environment, development plans should reflect the following principles:
>
> - the natural, built and historic environment should be conserved and enhanced by positive management and by protecting it from development likely to cause harm
> - all important aspects of the countryside, including individual features, special sites and the wider landscape should be protected for their own sake
> - regional and local distinctiveness and variety, based on a thorough assessment of local character and scrutinised in depth through the development plan system, should be conserved and enhanced whenever possible
> - planning for development should provide effective protection of the environment by integrating a site-based approach with a more broadly based concern for
> - awareness of biodiversity and other environmental issues, including light and noise pollution
> - damaged and lost environmental features should be restored whenever possible and a common approach should be taken to landscape and character issues which cross local planning authority boundaries.

Structure planning

Surrey Structure Plan (adopted 2004)

> **Policy SE10: River corridors and waterways**
>
> Development should conserve the character, setting, ecology and heritage of river corridors and waterways. Development ancillary to water-based recreation will be encouraged where consistent with the above
>
> The function of rivers and waterways as green corridors within and between urban areas should be safeguarded as part of a green space strategy for settlements and as valuable links in access between town and country.
>
> **Policy SE7: Nature conservation**
>
> Land or water habitats designated as of importance for nature at international, national, regional or county level will be conserved and enhanced and inappropriate development will be resisted.

A2.4 ENVIRONMENTAL PROTECTION: BIODIVERSITY

A2.4.1 Policy guidance

Guidelines on types of policies that must be considered:

- refuse development that may put biodiversity at risk
- need positive policies to ensure that future development serves to increase biodiversity of species and habitats within the region
- recognise the provision of nature conservation, with no net loss of conservation value in any scheme.

A2.4.2 Example planning policies

Regional planning

Regional Planning Guidance for East Anglia (RPG6)

> **Policy 41: Local Biodiversity Action Plans**
>
> Local planning authorities should take positive action to achieve the targets set in national and local Biodiversity Action Plans through planning decisions and by adopting appropriate policies and targets in development plans. They should also incorporate targets set in national and local Biodiversity Action Plans into existing initiatives and review their adopted land-use policies to ensure that they do not damage biodiversity. The development plan process should also be used as a mechanism to monitor the progress towards meeting the targets set in Biodiversity Action Plans.
>
> **Policy 42: Safeguarding and creating habitats**
>
> Local planning authorities should safeguard threatened habitats and create new habitats characteristic of East Anglia by including relevant policies and proposals in development plans and by working jointly with others on non-statutory management plans. Priority should be given to those habitats for which East Anglia has a significant proportion of the UK total.

Regional Planning Guidance for the South West (RPG10)

> **Policy EN 1: Landscape and biodiversity**
>
> Local authorities and other agencies in their plans, policies and proposals, should:
>
> - provide for the strong protection and enhancement of the region's internationally and nationally important landscape areas and nature conservation sites
> - draw up policies for the protection of nature conservation interests of regional and local significance;
> - encourage the maintenance and enhancement of the biodiversity resources of the region, having particular regard to the targets set out in tables 3, 4 and 5
> - promote the restoration and expansion of depleted and vulnerable biodiversity resources in order to reverse fragmentation and create continuous viable habitats
> - indicate that the protection and, where possible, enhancement of the landscape and biodiversity should be planned into new development
> - have regard to the significant landscape joint character areas of the region set out in this RPG (Map 4) and aim to conserve and enhance local character
> - take measures to protect the character of the countryside and the environmental features that contribute towards that character, including the minimisation of light pollution.

Structure planning

Surrey Structure Plan (adopted 2004)

Policy SE6: Biodiversity and development

Biodiversity within Surrey should be conserved and enhanced and development will be expected to contribute to action safeguarding and managing habitats identified as important through the UK and Surrey Biodiversity Action Plans or where they are protected by wildlife legislation. Species protection will contribute to safeguarding biodiversity. This will be secured by:

- ensuring that site evaluation is undertaken to establish the nature conservation value of proposed development sites
- providing for identification, safeguarding and management of existing and potential land for nature conservation as part of development proposals, particularly where a connected series of sites can be achieved.

Features within the landscape which are of importance for wild fauna and flora should be protected. Development should seek to retain such features and their management will be encouraged by agreements or conditions as appropriate.

Developers will be required to provide information on species or features present within sites, or on adjoining land and to propose how impacts on their conservation will be mitigated.

Staffordshire and Stoke-on-Trent Structure Plan (adopted 2001)

Policy NC5: Biodiversity

Planning authorities will seek to further the objectives of the UK and Staffordshire Biodiversity Action Plans through appropriate policies and proposals for safeguarding and increasing key habitats and species. Opportunities will be sought to achieve UK and Staffordshire Biodiversity Action Plan targets for key habitats and species.

A3   Case studies

This appendix contains selected case studies showing where sustainable water management practices have been successfully integrated into the planning/development system. These include:

A3.1   A sustainable development framework for the east of England 142

A3.2   Sustainable water management in California: success stories 146

A3.3   Flag Fen high-purity water production scheme 150

A3.4   Challenges to sustainable water management: Basingstoke case study 154

A3.5   Putting water into planning: "Water in Hampshire" 158

A3.1 A sustainable development framework for the east of England

A3.1.1 Summary

In October 2001, a joint working group comprising the East of England Regional Assembly and the Regional Development Round Table published *A Sustainable development framework for the east of England* (EERA and EESDRT, 2001) in response to the government wish (expressed in *A better quality of life* – DETR, 1999a) to see such frameworks in place throughout England. The east of England framework was based on contributions from a wide range of stakeholders and was widely endorsed and supported by regional government offices and agencies. The framework sets out a vision for sustainable development within the region, but it is recognised that "it is in the implementation of regional and local strategies that the sustainability of any development will really be determined". Nevertheless, the framework is presented here as an example of good practice at a macro scale.

A3.1.2 Purpose

The purpose of the Framework is...to:

- Promulgate a high-level vision for sustainable development in the East of England to which key partners can subscribe, distinctive to the region although linked to the UK strategy for sustainable development.

- Set out agreed sustainable development objectives for the region, and set priorities with the help of regional indicators.

- Provide a basis for monitoring whether progress is being made towards greater sustainability, and a benchmark for appraisal of regional strategies and plans.

- Influence and direct other regional and local strategies and contribute to the development of an integrated Regional Strategy.

Section 1.3, EERA and EESDRT, 2001

A3.1.3 Vision

The shared vision of those who have produced this Framework...[is]...to plan for an improving quality of life for the people of the East of England which is sustainable for the long-term future and, in particular:

- Enable its potential for economic growth to be achieved in a balanced way, in the interests of all the people of the region and the UK and beyond.

- Spread the benefits of growth more equally, so as to reduce poverty, crime, ill health and social exclusion and reduce inequalities.

- Foster a sense of well-being and self-worth by enabling people to achieve their full potential, and providing for rewarding employment, learning and leisure.

- Protect and enhance the quality of the region's natural and built environment.

- Manage the use of resources sustainably and innovatively, in order to minimise the region's global environmental impact.

Section 2.1, EERA and EESDRT, 2001.

A3.1.4 The issues

The framework first identifies 21 key sustainability issues for the east of England. These range from the economy, through crime and climate change to waste and minerals. Key water sustainability issues are highlighted in Section 4.20 of the framework (Water resources and quality), presented below as Box A3.1.

Box A3.1 *Water resources and quality issues (EERA and EESDRT, 2001)*

Context
The East of England is the driest UK region. It is also a region of high growth resulting in increasing demands for water. Water supplies already depend upon demand-management measures, transfers and re-use. Half of public water supply is provided from groundwater. The region's slow moving rivers and watercourses are often eutrophic, with damaging high levels of nutrients from agricultural run-off and the cumulative effect of many small discharges.
Regional strengths
Quality of bathing waters has improved steadily since 1987.
Quality of (raw) water has greatly improved.
Recent and ongoing dialogue with regional stakeholders and key players is achieving greater awareness and understanding of water issues in the region.
Estuaries and inland waterways attract recreational and tourism activities (eg boating).
Challenges
Managing demand for water amid rising material expectations, especially for irrigation and domestic use, driven by pressures such as supermarket quality standards.
Recognising that, locally, water supply acts as a constraint on growth.
Maintaining the integrity of water-dependent wildlife sites (wetlands), some of international importance (eg Norfolk Valley Fens), and archaeological sites against increased abstraction.
Increasing statutory responsibility to enforce or promote water efficiency, and introducing price incentives to save water.
Planning for impacts on water supplies arising from changing rainfall patterns, such as longer hotter summers as a result of climate change.
Achieving a shared understanding of water resource use in the region, as there is no widely shared and trusted information base.
Improving water quality, which is still too poor in some rivers, water bodies and estuaries, due to effluents and run-off from urban land, and pollution from agricultural run-off, exacerbated by the region's susceptibility to low flows of water.
Recognising that water transfers and purification are not energy efficient and may be environmentally damaging.
Key objectives
To regulate water supply to within reasonable limits, and manage demand.
To raise awareness to encourage water efficiency and conservation.
To develop and promote local water recycling initiatives for developments and buildings.
To encourage rainwater harvesting, to reduce significantly new development needs.
To anticipate situations in which local water supplies may be a constraint on development and where water transfers may be needed (eg Essex developments supplied from Norfolk).
To introduce domestic metering/innovative tariff charging whilst ensuring that the cost of water does not add to social deprivation.
To promote sustainable urban drainage systems to reduce flood risk and water loss from natural systems, and the use of natural techniques, eg reed bed technology, to clean water.
To improve quality and flow of rivers and reduce nitrate levels in groundwater.
To maintain or restore the integrity of the many water-dependent wildlife sites of the region.
To reduce pollution by managing supplied water and effluents in an integrated way.
To continue to improve the quality of bathing waters.
To encourage increased/innovative use of renewable energy for the treatment of water.

The above provides some good objectives for sustainably managing development with respect to water. Water sustainability issues also feature within several of the other categories identified, and this cross-cutting approach is one of the Framework's main strengths. Some of the main issues are summarised in Box A3.2.

Box A3.2   *Selected water sustainability challenges and key objectives within other issues (EERA and EESDRT, 2001)*

Location and growth	**Challenges** Reducing pressures on infrastructure, services and natural resources, eg water, arising from population/household growth and lower occupancy rates.
	Key objectives To direct growth to the most environmentally, economically and socially sustainable locations. To ensure development is not at risk from flooding and does not increase flood risk elsewhere. To protect landscape character and be sustainable in the use of resources, eg energy, water.
Agriculture, food and forestry	**Challenges** Managing the steady rise in competing demands for water generated by development and environmental factors, including landscape management and climate change.
	Key objectives To raise the level of understanding of the tension between economic, social and environmental requirements in achieving agriculture and food production that is sustainable. To recognise the environmental impacts of water abstraction and so encourage efficient use of water.
Natural environment	**Challenges** Increasing demands on land, aggregates and water supply from built development. Recognising natural resource use and climate change as key economic and political issues. Reducing diffuse pollution, which potentially has the greatest impact on river quality/biodiversity and associated decline in quality of groundwaters. Increasing public involvement and understanding of natural environmental issues.
	Key objectives To ensure appropriate planning policies are in place and implemented to minimise adverse environmental impacts, recognise and support environmental limits, and provide the highest level of protection for irreplaceable natural features. To support standards, regulations and economic instruments to safeguard and enhance environmental quality. To raise awareness of the link between use of natural resources and environmental impacts. To manage water quality and water resources to maximise value to people and wildlife.
Historic and built environment	**Challenges** Minimising energy/resource use and reducing waste in building construction/use/repair/ demolition. Improving skills and staff resources in decision-making bodies and the building industry.
	Key objectives To encourage thoughtful design, high- density housing and mixed-use developments which, for example, includes energy and water efficiency measures and incorporate sustainable drainage.
Living with climate change	**Challenges** Taking into account the special characteristics of the east of England when planning for climate change: • growing number of households • lowest average rainfall in the country and water resources under pressure • vulnerability to flooding.
	Key objectives To take decisions now that will reduce the impact of climate change in the future, such as not developing on areas at risk of flooding and allowing for managed retreat where necessary. To adopt lifestyle changes to cope with climate change, such as promoting water and energy efficiency. To encourage technological development to provide clean and efficient use of resources.

Together, these issues, challenges and key objectives provide a good basis for understanding and addressing the key water sustainability issues in planning future developments within the east of England. Perhaps the only area omitted is some reference to highway/runway runoff and the appropriate management of this to promote water quality and reduce flood risk.

In analysing priority sustainable development issues for the region, the Framework considers sustainability from a number of related angles:

- identification of the positive aspects of regional sustainability
- highlighting key unsustainable assets, activities and trends that are likely to continue as such without concerted action
- defining the key challenges that need to be faced if the region is to move towards a more sustainable future.

A set of regional high-level objectives were then proposed (see Box A3.3), together with associated indicators that could be used to measure progress.

Indicators for these high-level objectives relevant to sustainable water management include:

- populations of birds/areas of important habitats
- household water use and peak demand
- low flows in rivers
- margin between water supply and projected demand
- percentage of water lost to leakage
- rivers of good or fair quality
- proportion of water needs met by local water recycling in urban and rural areas.

Box A3.3   *Selected East of England sustainable development high-level objectives*

> To achieve sustainable levels of prosperity and growth.
>
> To deliver more sustainable patterns of location of development, including employment and housing.
>
> To protect and maintain our most valuable regional assets such as habitats and landscapes.
>
> To reduce our consumption of fossil fuels.
>
> To achieve a more equitable sharing of benefits of prosperity across all sectors of society.
>
> To use natural resources, both finite and renewable, as efficiently as possible and re-use finite resources or recycled alternatives wherever possible.
>
> To minimise our production of by-products or waste.
>
> To avoid using the global environment to underwrite our own unsustainable way of life.
>
> To revitalise town centres to promote a return to sustainable urban living.

A3.1.5 Using the Sustainable Development Framework

The framework is being promoted as the reference point for ensuring that regional and local strategies are consistent with the principles of sustainable development. An annex to the framework sets out who should be involved with implementing the objectives for each issue identified, together with the strategic documents that are relevant. The authors are committed to updating the framework regularly and, importantly, to reporting on progress towards the high-level objectives using the set of agreed indicators.

Particular activities within the region that the framework will support include:

- stakeholder workshops run by the Sustainable Development Round Table to raise awareness of key issues facing the region, on water resources, renewable energy, waste and climate change

- the adoption of environmental management systems by some influential regional businesses

- the establishment of local "green business forums" to share and promote good practice.

- the adoption of sustainable development principles by local authorities throughout the region

- adoption of planning policies that will protect urban and rural environments.

A3.2 Sustainable water management in California: success stories

A3.2.1 Background

The demand for water resources in this water-stressed area of the USA is high, so throughout the 20th century water policy in California has been characterised by intense political and legal battles. Alongside these debates, California is taking significant steps towards more sustainable water management and use. In 1995, the Pacific Institute for Studies in Development, Environment, and Security published *California water 2020: a sustainable vision* (Pacific Institute, 1995). This presented a positive vision of where California water resources could be in the year 2020, together with a detailed analysis of how to get there using existing and proven economic incentives, efficient water technologies, and innovative governmental and non-governmental management practices. That analysis offered compelling support for the argument that alternative approaches to water planning and use can be and have been very successful.

As a follow-up to the 1995 report, the Pacific Institute produced a second document, *Sustainable use of water: California success stories* (Pacific Institute, 1999). This describes 28 successful, informative and educational examples of collaborative water planning, effective institutional and governance structures, intelligent use of technology or economic incentives, and environmental protection and restoration in areas where deadlock and litigation used to be the norm. These "success stories" identify, describe and analyse examples of sustainable water policies and practices in California and show water managers, policy-makers and the public how to move towards more equitable and efficient water management and use.

These case studies may also offer lessons for stakeholders in the UK – in particular by demonstrating approaches to water sustainability that work (and why). A key factor in the success of this work has been adoption of a multi-faceted approach to water management engaging the land use planning process, environmental regulators, industry, institutions and the public throughout to maximise the effectiveness of the policy. Some of the approaches to improved water management are summarised below.

Innovative integrated resource management programmes

This has included a comprehensive integrated resource management plan linking phased development of new water supply to a sophisticated demand management programme. The implementation of conservation and water recycling programmes has, for example enabled Marin Municipal Water District to stabilise demand at close to 1980 levels, despite a substantial increase in population.

Promoting conservation within ascending block-rate structures

The appropriate use of differential water rates and prices can have a major effect on water use and efficiency. In 1991, Irvine Ranch Water District (IRWD) replaced its flat rate-per-unit charge with an innovative ascending block rate structure, which has produced a significant drop in per capita water use.

Effective public participation in the rate setting process

The formation of a citizens' committee to assist in the development of water rate structures has promoted wider understanding of rate-setting issues, eg who pays and how much and the use of rates to send signals on water use and to reflect the true cost of water, as well as public engagement in the process. This helped to address issues of fairness and equity and produced a rate structure that was eventually approved.

Reducing water use in residential, industrial and municipal landscapes

Urban landscapes consume a significant amount of water in California. Three separate programmes have identified how water efficiency can be promoted by better informing developers and users and through the use of proper incentives for efficient water use. These included the use of credits and rebates for reducing water use in landscape maintenance, voluntary audit programmes to develop proper irrigation scheduling and careful maintenance, and the use of progressive rate structure and outreach (educational) programmes.

Community–agency partnerships to promote water-saving measures

Water agencies have formed highly successful partnerships with community groups to distribute ultra-low-flush toilets (ULFTs) in cities throughout the state. By August 1998, these programmes had saved estimated annual 13 000 acre-feet of water. Agencies hire local unemployed residents to run their ULFT programmes. Revenues are invested in community activities. Participation has been greater than in similar programmes run by agencies alone, since residents are eager to support programmes managed by and benefiting their communities. Agencies benefit from improved public relations and a greater ability to meet their conservation goals.

An overview of water-efficiency potential in the CII sector

Commercial, industrial and institutional (CII) water users account for approximately 30 per cent of urban water use in California. A review has been carried out to demonstrate the potential for large-scale water-efficiency gains, illustrated using case studies, and identifying barriers and the factors that promote successful schemes.

Assessing commercial, industrial and institutional water-efficiency potential through audits

A major water-efficiency improvement programme was initiated by the Metropolitan Water District of Southern California (MWD), to provide water audits for the CII sector. A database of information from the 900 commercial, industrial and institutional water users audited provided a valuable source of information on water use. It not only helped identify potential areas for saving water but also aided implementation of conservation programmes.

Increasing institutional water-use efficiencies

This work has included the development of a comprehensive water-efficiency programme at the University of California, Santa Barbara, which has lead to significant water and cost-savings. Total campus water use was reduced by nearly 50 per cent between 1987 and 1994 (despite campus population increases), saving approximately $3.7 million between 1987 and 1996, excluding energy and maintenance savings. This type of flagship programme can help to demonstrate the operational viability of water-efficient systems as well as the cost incentives that can promote their use.

Reducing water use and solving wastewater problems with membrane filtration systems

The adoption of water-saving membrane filtration and by-product recovery systems can allow major environmental and economic benefits through water saving, particularly in the region's food processing industry. For example, in one case study a system enabled the reuse of 80 per cent of a plant's processing water, reducing the plant's daily groundwater pumping requirements by 91 per cent and eliminating wastewater discharges.

Changes in agricultural practice to benefit farmers and wildlife

Growing numbers of California farmers are changing their land management practices and allowing fields to flood to shallow depths each winter. This helps to decompose crop stubble and to provide habitat for the hundreds of thousands of waterfowl and shorebirds. This practice also offers a solution to the air-quality problem caused in some areas of the state when rice stubble is burned. It could also have the potential to reduce downstream flood risk.

Restoring urban streams to provide social, environmental, and economic benefits

Case study examples of stream restoration projects have been developed to demonstrate the potential social, economic and environmental benefits to urban communities. These have shown how urban rivers can provide major focal points for pedestrian/retail centres. In addition flood risk can be reduced by remediating culverts/concrete channels so that they are more environmentally acceptable, while also creating new riparian habitats and maintenance jobs.

A3.2.2　Key lessons learned

- Avoid splitting water stakeholders into "special interest groups" – the groups need to work together to develop solutions

- ensure that all stakeholders are identified and brought into the process as early as possible

- industry, public agencies and governments need to continue to invest in and support research and development of water-efficient and water-treatment technologies

- demonstration programmes, technical assistance and education initiatives that introduce water users to existing technologies and their effective application should be adequately funded and expanded

- financial incentive programmes should be implemented to assist with conversion to and adoption of new technologies

- regulations and standards should be considered important components of water policy reform

- policy-makers and the public should continue to look for effective regulatory tools in the water area. Such tools should be designed to allow flexibility in approach

- water providers should adopt prices that better reflect the costs of service, including capital costs and environmental costs

- water retailers should adopt pricing structures that encourage efficient use of water

- water agencies should adopt strategies that reduce economic risks associated with sustainable water projects

- governments and others need to be willing to fund and share in the economic risks of projects with multiple benefits

- gaps in water data and information must be filled by more active water data collection programmes. Available water data and information should be made more widely available

- comprehensive water-use efficiency drives are needed for all sectors, as fundamental components of water policy efforts. Existing voluntary conservation initiatives should be expanded in scope and their implementation accelerated

- manage agricultural land to improve wildlife habitat, reduce agricultural water requirements and improve air and water quality

- include agricultural values in environmental restoration efforts. This will work most effectively when environmentalists and growers work together

- urban water agencies must also consider the upstream and downstream environmental impacts of their activities. Co-operative actions with other users can increase environmental benefits.

A3.3 Flag Fen high-purity water production scheme

A3.3.1 Summary

Anglian Water Services Ltd provides water supply and sewage services to more than 5.4 million people living in the east and south-east of England. This geographic area has the lowest long-term rainfall in Britain, with an average of less than 600 mm a year, around half the current UK average. In the 1990s the Anglian Water region suffered four consecutive drought years, which put serious pressure on water resources, with groundwater falling to the lowest recorded levels.

Anglian Water undertook an extensive research programme to examine initiatives that could help sustain the long-term water supply for their customers. Items considered were desalination, leakage control, water-saving devices, improved efficiency at waterworks and the reuse of sewage effluent.

All the above helped to reduce water demand, but the most innovative successful scheme was the Flag Fen high-purity water production plant, where sewage effluent is treated to produce high-quality, high-value industrial water to supply a local power station.

The scheme saves Anglian Water 1200 m³/day of potable water, the power station save money on its operational costs, and the environment benefits from reduced water abstraction and reduced chemical loads being discharged to the environment.

This case study describes the development of the scheme from concept to reality and reviews the business and environmental benefits that have been achieved from two utilities working closely together.

A3.3.2 Background

In the east and south-east of England water resources are limited and pressure for additional supply is rising through increased demand and population growth. The Anglian Water region is also the fastest-growing part of the UK, with population estimated to expand at 0.7 per cent a year, twice the UK average.

Anglian Water is committed to sustainable development and aims fully to meet its legislative obligations while continuing to develop and improve its wider environmental performance. This is of particular importance so far as water resources are concerned because of the many wetland sites of conservation concern in the region, such as the Norfolk Broads, the UK's only wetland national park. Anglian Water is therefore aware that in the next 10 years major initiatives will be needed to ensure a long-term sustainable water supply for the region.

Improvements in sewage treatment, particularly at coastal sites, have led to large quantities of high-quality water being discharged to the sea or to tidal estuaries. If some of this water could be reused for industrial purposes, it could save significant amounts of potable water and avoid the customer perception of recycled effluent being used to support potable supplies. Anglian Water's Innovation department has spent more than three years evaluating and developing membrane technology to create treatment processes that can produce high-purity or potable-quality industrial water from sewage effluent.

To assess potential market demand for the technology, a survey was carried out of potential customers located near a sewage works who required high-purity process water. The best opportunity for a trial implementation of the technology was a gas-fired power station in Peterborough, owned by Texas Utilities (TXU). The station requires up to 1200 m3/day of potable water to produce the ultra-pure water required for flue gas injection and boiler feed make-up. It was ideally located, being adjacent to the Flag Fen sewage works that serves the city of Peterborough. The final effluent from Flag Fen is discharged to the tidal section of the River Nene and then makes its way into the North Sea.

A3.3.3   Business arrangements

After negotiations between the parties, in October 1999 TXU signed a long-term water supply contract with Alpheus Environmental, a wholly owned Anglian Water Group subsidiary company. As part of the contract, TXU was required to supply the new plant with low-cost energy directly from its generators, via a cable laid in the pipe trench. Construction started in the spring of 2000, the plant was completed in the late summer and the high-purity water supply started at the beginning of October 2000.

Details of the average water quality delivered by the plant are shown in Table A3.1 below.

Table A3.1   *Typical water quality delivered*

	Min	Mean	Max
Conductivity (uS/cm)	17	32	38.8
Silica (mg/l)	0.2	0.24	0.4
TOC (mg/l)	< 0.2	0.23	0.3
Sodium (mg/l)	5.5	7.4	10
Calcium (mg/l)	< 0.4	0.8	1

A3.3.4   Process technology

The effluent discharged from Flag Fen sewage works varies in quality during the year. The treatment process had to be capable of dealing with the occasional high solid ratios during flood conditions and occasional high loads from local industries. The impact of effluent discharged from a vegetable-processing factory during the pea-processing season was one example of the problems faced.

Table A3.2   *Typical sewage treatment works effluent quality*

	Min	Mean	Max
BOD (mg/l O)	2	3.2	7.6
Ammonia (mg/l N)	0.03	0.36	2.3
TON (mg/l N)	9.3	17.5	23.8
TSS @ 105°C (mg/l)	2.4	8.3	17
Oils and fats (mg/l)	< 5	6.5	16.6

The treatment process comprises pre-screening, microfiltration and reverse osmosis, as shown on the process schematic diagram below.

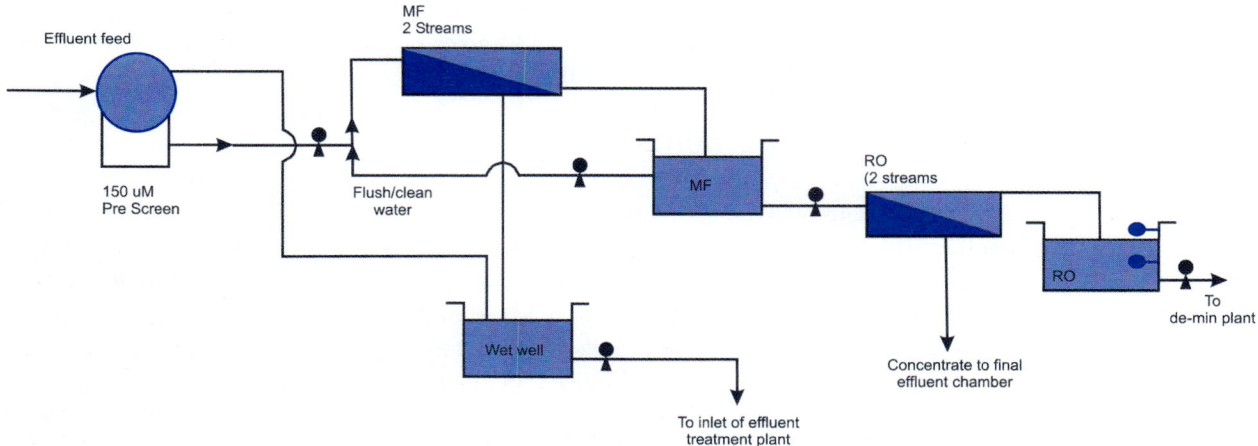

Figure A3.1   *Flag Fen high-purity water treatment process schematic*

A3.3.5   Pre-screening

All the incoming effluent is screened to remove any particles larger than 150 micro-metres. The screen is self-cleaning, rotating and removing solids by back-flushing with screened water. All wastewaters produced from this process are returned to the head of the sewage works.

A3.3.6   Microfiltration

The screened effluent is treated by a Pall "Microza" microfiltration (MF) plant. The plant has two streams, each 60 per cent of design output. The MF plant polishes and physically disinfects the water by removing all particles, virus and bacteria > 0.1 micrometre. The microfiltration plant operates in a semi-dead-end mode with air, water and chemicals used to clean the membranes automatically on a timed basis. In addition to the automatic cleans, every two weeks each stream is chemically cleaned via a "clean in place" (CIP) plant. The wastewaters from the back-flushing and chemical cleans are returned to the head of the sewage works.

Figure A3.2   *Flag Fen microfiltration plant*

A3.3.7 Reverse osmosis

The reverse osmosis (RO) plant comprises two streams, each 60 per cent of design output operating at 80 per cent recovery. Each stream is a 4:2 array with four 200 mm-diameter TFC ULP magnum membrane elements and one standard element per pressure vessel. The concentrated waste stream is discharged by blending with the final effluent. The membranes are cleaned periodically (about every three months) to remove organic and inorganic foulants from the membrane surface. The waste-cleaning solutions are discharged to the head of the sewage works.

Figure A3.3 *Flag Fen reverse osmosis plant*

A3.3.7 Benefits of the high-purity water scheme

This scheme contributes to sustainable development by delivering business, environmental and community benefits. Some of these are summarised below.

TXU has seen a large saving in the operation of its existing de-min plant; operating times between regeneration have increased from eight hours to more than 60 hours. This has led to big savings in hydrochloric acid, caustic soda, energy and rinse water. The improvement in the efficiency of the de-min plant has increased its ultra-pure water capacity and reduced the wastewater and chemicals that would normally be discharged into the environment.

Anglian Water is saving up to 1200 m³/day of potable water, which can now be used to meet the increase in demand in the Peterborough area, one of the fastest-growing towns in the country. The water saved is sufficient to supply more than 6500 new customers without needing to extend the water treatment plant or distribution network.

Alpheus Environmental has a long-term water supply contract that will enable all capital and operating costs to be met and an acceptable profit margin achieved in this novel scheme.

The local environment has been improved by reducing the abstraction from the river, helping to maintain river flow during dry periods of the year. The water quality of the river is improved through reduced disposal of waste power station chemicals. Before the high-purity water supply arrangement the power station was using one tanker of acid every two weeks and one tanker of caustic soda every three weeks. In the last five months only two deliveries of acid and one of caustic soda have been made. This reduction helps to reduce traffic nuisance and the risk of spillage during unloading of these aggressive, highly corrosive chemicals.

A3.3.8 The future for recycling effluent

Flag Fen high-purity water production plant is the first of its type in Europe. The success of the scheme has led to numerous enquiries in the UK and around the world. Anglian Water is investigating several potential schemes for implementing similar technology initiatives in the east of England with outputs totalling 28 400 m³/day. If these schemes proceed, the water saved would be sufficient to supply a conurbation of more than 150 000 people.

Current research work at Flag Fen will also establish the optimum treatment processes required and will confirm the associated long-term costs of producing potable quality water from sewage effluent.

A3.4 Challenges to sustainable water management: Basingstoke case study

River water quality, unlike water resources, has not been a significant material consideration in planning for new development. This case study highlights the problems faced by Thames Water in fulfilling its statutory duty both as a sewerage undertaker to provide for continuing development and in meeting the standards necessary to maintain and improve river quality. Basingstoke is one of several conurbations within TW's operational area that are at or near the headwaters of receiving rivers where available dilution is therefore limited, where discharge consent limits are already very stringent and that have been earmarked for continuing development.

A3.4.1 Early development

Basingstoke, situated in the north-east of Hampshire, originated as a Saxon settlement and expanded over the centuries to cover the hills on both sides of the headwaters of the River Loddon. The market place, established in the 13th century, became the centre of the town and trade grew around that area. Construction of the Basingstoke Canal occurred in the late 18th century and that of the railway began in 1839. In the 1930s Basingstoke was a market town of some 15 000 people.

In 1944 the Greater London Plan provided for one million people to be dispersed from the London area to regions such as Hampshire and Hertfordshire. The Plan recommended an allocation of 20 000 people for decentralisation to Basingstoke. Following the passing of the Town Development Act of 1952 to assist this process of relieving congestion on London and elsewhere, discussions took place between London County Council (LCC) and the Basingstoke Borough to accommodate the overspill. However, in 1958 the LCC proposed the development of a new town at Hook, just to the east of Basingstoke. On 10 000 acres of mainly agricultural land, it was intended that this would initially accommodate 60 000 people.

To counter this greenfield development, Hampshire County Council responded with its own proposal centred on Basingstoke. In 1961 Hampshire County Council, London County Council and Basingstoke Borough Council signed the Town Development Agreement. The ensuing formation of the Basingstoke Development Group to take overspill from the London area, set the trend for Basingstoke's expanding population.

Basingstoke's population increased to 26 000 in 1961 and to 33 000 by 1965. By 1989 it had grown to 90 400 and current projections are for it to increase to 101 500 in 2011 (Table A3.3). These figures do not include the latest SERPLAN projections that are likely to increase the housing allocation for Basingstoke.

Table A3.3   *Domestic population data for the Basingstoke sewerage catchment, 1935–2011*

1935	1961	1965	1988	1991	1995	2000	2006	2111
15 000	25 980	33 000	90 403	92 706	93 579	96 229	99 142	101 516

A3.4.2   Water and sewerage

The Basingstoke conurbation is located at the watershed of the River Loddon in the Thames Basin and the southern groundwater catchments of the Rivers Test and Itchen.

Water, supplied to the area by South East Water, is drawn via boreholes from the groundwaters of both the Thames and southern basins. The potential exists for providing for future development from the River Thames at Bray, and water resources are not therefore perceived to be a constraint within current planning horizons.

Sewage treatment is provided by Thames Water, and effluent is discharged via the works at Chineham, to the north-east of the town, to the River Loddon, a tributary of the Thames.

A3.4.3   River quality

To gain a better understanding of the implications of further development in the Basingstoke area, Thames Water and the Environment Agency in conjunction with WRc co-operated to carry out detailed auditable modelling studies. These examined the effects of increases in flows from Basingstoke and surrounding STWs on the watercourses receiving effluent.

Under the Environment Agency's River Ecosystem Classification, the river quality objective for the River Loddon is RE2 for 18.2 km downstream of Basingstoke to the confluence with the River Blackwater.

This reach of the River Loddon is also classified as a salmonid fishery under the Freshwater Fish Directive (78/6/59/EEC). Under the Asset Management Plan 3 (AMP3) periodic review process, a I mg/I limit for ammonia is to be imposed on the consent for the discharge from Basingstoke STW to achieve the more stringent operational standard under the Directive. The River Loddon has also been designated as a sensitive area (eutrophic) under the Urban Wastewater Treatment Directive (91/271/EEC). The population equivalent for Basingstoke STW exceeds the threshold in the Directive for STWs requiring phosphorus reduction.

At Standford End, 13.5 km downstream of Basingstoke STW, 4 km of the River Loddon is designated under Section 22(3) of the Water Act 1973 (as amended by Section 48 of the Wildlife and Countryside Act 1981) as a site of special scientific interest. This is to protect the Loddon pondweed (*Potamogeton nodosus*), a rare aquatic species for which this reach of the Loddon is a national stronghold, and the river reach as a whole, an all-too-rare example of a high-quality chalk stream in a rural setting that supports a wide variety of wildlife.

Sewage treatment implications

The rigorous standards of water quality demanded by these designations require that Basingstoke's sewage treatment processes are consistently robust to ensure the effluent quality guarantees the necessary level of compliance and protection.

The discharge from Basingstoke STW to the River Loddon is just 7.81 km from its source at West Ham, near the centre of Basingstoke. The 1995–98 mean river flow data 2.36 km upstream of the discharge at Pyotts Bridge (37.30 Mld) and mean flow from the STW (27.83 Mld), indicate dilution by the river is 1.34:1. Under the 95 percentile low flow conditions (17.7 Mld) and dry weather flow from the works (23.50 Mld) for the same period, the ratio of dilution is reversed to 0.72:1.

Flow, and therefore water quality, in the upper reaches of the River Loddon is heavily influenced by the discharge of sewage effluent from Basingstoke STW. As a result of the AMP2 periodic review process (1995–2000), the discharge from Thames Water's activated sludge treatment process is consistently required to guarantee compliance with limits for biochemical oxygen demand and ammonia (respectively 10, 2 mg/l as 95 percentiles), which are already amongst the tightest imposed for any sewage treatment works in England and Wales.

At current levels of populations and dwellings in the Basingstoke area, achievement of the new limits of 1 mg/l ammonia and 1 mg/l total phosphorus to be imposed as a result of the AMP3 periodic review process (2000–2005) will be a significant challenge for the company (Table A3.4).

Table A3.4   *Basingstoke STW discharge consent, 1989–2005*

	SS	BOD	AmmN	P
AMP1 (1989–1995)	10*15	10*10	3*10	–
AMP2 (1995–2000)	10	10	2	–
AMP3 (2000–2005)	10	10	1	1
AMP4 (2005-2010?)	?	?	?	1

Note: All limits – mg/l as 95 percentiles summer*winter

The Environment Agency will not accept any degradation in river quality, particularly in rivers designated under the Freshwater Fish directive. Increases in flow from sewage treatment works due to increases in population may require the tightening of consent limits for those works. This "load standstill" or no deterioration policy may be interpreted as meaning that the quality in a river downstream that would be delivered by a current consent must be maintained after a population increases. This may not take account of additional improvements in river quality that may be required as a result of further regulatory designations during AMP4.

Thames Water has a statutory duty to provide the necessary infrastructure for sewerage and sewage treatment arising from new development and is regulated in this duty by Ofwat. The prospect of additional development in the Basingstoke area with the implications for further tightening of consent limits is therefore a considerable cause for concern.

In fulfilling its statutory duty, and in addition to seeking new technical solutions to treatment at its Basingstoke STW, the company considered various alternatives, which are outlined below and in Figure A3.4.

1 **Diversion of flows to other local sewage treatment works.**

Those within reasonable proximity to Basingstoke, eg Sherborne St John, Sherfield-on-Loddon, discharge to tributaries of the upper reaches of the River Loddon and may themselves be subject to more stringent limits due to load standstill.

2 **Diversion of flows over significant distances outside the catchment area to treatment works that may have available capacity, eg Hartley Wintney.**

Pumping of sewage over long distances has the attendant risk of septicity within the sewerage network.

3 **The construction of new treatment works.**

To the west of Basingstoke, where much development is proposed, there are no watercourses to receive treated effluent. The Environment Agency has indicated that discharges to ground would not be permitted, to protect groundwater supplies drawn from boreholes down-gradient at Basingstoke.

4 **The piping of treated effluent over long distances to suitable discharge points down the River Loddon, where more dilution may be afforded.**

The construction of such a pipeline may in itself cause significant environmental damage.

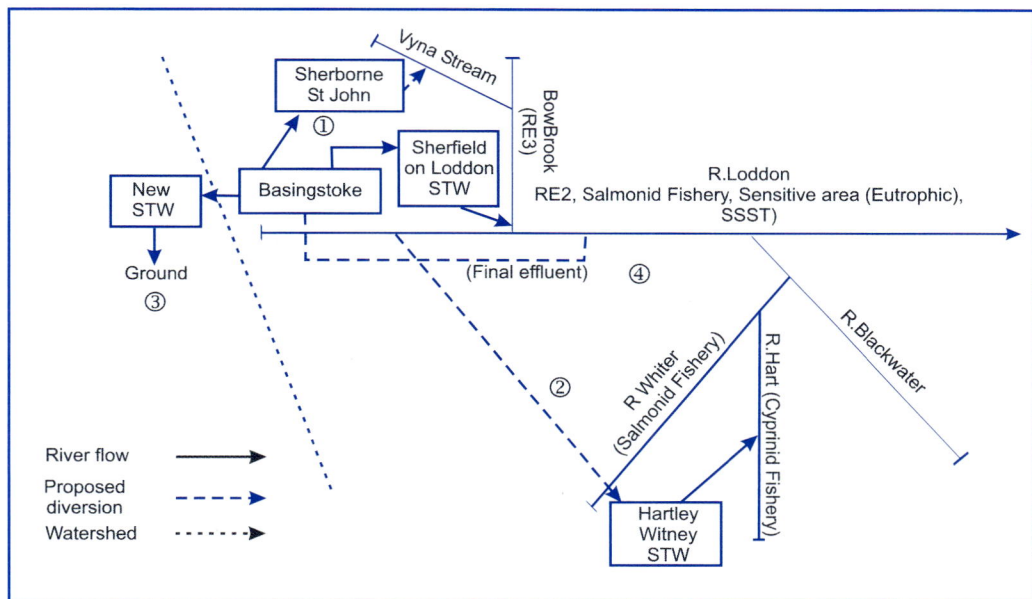

Figure A3.4   *Basingstoke alternatives*

These alternatives have to be considered not only in terms of feasibility, practicality and cost, but also their environmental, social and economic impacts. On a catchment-specific basis, the alternatives will be subject to varying degrees of constraint, some of which may be considered absolute.

The ultimate solution adopted for Basingstoke is likely to incur both capital and operating costs that are significantly greater than for other areas of Thames Water's operations. To date, the cost of delivering sewerage and sewage treatment services has conventionally been spread across the company's whole customer base. However, for conurbations such as Basingstoke where the carrying capacity of the environment is at or near saturation, the consequence of pursuing what could be considered unrealistic levels of development might be that local customers are asked to pay a premium that reflects the proportionately higher cost of conserving the environment of which they are the beneficiaries.

A3.5　Putting water into planning: "Water in Hampshire"

A3.5.1　Summary

Hampshire County Council established the Water in Hampshire project in response to the substantial and increasing pressures being placed on the county's water environment. The council saw such pressures to include new development, climate change and increasing domestic water consumption. The project aims to raise the profile of water; gain a better understanding of the environmental, planning and management issues associated with the county's water environment; and to develop sustainable solutions through working in partnership with other organisations that have an influence on or statutory responsibility for water management.

A3.5.2　Background

Hampshire has a rich diversity of rivers and wetlands, many of which are of international importance but are facing substantial and increasing pressures such as new development. In response to the pressures, the county council's planning department set up, and is continuing to co-ordinate, the innovative multi-agency Water in Hampshire project. The project's focus is on freshwater issues, particularly rivers and groundwater. The project is being undertaken in a number of stages, as summarised below.

A3.5.3　"Water in Hampshire – a comprehensive review"

The first phase was completed in February 2000, with the publication of *Water in Hampshire: a comprehensive review* (HCC, 2000b). Compiled with assistance from the Environment Agency and the local water companies, this publication represented the first attempt at putting together a picture of the complex water situation in the county. It concluded that while water resources are relatively plentiful in Hampshire and that water quality is generally good, the county cannot be complacent. The publication identified that the county's water environment is already under severe stress in places and, if current trends continue, the situation can only worsen if Hampshire does not adapt accordingly.

A3.5.4　National conference "Water: challenges for the 21st century"

The review document was followed on 28 March 2000 by the county council and the Environment Agency hosting the national conference "Water: challenges for the 21st century" at the Winchester Guildhall. Speakers from each of the key sectors involved in the water debate addressed a diverse audience of more than 300 delegates. A range of issues were raised during the speeches and discussion times, complementing and adding to those identified in the *Comprehensive review*.

A3.5.5　Corporate Water Action Plan

The first two stages laid the foundations of the Water in Hampshire project. This has been taken forward by the preparation of water strategies for taking co-ordinated action, either directly or through partnerships, to tackle the issues identified from the document, the conference and beyond.

The first strategy is the internal Corporate Water Action Plan prepared for the operations of Hampshire County Council (HCC, 2001). As a major employer and landowner in the county with a wide range of responsibilities, the council has significant direct and indirect links with the water environment. These links are detailed in the document, which culminates in a policy statement for the county council. The document sets the context for the action the county council will take and provides a detailed action plan. The list of actions is detailed in a separate document, which is monitored and updated regularly (HCC, 2002).

The overall aim of the action plan is to make Hampshire County Council a model for excellence in its stewardship of the water environment.

The plan sets the following broad objectives to help meet the overall aims to:

- set an excellent example to other organisations both within Hampshire and beyond
- raise the profile of water issues amongst staff and councillors, leading to better-informed decisions
- improve cross-department co-ordination and co-operation
- challenge existing practices and implement changes where necessary
- develop innovative solutions
- set and monitor ambitious targets for continuous improvement and to revise them regularly.

This is strengthened by the following policy statement contained within the document.

> *The County Council will ensure that the implications of its decisions and actions on the water environment are taken into account. In line with the 'Stewardship of the Environment' aim of the Corporate Strategy, the County Council will ensure that its unavoidable adverse impacts on the water environment are kept to an absolute minimum, and that it takes opportunities to maintain and enhance the water environment wherever possible. To achieve this, the County Council will set and monitor ambitious targets for continuous improvement.*

> (HCC, 2001)

The plan includes some very specific and measurable actions covering management actions to identify and better control water use within the county council premises, specific policy enhancements or links to include water issues in future planning, improved education on water issues and a focus on consultation with other stakeholders in the planning and management of water issues. Examples of these are given in Table A3.5.

A3.5.6   Hampshire Water Strategy

In developing the Hampshire Water Strategy, the county council, in partnership with organisations involved in the management of the county's water environment, aims to address key issues such as resource management, the impact of new development and flooding.

The aim of the strategy is:

> *To establish a framework for safeguarding and enhancing the water resources, water quality and biodiversity of Hampshire's freshwater environment by adopting a holistic partnership approach to the water issues faced in the county.*

> (Hampshire's Water Project, 2003)

The strategy is being developed by a steering group made up of representatives from a cross-section of organisations involved in the management of the county's water environment. These representative organisations are Bryant Homes, the Environment Agency, Hampshire and Isle of Wight Wildlife Trust, Hampshire County Council, New Forest District Council, Southampton City Council, the National Farmers Union, Southern Water and the Hampshire Association of Parish and Town Councils.

To encourage a wider ownership of the HWS, a stakeholder event was held in September 2001 to help scope the work. The 55 delegates from more than 40 organisations who attended represented a diverse range of interests across the public, private and voluntary sectors. The ideas generated by delegates at the stakeholder event were used by the project steering group as a basis for developing a first draft of the Hampshire Water Strategy. The final version of the Strategy was launched in March 2003 with a strong commitment from all involved to carry through the actions recommended and to review and update the strategy after three years.

The Strategy outlines the issues and current actions being taken before setting out a future action plan for more co-ordinated management of the water environment of Hampshire.

A3.5.7 Water issues in planning documents within Hampshire

Water in Hampshire is an ongoing project, but there are already clear demonstrations of where the work completed to date has been taken into the mainstream planning environment.

The *Hampshire county structure plan 1996–2011*, adopted 2000 (HCC, 2000a), includes a section on water issues (see Box A3.6) and two policy statements covering constraints on developments designed to promote sustainable water management. Significantly, the county plan also covers the unitary authorities of Southampton and Portsmouth and so provides a co-ordinated approach to water management through the region's big urban centres and rural areas.

Table A3.5   *Selected Water in Hampshire actions and performance targets (HCC, 2003)*

	No	Action		Target/performance indicator
General	2	Take the year 2000/2001 as the County Council's baseline for water consumption, and from this date onwards publish total water usage, broken down by Departments on an annual basis.		1. Produce annual report.
	3	Undertake feasibility study into major corporate water efficiency exercise with the aim of reducing the County Council's total annual water consumption (excluding schools – see Action 4).		1. Complete study by September 2002. 2. By 5% of 2000/01 absolute level by 2002/03 By 10% of 2000/01 absolute level by 2003/04 By 15% of 2000/01 absolute level by 2004/05
	4	Raise awareness of water consumption in schools with the aim of setting a target to reduce total annual water consumption		Set targets for reducing water consumption in schools by March 2003.
	8	Audit the county council's use of pesticides that go into the water cycle, providing a baseline from which to reduce adverse impacts on water quality.		Carry out annual audit and disseminate results to each department.
Highways	26	Include SUDS solutions in standard details for new builds.		By July 2002.
	27	Produce guidelines for implementation of SUDS in typical Hampshire geology.		By March/April 2002.
	28	Encourage inclusion of SUDS schemes in major new developments via Section 38/278 agreements.		Four more schemes to include SUDS by the end of 2002.
Hampshire	35	Overhaul water section in the next review of the County Structure Plan (this should include policies covering water resources; the inclusion of water-efficient technology in new developments; and sustainable urban drainage systems).		Water element of County Structure Plan to be a national model of excellence.
Influencing development	51	Ensure all development briefs prepared by the county council address water resource and water quality issues.		Prepare guidance note for officers by end 2002.
	52	Additional detail on water issues to be given in the guidance for major development areas implementation to ensure innovative development takes place.		Section on water resources and water quality in the guidance (timetable yet to be agreed).
	53	Promote incorporation of sustainable drainage systems into all new developments where appropriate.		Prepare guidance note for officers by end 2002.

Box A3.4   *Water-related policy statements from the* Hampshire county structure plan 1996–2011 *(review) (HCC, 2000a)*

Water is an essential part of everyone's daily life, domestically and for industry. It also has a vital role to play in supporting the natural environment. In recognition of this, Hampshire County Council, with the key regulatory authorities and utilities, has undertaken a comprehensive study of water resources to develop a joint strategy for the future. This recognises that all players must operate together, at as early a stage as possible, to ensure efficient use of water resources without compromising the natural environment.

Climate change may have an increasing effect on water resources, with predicted increase in winter rainfall, drier summers and rising sea levels. Together with increasing usage per head and the scale of new development required in the Plan, water management issues are likely to become increasingly important.

E1 Development will not be permitted where it is likely to lead to the deterioration of the quality of groundwater or surface water.

National guidance on water quality, contaminated land and land drainage is largely set out in PPG12, PPG23, EC Bathing Water and Urban Waste Water Treatment Directives and various Environment Agency documents, in particular the Policy and Practice for the Protection of Ground Water.

In Hampshire, investigations have indicated that, overall, there are currently no major constraints on new development imposed by water supply or water quality considerations, but awareness of the implications of development on the water environment is evolving rapidly and a precautionary approach must be adopted. There are also some potential local capacity thresholds and water quality concerns which, although they may be overcome by investment, require careful and early integration with the development plan process.

Local planning authorities must not, therefore, be complacent. As a result of the additional pressures on the resource they should, through the promotion, control and design of new development, try to raise water quality standards, deter profligate use of water resources through the use of efficient installation and drainage systems; and continue to have regard to the various means for protecting aquifers.

Unless carefully sited, new development can exacerbate problems of water supply, flooding, pollution in watercourses and groundwater and water levels in surface ponds and streams. Effective liaison between the local planning authorities and the Environment Agency will be essential if the water environment is to be protected. To assist in this process at a strategic level Hampshire County Council has established a Water Consultation Group on which the authorities, the EA regional offices, and all the water utilities operating in the area are represented.

E2 Development, other than change of use, which would be at direct risk of flooding or likely to increase risk of flooding elsewhere, will not be permitted. Within defined flood risk areas, any development permitted should incorporate flood containment or public safety measures justified on that account. New development, or the extension or intensification of existing development along the coast, must take into account areas identified as being at risk from coastal flooding or coastal erosion.

National guidance on flood and coastal defence policies for risk areas is set out in the Strategy for Flood and Coastal Defence in England and Wales, PPG20 and PPG25, plus various Environment Agency documents.

The risk to people, buildings and the environment from flooding and coastal erosion must be reduced. This objective will be met by encouraging the provision of technically, environmentally and economically sound flood defence measures. At the same time, development will be discouraged in areas at risk from flooding and erosion.

Local planning authorities will need to adopt policies to avoid, rather than mitigate, the undesirable effects of development within areas liable to flood and prevent an increase in surface water run-off.

Sea defence planning is undertaken by the Environment Agency and coastal district councils. The Agency is currently planning its sea defence programme based on an annual rise in sea level of 6 mm a year and has defined coastal flood risk areas in accordance with the Water Resources Act. Local plans will need to show these flood risk areas and those stretches of the coastline which are prone to coastal erosion.

This guidance and these policies should in time feed through to local plans, supplementary planning guidance and development briefs.

Conversely, some local plans that are being developed within Hampshire have not yet included within their texts the latest thinking on water from the Water in Hampshire project. This may be a matter of timing of information or a question of priorities. For example, the Basingstoke and Deane local plan review – issues report, published in late 2000 sought local views on the proposed major developments in/around Basingstoke. The document covered many issues, but made no specific reference to water management issues, despite the fact that these are potentially major constraints that would be recognised by the policy in the structure plan.

HCC has also worked with the local district councils on the implementation of planned major development areas to ensure that water issues are considered in the detailed planning for these areas.

A3.5.8   Hampshire Water Consultative Group

The HWCG is co-ordinated by the county council and is made up primarily of representatives of water companies, district and unitary authorities and the EA. Its aim is to discuss issues in the development of the structure and local plans and ensure that there is early dialogue on any areas where potentially there may be problems for water management. The main areas of debate are water supply to new development areas and subsequent removal of wastewater, drainage issues and updating of progress on each organisation's emerging planning documents. This work links with the wider work on the emerging Hampshire Water Strategy.

A4 Stakeholder website addresses

A4.1 Web addresses for sustainable water management

National policy and regulation	
Department for the Environment, Food and Rural Affairs	<www.defra.gov.uk>
Welsh Assembly Government	<www.wales.gov.uk>
Environment Agency	<www.environment-agency.gov.uk>
Water resources	<www.environment-agency.gov.uk/subjects/waterres/?lang=_e>
Office of the Deputy Prime Minister	<www.odpm.gov.uk>
Department for Transport	<www.dft.gov.uk>
Transport, Planning and Environment Group	<www.wales.gov.uk/keypubassemeplantrans/index.htm>
Local Government Association	<www.lga.gov.uk>
Links to local authority websites	<www.lga.gov.uk/Briefing.asp?lsection=329&id=SX9D0B-A77FE3B1&ccat=329>
Planning Inspectorate	<www.planning-inspectorate.gov.uk>
Water supply and sewerage companies	
Regulatory organisations	
Office of Water Services (Ofwat)	<www.ofwat.gov.uk>
Drinking Water Inspectorate (DWI)	<www.dwi.gov.uk>
Conservation	
English Nature (EN)	<www.english-nature.org.uk>
Countryside Agency (CA)	<www.countryside.gov.uk>
Countryside Council for Wales (CCW)	<www.ccw.gov.uk>
Royal Society for the Protection of Birds (RSPB)	<ww.rspb.org.uk>
Drainage	
Association of Drainage Authorities	<www.ada.org.uk>
Highways Agency (HA)	<www.highways.gov.uk>

References

Publications

BASINGSTOKE AND DEANE BOROUGH COUNCIL (2000). *Basingstoke and Deane local plan review. Issues report*. Basingstoke and Deane BC, Basingstoke

DEFRA (2002). *Directing the flow – priorities for future water policy*. Department for Environment, Food and Rural Affairs, London

DETR (1998a). *Planning for sustainable development – towards better practice*. GPG22, Department of the Environment, Transport and the Regions, Norwich (ISBN 0-11-753406-4)

DETR (1998b). *Planning and development briefs – a guide to better practice*. GPG20, Department of the Environment, Transport and the Regions, London (ISBN 1-85112-069-6)

DETR (1999a). *A better quality of life – a strategy for sustainable development for the United Kingdom*. Cm 4345, Stationery Office, London (ISBN 0-10-143452-9)

DETR (1999b). *Environmental impact assessment*. Circular 02/99, Department of the Environment, Transport and the Regions, Norwich (ISBN 0-11-753493-5)

DETR (1999c). *Water Supply (Water Fittings) Regulations 1999: guidance document relating to Schedule 1: fluid categories and Schedule 2: requirements for water fittings*. Department of the Environment, Transport and the Regions, Norwich

DETR (1999d). *Planning requirements in respect of the use of non-mains sewerage incorporating septic tanks in new development*. Circular 03/99, Department of the Environment, Transport and the Regions, Norwich

DETR (1999e). *Planning and waste management*. PPG10, Department of the Environment, Transport and the Regions, Norwich (ISBN 1-85112-318-0)

DETR (2000a). *Sustainable development – what it is and what you can do*. Department of the Environment, Transport and the Regions, Sustainable Development Unit, London

DETR (2000b). *Development plans*. PPG12, Department of the Environment, Transport and the Regions, London (ISBN 0-18-5112349-0)

DETR (2000c). *Regional planning*. PPG11, Department of the Environment, Transport and the Regions, Norwich (ISBN 0-11-753557-5)

DETR (2000d). *Sustainability appraisal of regional planning guidance – a good practice guide*. GPG25, Department of the Environment, Transport and the Regions, Norwich (ISBN 0-11-753568-0)

DETR (2000e). *Housing*. PPG3, Department of the Environment, Transport and the Regions, Norwich (ISBN 0-11-753546-X)

DETR (2000f). *Water Bill – consultation on draft legislation*. Department of the Environment, Transport and the Regions, Norwich

DETR and Welsh Office (1999). *Taking water responsibly: government decisions following consultation on changes to the water abstraction licensing system in England and Wales*. The Stationery Office, London

DoE (1991). *Water industry investment: planning considerations*. Circular 17/91, Department of the Environment, London (ISBN 0-11-752452-2)

DoE (1992a). *Coastal planning*. PPG20, HMSO, London (ISBN 0-11-752711-4)

DoE (1992b). *Local development plans and unitary development plans – best practice*. GPG18, HMSO, London

DoE (1992c). *Development plans – a good practice guide*. GPG13, HMSO, London (ISBN 0-11-752689-4)

DoE (1993). *Environmental appraisal of development plans – a good practice guide*. GPG15, HMSO, London (ISBN 0-11-752866-8)

DoE (1994a). *Planning and pollution control*. PPG23, Department of the Environment, London (ISBN 0-11-752947-8)

DoE (1994b). *Evaluation of environmental information for planning projects – a good practice guide*. GPG16, HMSO, London (ISBN 0-11-753043-3)

DoE (1995). *Preparation of environmental statements for planning projects that require environmental assessment – a good practice guide*. GPG24, HMSO, London (ISBN 0-11-753207-X)

DoE (1997). *General policy and principles*. PPG1, Department of te Environment, Norwich (ISBN 0-11-753368-8)

DoE and Department of Transport (1994). *Transport*. PPG13, HMSO, London

DoE and Department of Transport (1995). *PPG13 – guide to better practice*. GPG23, HMSO, London (ISBN 0-11-753144-8)

DTLR (2001a). *Development and flood risk*. PPG25, Department for Transport, Local Government and the Regions, London (ISBN 0-11-753611-3)

DTLR (2001b). *Planning: delivering a fundamental change*. Planning Green Paper, Department for Transport, Local Government and the Regions, London

DTLR (2001c). *Building Regulations 2000 – drainage and waste disposal. Approved Document H, 2002 edition*. Department for Transport, Local Government and the Regions, London (ISBN 0-11-753607-5)

DWI (2001). *List of approved products and processes*. Drinking Water Inspectorate, London

EERA AND EESDRT (2001). *A sustainable development framework for the east of England*. East of England Regional Assembly, Flempton; East of England Sustainable Development Round Table, Cambridge

ENVIRONMENT AGENCY (1998). *Thames environment 21 – the Environment Agency strategy for land use planning in Thames Region*. Environment Agency, Reading

ENVIRONMENT AGENCY (2001a). *Water resources for the future: a water resources strategy for England and Wales*. Environment Agency, Bristol (ISBN 1-85705-508-X)

ENVIRONMENT AGENCY (2001b). *Managing water abstraction – the catchment abstraction management strategy process*. Environment Agency, Reading (ISBN 1-85705-554-3)

ENVIRONMENT AGENCY (2001c). *Constructive thinking – save water, save the environment*. Environment Agency, Worthing

ENVIRONMENT AGENCY (2001d). *Conserving water in buildings*. <www.environment-agency.gov.uk/subjects/waterres/286587/286599/286911/548861/?version=1&lang=_e>

ENVIRONMENT AGENCY (2002a). *Waterwise – good for business and good for the environment* <www.environment-agency.gov.uk/subjects/waterres/286587/286599/286911/878032/?lang=_e>

ENVIRONMENT AGENCY (2002b). *Savewater web site* <www.environment-agency.gov.uk/subjects/waterres/286587/?version=1>

ENVIRONMENT AGENCY and LGA (1999). *Protocol between the Local Government Association and the Environment Agency (Part 1). Working better together in town and country planning.* Local Government Association, London

ENVIRONMENT AGENCY AND SEERA. *Preparing for growth in the south-east*

ENVIRONMENT, TRANSPORT AND REGIONAL AFFAIRS COMMITTEE (2001). *Water Bill.* 9th report of House of Commons Environment, Transport and Regional Affairs Committee, HC 145-I, The Stationery Office, London (ISBN 0-10-223601-1)

ESSEX COUNTY COUNCIL (2001). *Essex county structure plan.* Essex County Council, Colchester

GO-EAST (2000). *Regional planning guidance for East Anglia to 2016.* RPG6, Government Office for East Anglia, Cambridge (ISBN 0-11-753561-3)

GOEM (2002). *Regional planning guidance for the East Midlands.* RPG8, Government Office for the East Midlands, Nottingham (ISBN 0-11-753626-1)

GO-SE (2001). *Regional planning guidance for the South East.* RPG9, Government Office for the South East, Guildford (ISBN 0-11-753562-1)

GOSW (2001). *Regional planning guidance for the South West.* RPG10, Government Office for the South West, Bristol (ISBN 0-11-753603-2)

GOYH (2001). *Regional planning guidance for Yorkshire and the Humber.* RPG12, Government Office for Yorkshire and the Humber, Leeds (ISBN 0-11-753618-0)

HAMPSHIRE COUNTY COUNCIL (2000a). *Hampshire county structure plan.* Hampshire County Council, Winchester

HAMPSHIRE COUNTY COUNCIL (2000b). *Water in Hampshire – a comprehensive review.* Hampshire County Council, Winchester (ISBN 1-85975-352-3)

HAMPSHIRE COUNTY COUNCIL (2001). *Corporate water action plan.* Hampshire County Council, Winchester

HAMPSHIRE COUNTY COUNCIL (2002). *Corporate water action plan.* Hampshire County Council, Winchester

HAMPSHIRE COUNTY COUNCIL (nd). *Water in Hampshire website.* <www.hants.gov.uk/environment/water/index.html>

HAMPSHIRE'S WATER (nd). Website <www.hampshireswater.org.uk>

HAMPSHIRE'S WATER PROJECT (2003). *Hampshire water strategy.* Hampshire County Council, Winchester

HERTFORDSHIRE COUNTY COUNCIL (2003). *Hertfordshire structure plan 2001-2016.* Deposit draft, Hertfordshire County Council, Hertford

HULME, M, JENKINS, G J, LU, X, TURNPENNY, J R, MITCHELL, T D, JONES, R G, LOWE, J, MURPHY, J M, BOORMAN, D, McDONALD, R AND HILL, S (2002). *Climate change scenarios for the United Kingdom – the UKCIP02 scientific report.* Tyndall Centre for Climate Change Research, Norwich

ICE (2003). *State of the nation 2003.* Institution of Civil Engineers, London

LAND USE CONSULTANTS (2005). *A toolkit for delivering water management climate change adaptation through the planning system.* Land Use Consultants (for Environment Agency and SEERA), London

LEGGETT, D, BROWN, R, BREWER, D, STANFIELD, G AND HOLLIDAY, E (2001). *Rainwater and greywater use in buildings. Best practice guidance.* C539, CIRIA, London (ISBN 0-86017-539-1)

MARTIN, P, TURNER, B, WADDINGTON, K, DELL, J, PRATT, C, CAMPBELL, N, PAYNE, J AND REED, B (2000). *Sustainable urban drainage systems – design manual for England and Wales*. C522, CIRIA, London (ISBN 0-86017-522-7)

MARTIN, P, TURNER, B, DELL, J, PAYNE, J, ELLIOTT, C AND REED, B (2001). *Sustainable urban drainage systems – best practice manual for England, Scotland, Wales and Northern Ireland*. C523, CIRIA, London (ISBN 0-86017-523-5)

NSWG (2004). *Interim code of practice for sustainable drainage systems*. National SUDS Working Group, London (ISBN 0-86017-904-4)

ODPM (2003a). *Sustainable communities: building for the future*. 02HC00964, Office of the Deputy Prime Minister, London

ODPM (2003b). *The relationships between community strategies and local development frameworks*. Entec (for Office of the Deputy Prime Minister), London

ODPM (2004a). *Regional spatial strategies*. PPS11, Office of the Deputy Prime Minister, London (ISBN 0-11-753925-2)

ODPM (2004b). *Sustainability appraisal of regional spatial strategies and local development frameworks*. Consultation paper, Office of the Deputy Prime Minister, London

ODPM (2004c). *Local development frameworks*. PPS12, Office of the Deputy Prime Minister, London (ISBN 0-11-753926-0)

ODPM (2004d). *Planning and climate change – a guide to better practice*. Office of the Deputy Prime Minister, London

ODPM (2004e). *Planning and pollution control*. PPS23, Office of the Deputy Prime Minister, London (ISBN 0-11-753927-9)

ODPM (2004f). *Planning and pollution control. Pollution control, air and water quality*. PPS23 Annex 1, Office of the Deputy Prime Minister, London (ISBN 0-11-753931-7)

ODPM (2004g). *Planning and pollution control. Development on land affected by contamination*. PPS23 Annex 2, Office of the Deputy Prime Minister, London (ISBN 0-11-753932-5)

ODPM (2005a). *Creating sustainable communities*. PPS1, Office of the Deputy Prime Minister, London (ISBN 0-11-753939-2)

ODPM (2005b). *Controlling and mitigating the environmental effects of minerals extraction in England*. MPS2, Office of the Deputy Prime Minister, London (ISBN 1-85112-780-1)

OXFORDSHIRE COUNTY COUNCIL (2003). *Oxfordshire structure plan review*. Revised deposit draft. Oxfordshire County Council, Oxford

PACIFIC INSTITUTE (1995). *California water 2020: a sustainable vision*. Pacific Institute for Studies in Development, Environment, and Security, Oakland, California

PACIFIC INSTITUTE (1999). *Sustainable use of water: California success stories*. Pacific Institute for Studies in Development, Environment, and Security, Oakland, California

PLANNING CO-OPERATIVE (2001). *Regional planning guidance for the South East. Environment Agency's users' manual*

PRATT, C, WILSON, S AND COOPER, P (2002). *Source control using constructed pervious surfaces. Hydraulic, structural and water quality performance issues*. C582, CIRIA, London (ISBN 0-86017-582-7)

ROTHER DISTRICT COUNCIL (2003). *Rother District local plan*. Revised deposit draft. Rother District Council, Bexhill-on-Sea

RCEP (2002). *Environmental planning*. 23rd report, Royal Commission on Environmental Pollution, London

SHAFFER, P, ELLIOTT, C, REED, J, HOLMES, J AND WARD, M (2004). *Model agreements for sustainable water management systems. Model agreements for SUDS*. C625, CIRIA, London (ISBN 0-86017-625-8)

SOUTH BEDFORDSHIRE DISTRICT COUNCIL (2004). *South Bedfordshire local plan review. Adopted January 2004*. South Bedfordshire District Council, Dunstable

SOUTH CAMBRIDGESHIRE DISTRICT COUNCIL (2004). *South Cambridgeshire local plan. Adopted February 2004*. South Cambridgeshire District Council, Cambourne (ISBN 0-906016-24-X)

SOUTH GLOUCESTERSHIRE COUNCIL (2002). *South Gloucestershire local plan*. South Gloucestershire Council, Thornbury

STAFFORDSHIRE COUNTY COUNCIL and STOKE-ON-TRENT CITY COUNCIL (2001). *Staffordshire and Stoke-on-Trent structure plan 1996–2011*. Staffordshire County Council, Stafford

SURREY COUNTY COUNCIL (2004). *Shaping Surrey's future. Surrey structure plan 2004*. Surrey County Council, Kingston-upon-Thames (ISBN 1-899706-77-1)

TRANSPORT, LOCAL GOVERNMENT AND THE REGIONS COMMITTEE (2002). *Planning green paper*. HC 476-1, Session 2001–02, 13th report, House of Commons Transport, Local Government and the Regions Committee, vol I, Stationery Office, London (ISBN 0-21-500410-8)

WCED (1987). *Our common future*. Report of the 1987 World Commission on Environment and Development (the Brundtland Report), Oxford University Press, Oxford (ISBN 0-19-282080-X)

WELWYN HATFIELD COUNCIL (2002). *Welwyn Hatfield district plan*. Revised deposit draft. Welwyn Hatfield Council, Welwyn Garden City

WILSON, S, BRAY, R AND COOPER, P (2004). *Sustainable drainage systems. Hydraulic, structural and water quality advice*. C609, CIRIA, London (ISBN 0-86017-609-1)

WRAS (nd). *Water fittings and materials directory*. Biannual. Water Regulations Advisory Scheme, Oakdale

WRAS (2000). *Water regulations guide*. Water Regulations Advisory Scheme, Oakdale (ISBN 0-953970-80-9)

WRc (2001). *Sewers for adoption: a design and construction guide for developers*. 5th edition, WRc, Swindon (ISBN 1-898920-43-5)

Environmental and planning guidance

Circulars

17/91   *Water industry investment: planning considerations* (DoE, 1991)

02/99   *Environmental impact assessment* (DETR, 1999b)

03/99   *Planning requirements in respect of the use of non-mains sewerage incorporating septic tanks in new development* (DETR, 1999d)

Good Practice Guides

GPG13   *Development plans* (DoE, 1992c)

GPG15   *Environmental appraisal of development plans* (DoE, 1993)

GPG16   *Evaluation of environmental information for planning projects* (DoE, 1994b)

GPG18   *Local development plans and unitary development plans* (DoE, 1992b)

GPG20   *Planning and development briefs* (DETR, 1998b)

GPG22   *Planning for sustainable development – towards better practice* (DETR, 1998a)

GPG23   *PPG13 – guide to better practice* (DoE and DoT, 1995)

GPG24   *Preparation of environmental statements for planning projects that require environmental assessment* (DoE, 1995)

GPG25   *Sustainability appraisal of regional planning guidance* (DETR, 2000d)

Minerals Policy Statement

MPS2   *Controlling and mitigating the environmental effects of minerals extraction in England* (ODPM, 2005b)

Planning Policy Guidance Notes

* Withdrawn and replaced by a PPS with the same number (eg PPG1 has been replaced by PPS1)

PPG1   *General policy and principles* (DoE, 1997)*

PPG3   *Housing* (DETR, 2000e)

PPG10   *Planning and waste management* (DETR, 1999e)

PPG11   *Regional planning* (DETR, 2000c)*

PPG12   *Development plans* (DETR, 2000b)*

PPG13   *Transport* (DoE and DoT, 1994)

PPG20   *Coastal planning* (DoE, 1992a)

PPG23   *Planning and pollution control* (DoE, 1994a)*

PPG25   *Development and flood risk* (DTLR, 2001a)

Planning Policy Statements

PPS1   *Delivering sustainable development* (ODPM, 2005a)

PPS11   *Regional spatial strategies* (ODPM, 2004a)

PPS12   *Local development frameworks* (ODPM, 2004c)

PPS23   *Planning and pollution control. Development on land affected by contamination* (ODPM, 2004g)

Regional Planning Guidance

RPG6   *East Anglia* (GO-EAST, 2000)

RPG8   *East Midlands* (GOEM, 2002)
To be replaced by: *Regional planning guidance for the East Midlands to 2021. Towards a regional spatial strategy.* Revised drafts (East Midlands Regional Local Government Association, Melton Mowbray, 2003)

RPG9   *South East* (GO-SE, 2001)

RPG10   *South West* (GOSW, 2001)

RPG12   *Yorkshire and the Humber* (GOYH, 2001)

Legislation

UK legislation

The following UK Acts and Regulations are available from The Stationery Office.

Building Act 1984. 1984 c. 55 (ISBN 0-10-545584-9)

Building (Amendment) Regulations 2001. SI 2001/3335 (ISBN 0-11-038645-0)

Building Regulations 2000. SI 2000/2531 (ISBN 0-11-753607-5)

Conservation (Natural Habitats, &c.) Regulations 1994. SI 1994/2716 (ISBN 0-11-045716-1)

Environment Act 1995. 1995 c. 25 (ISBN 0-10-542595-8)

Environmental Assessment of Plans and Programmes Regulations 2004. SI 2004/1633
(ISBN 0-11-049455-5)

Environmental Impact Assessment (Land Drainage Improvement Works) Regulations 1999.
SI 1999/1783 (ISBN 0-11-082920-4)

Environmental Protection Act 1990. 1990 c. 43 (ISBN 0-10-544390-5)

Highways Act 1980. 1980 c. 66 (ISBN 0-10-546680-8)

Land Drainage Act 1991. 1991 c. 59 (ISBN 0-10-545991-7)

Land Drainage Act 1994. 1994 c. 25 (ISBN 0-10-542594-X)

Planning and Compensation Act 1991. 1991 c. 34 (ISBN 0-10-543491-4)

Planning and Compulsory Purchase Act 2004. 2004 c. 5 (ISBN 0-10-540504-3)

Planning (Listed Buildings and Conservation Areas) Act 1990 (c. 9), ISBN 0-10-540990-1

Pollution Prevention and Control Act 1999. 1999 c. 24 (ISBN 0-10-542499-4)

Salmon and Freshwater Fisheries Act 1975. 1975 c. 51

Surface Waters (Fishlife) (Classification) Regulations 1997. SI 1997/1331 (ISBN 0-11-063707-0)

Surface Waters (River Ecosystem) (Classification) Regulations 1994. SI 1994/1057
(ISBN 0-11-044057-9)

Town and Country Planning Act 1990. 1990 c. 8 (ISBN 0-10-540890-5)

Town and Country Planning (Environmental Impact Assessment) (England and Wales) Regulations
1999. SI 1999/293 (ISBN 0-11-080474-0)

Town and Country Planning (General Development Procedure) Order 1995. SI 1995/419
(ISBN 0-11-052498-5)

Town and Country Planning (General Permitted Development) Order 1995. SI 1995/418
(ISBN 0-11-052506-X)

Town and Country Planning (Local Development) (England) Regulations 2004. SI 2004/2204
(ISBN 0-11-049748-1)

Town Development Act, 1952. 1952: 15 & 16 Geo. 6 & 1 Eliz.2 Ch.54

Urban Wastewater Treatment (England and Wales) Regulations 1994. SI 1994/2841
(ISBN 0-11-045841-9)

Water Act 1989. 1989 c. 15 (ISBN 0-10-541589-8)

Water Act 2003. 2003 c. 37 (ISBN 0-10-543703-4)

Water Environment (Water Framework Directive) (England and Wales) Regulations 2003.
SI 2003/3242 (ISBN 0-11-048355-3)

Water Industry Act 1991. 1991 c. 56 (ISBN 0-10-545691-8)

Water Resources Act 1963. 1963 c. 38

Water Resources Act 1991. 1991 c. 57 (ISBN 0-10-545791-4)

Water Resources (Environmental Impact Assessment) (England and Wales) Regulations 2003. SI
2003/164 (ISBN 0-11-044793-X)

Water Supply (Water Fittings) Regulations 1999. SI 1999/1148 (ISBN 0-11-082552-7)

Water Supply (Water Quality) Regulations 2000. SI 2000/3184 (ISBN 0-11-018878-0

Wildlife and Countryside Act 1981. 1981 c. 69 (ISBN 0-10-546981-5)

EC legislation

The following European Community Directives are published by the Office for Official Publications of the European Communities, Luxembourg. They are listed by Directive number. Where appropriate, the short title is given in parenthesis. OJ = Official Journal of the European Communities.

Council Directive 76/160/EEC of 8 Dec 1975 on the quality of bathing water ("the Bathing Water Directive"). *OJ* L031, P. 0001–0007

Council Directive 76/464/EEC of 4 May 1976 on pollution caused by certain dangerous substances discharged into the aquatic environment of the Community ("the Surface Waters (Dangerous Substances) (Classification) Directive"). *OJ* L129, P. 0023–0029

Council Directive 78/659/EEC of 18 Jul 1978 on the quality of fresh waters needing protection or improvement in order to support fish life ("the Freshwater Fish Directive"). *OJ* L222, P. 0001–0010

Council Directive 79/409/EEC of 2 Apr 1979 on the conservation of wild birds ("the Birds Directive"). *OJ* L103, P. 0001–0018

Council Directive 79/923/EEC of 30 Oct 1979 on the quality required of shellfish waters ("the Shellfish Waters Directive"). *OJ* L073, P. 0047–0052

Council Directive 85/337/EEC of 27 Jun 1985 on the assessment of the effects of certain public and private projects on the environment ("the Environmental Impacts Assessment Directive"). *OJ* L175, P. 0040–0048

Council Directive 91/271/EEC of 21 May 1991 concerning urban wastewater treatment ("the Urban Wastewater Treatment Directive"). *OJ* L135, P. 0040–0052

Council Directive 91/676/EEC of 12 Dec 1991 concerning the protection of waters against pollution caused by nitrates from agricultural sources ("the Nitrates Directive"). *OJ* L375, P. 0001–0008

Council Directive 92/43/EEC of 21 May 1992 on the conservation of natural habitats and of wild fauna and flora ("the Habitats Directive"). *OJ* L206, P. 0007–0050

Council Directive 97/11/EC of 3 Mar 1997 amending Directive 85/337/EEC on the assessment of the effects of certain public and private projects on the environment. *OJ* L073, P. 0005–0015

Council Directive 2000/60/EC of 23 Oct 2000 establishing a framework for Community action in the field of water policy ("the Water Framework Directive"). *OJ* L327, P. 0001–0073

Council Directive 2001/42/EC of 27 Jun 2001 on the assessment of certain plans and programmes on the environment ("the Strategic Environmental Assessment Directive"). *OJ* L197, P. 0030–0037

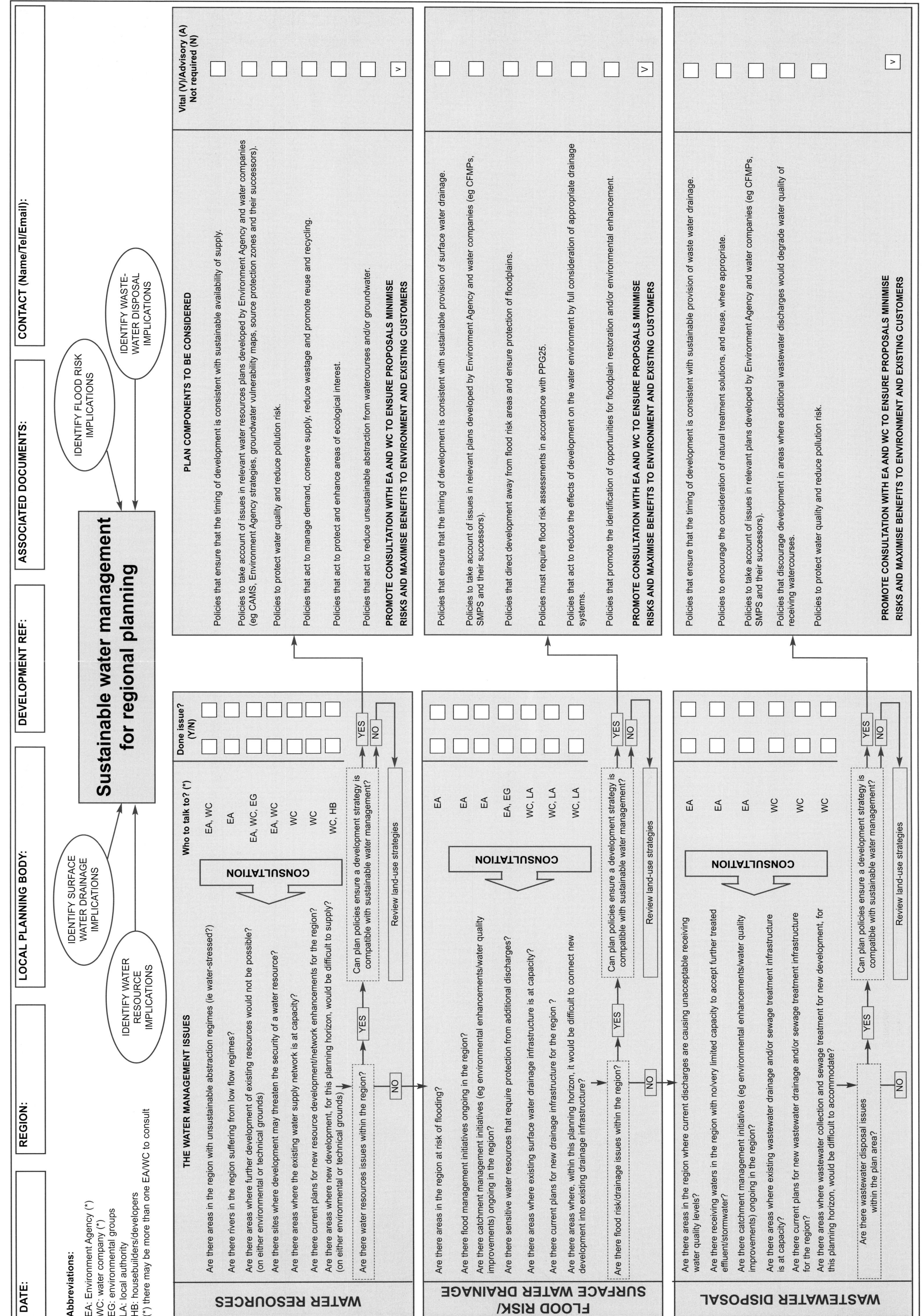

Sustainable water management for regional planning

DATE: | REGION: | LOCAL PLANNING BODY: | DEVELOPMENT REF: | ASSOCIATED DOCUMENTS: | CONTACT (Name/Tel/Email):

Abbreviations:
EA: Environment Agency (*)
WC: water company (*)
EG: environmental groups
LA: local authority
HB: housebuilders/developers
(*) there may be more than one EA/WC to consult

IDENTIFY SURFACE WATER DRAINAGE IMPLICATIONS
IDENTIFY WATER RESOURCE IMPLICATIONS
IDENTIFY FLOOD RISK IMPLICATIONS
IDENTIFY WASTE-WATER DISPOSAL IMPLICATIONS

Vital (V)/Advisory (A)
Not required (N)

Done Issue? (Y/N)

WATER RESOURCES

THE WATER MANAGEMENT ISSUES — Who to talk to? (*)

- Are there areas in the region with unsustainable abstraction regimes (ie water-stressed)? — EA, WC
- Are there rivers in the region suffering from low flow regimes? — EA
- Are there areas where further development of existing resources would not be possible? (on either environmental or technical grounds) — EA, WC, EG
- Are there sites where development may threaten the security of a water resource? — EA, WC
- Are there areas where the existing water supply network is at capacity? — WC
- Are there current plans for new resource development/network enhancements for the region? — WC
- Are there areas where new development, for this planning horizon, would be difficult to supply? (on either environmental or technical grounds) — WC, HB

CONSULTATION

Are there water resources issues within the region? — YES / NO

Can plan policies ensure a development strategy is compatible with sustainable water management? — YES / NO

Review land-use strategies

PLAN COMPONENTS TO BE CONSIDERED

- Policies that ensure that the timing of development is consistent with sustainable availability of supply.
- Policies to take account of issues in relevant water resources plans developed by Environment Agency and water companies (eg CAMS, Environment Agency strategies, groundwater vulnerability maps, source protection zones and their successors).
- Policies to protect water quality and reduce pollution risk.
- Policies that act to manage demand, conserve supply, reduce wastage and promote reuse and recycling.
- Policies that act to protect and enhance areas of ecological interest.
- Policies that act to reduce unsustainable abstraction from watercourses and/or groundwater.

PROMOTE CONSULTATION WITH EA AND WC TO ENSURE PROPOSALS MINIMISE RISKS AND MAXIMISE BENEFITS TO ENVIRONMENT AND EXISTING CUSTOMERS

FLOOD RISK/ SURFACE WATER DRAINAGE

- Are there areas in the region at risk of flooding? — EA
- Are there flood management initiatives ongoing in the region? — EA
- Are there catchment management initiatives (eg environmental enhancements/water quality improvements) ongoing in the region? — EA
- Are there sensitive water resources that require protection from additional discharges? — EA, EG
- Are there areas where existing surface water drainage infrastructure is at capacity? — WC, LA
- Are there current plans for new drainage infrastructure for the region? — WC, LA
- Are there areas where, within this planning horizon, it would be difficult to connect new development into existing drainage infrastructure? — WC, LA

CONSULTATION

Are there flood risk/drainage issues within the region? — YES / NO

Can plan policies ensure a development strategy is compatible with sustainable water management? — YES / NO

Review land-use strategies

PLAN COMPONENTS TO BE CONSIDERED

- Policies that ensure that the timing of development is consistent with sustainable provision of surface water drainage.
- Policies to take account of issues in relevant plans developed by Environment Agency and water companies (eg CFMPs, SMPS and their successors).
- Policies that direct development away from flood risk areas and ensure protection of floodplains.
- Policies must require flood risk assessments in accordance with PPG25.
- Policies that act to reduce the effects of development on the water environment by full consideration of appropriate drainage systems.
- Policies that promote the identification of opportunities for floodplain restoration and/or environmental enhancement.

PROMOTE CONSULTATION WITH EA AND WC TO ENSURE PROPOSALS MINIMISE RISKS AND MAXIMISE BENEFITS TO ENVIRONMENT AND EXISTING CUSTOMERS

WASTEWATER DISPOSAL

- Are there areas in the region where current discharges are causing unacceptable receiving water quality levels? — EA
- Are there receiving waters in the region with no/very limited capacity to accept further treated effluent/stormwater? — EA
- Are there catchment management initiatives (eg environmental enhancements/water quality improvements) ongoing in the region? — EA
- Are there areas where existing wastewater drainage and/or sewage treatment infrastructure is at capacity? — WC
- Are there current plans for new wastewater drainage and/or sewage treatment infrastructure for the region? — WC
- Are there areas where wastewater collection and sewage treatment for new development, for this planning horizon, would be difficult to accommodate? — WC

CONSULTATION

Are there wastewater disposal issues within the plan area? — YES / NO

Can plan policies ensure a development strategy is compatible with sustainable water management? — YES / NO

Review land-use strategies

PLAN COMPONENTS TO BE CONSIDERED

- Policies that ensure that the timing of development is consistent with sustainable provision of waste water drainage.
- Policies to encourage the consideration of natural treatment solutions, and reuse, where appropriate.
- Policies to take account of issues in relevant plans developed by Environment Agency and water companies (eg CFMPs, SMPS and their successors).
- Policies that discourage development in areas where additional wastewater discharges would degrade water quality of receiving watercourses.
- Policies to protect water quality and reduce pollution risk.

PROMOTE CONSULTATION WITH EA AND WC TO ENSURE PROPOSALS MINIMISE RISKS AND MAXIMISE BENEFITS TO ENVIRONMENT AND EXISTING CUSTOMERS

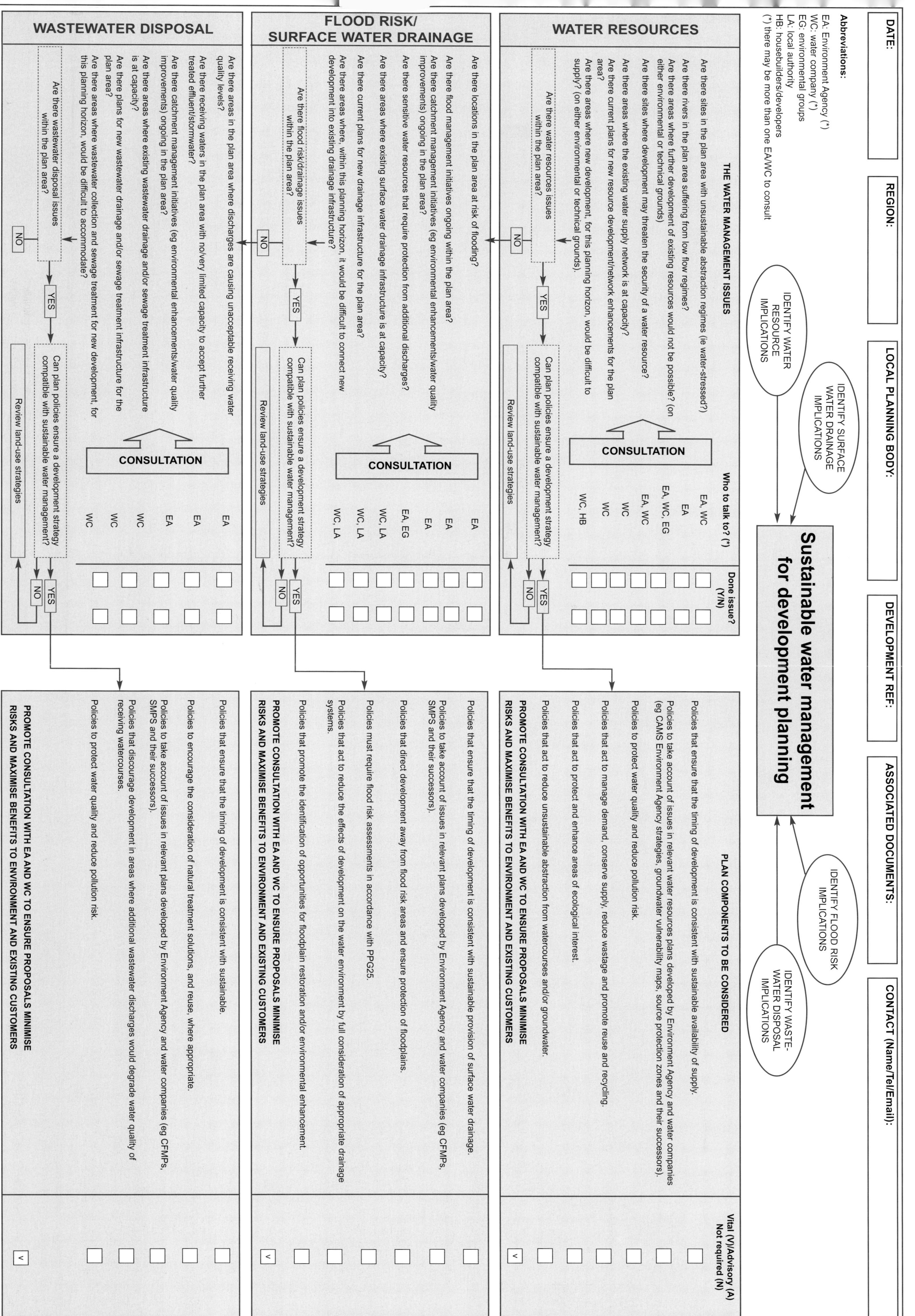

The page is a landscape-oriented planning checklist/flowchart titled "Sustainable water management for development planning."

Abbreviations:
EA: Environment Agency (*)
WC: water company (*)
EG: environmental groups (*)
LA: local authority
HB: housebuilders/developers
(*) there may be more than one EAWC to consult

Sustainable water management for development planning

IDENTIFY WATER RESOURCE IMPLICATIONS

IDENTIFY SURFACE WATER DRAINAGE IMPLICATIONS

IDENTIFY FLOOD RISK IMPLICATIONS

IDENTIFY WASTE-WATER DISPOSAL IMPLICATIONS

THE WATER MANAGEMENT ISSUES

WATER RESOURCES

Are there sites in the plan area with unsustainable abstraction regimes (ie water-stressed?)

Are there rivers in the plan area suffering from low flow regimes?

Are there areas where further development of existing resources would not be possible? (on either environmental or technical grounds)

Are there sites where development may threaten the security of a water resource?

Are there areas where the existing water supply network is at capacity?

Are there current plans for new resource development/network enhancements for the plan area?

Are there areas where new development, for this planning horizon, would be difficult to supply? (on either environmental or technical grounds).

Are there water resources issues within the plan area?

NO / YES

CONSULTATION

Can plan policies ensure a development strategy compatible with sustainable water management?

Review land-use strategies

Who to talk to? (*)

EA, WC
EA
EA, WC, EG
WC
EA, WC
WC
WC
WC, HB

Done issue? (Y/N)

FLOOD RISK/ SURFACE WATER DRAINAGE

Are there locations in the plan area at risk of flooding?

Are there flood management initiatives ongoing within the plan area?

Are there catchment management initiatives (eg environmental enhancements/water quality improvements) ongoing in the plan area?

Are there sensitive water resources that require protection from additional discharges?

Are there areas where existing surface water drainage infrastructure is at capacity?

Are there current plans for new drainage infrastructure for the plan area?

Are there areas where, within this planning horizon, it would be difficult to connect new development into existing drainage infrastructure?

Are there flood risk/drainage issues within the plan area?

NO / YES

CONSULTATION

Can plan policies ensure a development strategy compatible with sustainable water management?

Review land-use strategies

EA
EA
EA
EA, EG
WC, LA
WC, LA
WC, LA

WASTEWATER DISPOSAL

Are there areas in the plan area where discharges are causing unacceptable receiving water quality levels?

Are there receiving waters in the plan area with no/very limited capacity to accept further treated effluent/stormwater?

Are there catchment management initiatives (eg environmental enhancements/water quality improvements) ongoing in the plan area?

Are there areas where existing wastewater drainage and/or sewage treatment infrastructure is at capacity?

Are there plans for new wastewater drainage and/or sewage treatment infrastructure for the plan area?

Are there areas where, within this planning horizon, would be difficult to accommodate?

Are there wastewater disposal issues within the plan area?

NO / YES

Can plan policies ensure a development strategy compatible with sustainable water management?

Review land-use strategies

EA
EA
EA
WC
WC
WC

NO / YES

PLAN COMPONENTS TO BE CONSIDERED

WATER RESOURCES

PROMOTE CONSULTATION WITH EA AND WC TO ENSURE PROPOSALS MINIMISE RISKS AND MAXIMISE BENEFITS TO ENVIRONMENT AND EXISTING CUSTOMERS

Policies that act to reduce unsustainable abstraction from watercourses and/or groundwater.

Policies that act to protect and enhance areas of ecological interest.

Policies that act to manage demand, conserve supply, reduce wastage and promote reuse and recycling.

Policies to protect water quality and reduce pollution risk.

Policies to take account of issues in relevant water resources plans developed by Environment Agency and water companies (eg CAMS Environment Agency strategies, groundwater vulnerability maps, source protection zones and their successors).

Policies that ensure that the timing of development is consistent with sustainable availability of supply.

Vital (V)/Advisory (A) Not required (N)

FLOOD RISK/ SURFACE WATER DRAINAGE

PROMOTE CONSULTATION WITH EA AND WC TO ENSURE PROPOSALS MINIMISE RISKS AND MAXIMISE BENEFITS TO ENVIRONMENT AND EXISTING CUSTOMERS

Policies that promote the identification of opportunities for floodplain restoration and/or environmental enhancement.

Policies that act to reduce the effects of development on the water environment by full consideration of appropriate drainage systems.

Policies must require flood risk assessments in accordance with PPG25.

Policies that direct development away from flood risk areas and ensure protection of floodplains.

Policies to take account of issues in relevant plans developed by Environment Agency and water companies (eg CFMPs, SMPs and their successors).

Policies that ensure that the timing of development is consistent with sustainable provision of surface water drainage.

WASTEWATER DISPOSAL

PROMOTE CONSULTATION WITH EA AND WC TO ENSURE PROPOSALS MINIMISE RISKS AND MAXIMISE BENEFITS TO ENVIRONMENT AND EXISTING CUSTOMERS

Policies to protect water quality and reduce pollution risk.

Policies that discourage development in areas where additional wastewater discharges would degrade water quality of receiving watercourses.

Policies to take account of issues in relevant plans developed by Environment Agency and water companies (eg CFMPs, SMPs and their successors).

Policies to encourage the consideration of natural treatment solutions, and reuse, where appropriate.

Policies that ensure that the timing of development is consistent with sustainable.

Sustainable water management for development control

Abbreviations:
EA: Environment Agency (*)
WC: water company (*)
EG: environmental groups
LA: local authority
HB: housebuilders/developers
(*) there may be more than one EA/WC to consult

WATER RESOURCES

IDENTIFY WATER RESOURCE IMPLICATIONS

IDENTIFY SURFACE WATER DRAINAGE IMPLICATIONS

IDENTIFY FLOOD RISK IMPLICATIONS

IDENTIFY WASTE WATER DISPOSAL IMPLICATIONS

PLAN COMPONENTS TO BE CONSIDERED

Vital (V)/Advisory (A) / Not required (N)

Policies that ensure that the timing of development is consistent with sustainable availability of supply.

Policies to take account of issues in relevant water resources plans developed by Environment Agency and water companies (eg CAMS, Environment Agency strategies, groundwater vulnerability maps, source protection zones and their successors).

Policies to protect water quality and reduce pollution risk.

Policies that act to manage demand, conserve supply, reduce wastage and promote reuse and recycling.

Policies that act to protect and enhance areas of ecological interest.

Policies that act to reduce unsustainable abstraction from watercourses and/or groundwater.

PROMOTE CONSULTATION WITH EA AND WC TO ENSURE PROPOSALS MINIMISE RISKS AND MAXIMISE BENEFITS TO ENVIRONMENT AND EXISTING CUSTOMERS

FLOOD RISK/ SURFACE WATER DRAINAGE

Policies that ensure that the timing of development is consistent with sustainable provision of surface water drainage.

Policies to take account of issues in relevant plans developed by Environment Agency and water companies (eg CFMPs, SMPS and their successors).

Policies that direct development away from flood risk areas and ensure protection of floodplains.

Policies must require flood risk assessments in accordance with PPG25.

Policies that act to reduce the effects of development on the water environment by full consideration of appropriate drainage systems.

Policies that promote the identification of opportunities for floodplain restoration and/or environmental enhancement.

PROMOTE CONSULTATION WITH EA AND WC TO ENSURE PROPOSALS MINIMISE RISKS AND MAXIMISE BENEFITS TO ENVIRONMENT AND EXISTING CUSTOMERS

V

WASTE WATER DISPOSAL

CONSULTATION

Do the proposals place the water environment under increased pressure/unacceptable risk? EA

Do the proposals have WC commitment to the timely provision of sustainable wastewater disposal, and has the EA approved the solutions? EA, WC

Do the proposals mitigate effectively for any possible environmental damage that they contribute towards? EA

Do the proposals ensure the security of all water-related sites of environmental importance? EA, EG

Do the proposals contribute towards enhancement of the water environment? EA, EG

Are there risks to wastewater disposal remaining? → NO / YES

Can planning conditions ensure the proposals are compatible with sustainable water management? NO / YES

Review development proposals